Rooney Eats It! A Brit's Take on Pimps, Child Deaths and Other Fun Movie Stuff

Iceberg Movies Guide, Volume 3

Dave Franklin

Published by Baby Ice Dog Press, 2023.

While every precaution has been taken in the preparation of this book, the publisher assumes no responsibility for errors or omissions, or for damages resulting from the use of the information contained herein.

ROONEY EATS IT! A BRIT'S TAKE ON PIMPS, CHILD DEATHS AND OTHER FUN MOVIE STUFF

First edition. January 26, 2023.

Copyright © 2023 Dave Franklin.

ISBN: 978-0958006194

Written by Dave Franklin.

Table of Contents

The Gleeful Slaughter of Children 1

The Hidden (1987) 11

Grovel Before God, You Maggots! 15

Boogie Nights (1997) 29

Say Hello to My Leetle Frend 35

The Not Quite #1: Wolfen (1981) 49

Sexy Blind Chicks in Peril 53

Disaster, 70's Style 63

Blaxploitation #8: Coffy (1973) 83

The Return of Graham Chapman 87

This is Spinal Tap (1984) 101

Men Gotta Have Fun 105

Blaxploitation #9: Foxy Brown (1974) 125

Nasty Fuckers 129

The Not Quite #2: Demon Seed (1977) 139

Teacher Types 143

The Not Quite #3: Mad Max (1979) 161

Here We Go Again 165

Inflatable Bikinis, Erotic Soup Bowls and Randy Nignogs 189

The Not Quite #4: Paper Mask (1990) 199

Abusive Flesh Peddlers 203

The Not Quite #5: The Devils (1971).. 217

Thirty Odd Years of Walken 221

The Not Quite #6: The King of Comedy (1982) 241

Hodgespodge.. 245

The Not Quite #7: Dead Man's Shoes (2004) 253

Good God, What Were You Thinking, Girl? 257

Spinning Plates 263

The Gleeful Slaughter of Children

Being an ex-teacher, I naturally hate kids.

For almost four years I had to endure their relentless energy, selfishness, demands, spite and mediocrity, leaving me with the impression that the average child shares a lot in common with a small, intoxicated, unruly visitor from outer space. Think of a half-cut E.T. kicking your shins and then retreating to a corner to snigger with its mates. That was my working day. Honestly, there's no better contraceptive out there than classroom contact.

Those four long years also left me baffled why people reproduce. For a start, I can't think of anything worse than having to spend money on stuff like nappies. You're literally handing over precious cash for someone else to shit on what you've just bought. That's why I'm amused by those Facebook groups set up for parents who regret having taken the plunge. Sure, most of 'em still love their crotch spawn, but they can't help recalling what life was like before the pitter-patter of tiny talons. Parenting, they feel, is an expensive, exhausting and *unfulfilling* slog. Or as Johnny Rotten once muttered: "Ever get the feeling you've been cheated?" Such simmering discontent sure does allow me to indulge in a smug smile or two, fuelling the belief I've dodged a bullet rather than face the fact that no woman in her right mind would sleep with me.

Anyhow, you only have to look to cinema for confirmation of how irritating the average kid is. How many flicks have they polluted with their wholesomeness, whining or woeful lack of acting ability? Sure, we occasionally get Jodie Foster in *Taxi Driver*, River Phoenix in *The Mosquito Coast* or the magnificently creepy siblings in *The Innocents*, but most of the time we're lumbered with the equivalent of that irritating fuckwad Short Round in *Temple of Doom*. Look at *Terminator 2*. It's a fine movie that boasts the shape-shifting T-1000, a pumped-up Linda Hamilton and some ultra-cool stunts, but it has one abiding flaw: Mankind's future saviour, John Connor, is a dick. After spending a few minutes in the company of this pubescent cunt dropping, in which he *forbids* Arnie from killing anyone, I can't help praying for the machines to triumph.

I also get irked by filmmakers shying away from (or plain refusing) to kill the wee ones. Things started so well back in 1931 when Frankenstein's monster innocently chucked a girl into the drink to see if she'd float like a flower, but it wasn't long before that scene was hacked out by those child-revering censors. What the hell's so bad about splatting kids? Why's it still such a taboo? Look how James Cameron wimped out by not killing the doll-clutching Newt in *Aliens*, even when the xenomorph reared up behind her. When are we going to see the renowned child killer Freddy Krueger carve up a poppet rather than a bunch of over-aged teens? Am I the only one gutted by Tom Cruise's hateful daughter in *War of the Worlds* escaping the aliens' desiccating ray guns?

Thankfully, there are some directors happy to serve up soggy children on toast in flicks like *Don't Look Now*. Romero did his bit by having two zombie kids shot at close range during *Dawn of the Dead*. Irwin Allen upped the ante by getting into double figures in *The Swarm*. Graham Baker struck a momentous blow for good taste while butchering hundreds of newborns in *Omen III: The Final Conflict*. Then again, someone like Alfonso Cuaron got awfully confused in 2006's dystopian *Children of Men* by thinking he was presenting human infertility as a bad thing.

Ladies and gentlemen, a dearth of kiddiewinks is *exactly* what we should be aiming for.

Timmy failing to get a wriggle on in *Once Upon a Time in the West* (1968)

What would you do if you popped inside your house to freshen up for an al fresco lunch to welcome your new step-mum and came back outside to find your dad and older siblings lying dead in the dust?

Well, poor little Timmy (Enzo Santaneillo) doesn't do much at all. He just stands there clutching a bottle of drink as the hired gun Frank (Henry Fonda) and his four cohorts emerge from the bushes and advance.

Timmy obviously can't get a handle on what's happened, no doubt oblivious to the value of the bloodstained land he's standing on and what some men in big business will do to get their grasping hands on it. A few minutes earlier he'd been running around the arid terrain collecting grouse his father shot down. Everything was cool, even if his sister had just warned him not to touch that yummy, freshly baked apple pie.

And now... *this*?

OK, there were those odd couple of moments when the incessant cicada song stopped, as if the insects knew something bad was afoot, but that wasn't much of a warning for such carnage.

Timmy remains frozen to the spot as director Sergio Leone gives us a trademark close-up of his freckled, uncomprehending face, accompanied by a typically brilliant burst of searing guitar and harmonica to heighten the suspense. The lone survivor seems to know there's not much point fleeing. He's never gonna outrun five armed outlaws anyway. All he can do is rely on his tender age being a case for mercy, but given the look in Frank's ice-cold blue eyes his chances appear slim.

"What are we gonna do with this one, Frank?" a fellow gang member asks. Frank merely glances at him and spits. "Now that you've called me by name..." he replies, pushing aside his coat to unholster his pistol while subtly shifting the blame for what he's about to do.

Two things are for sure: Leone knows how to direct and Frank's one pitiless motherfucker.

Alex the floating fish bait in *Jaws* (1975)

The second killing in Spielberg's classic isn't quite in the same horrifying league as the half-drunk, early-morning skinny-dipper who gets chomped in the opening five minutes, but its victim (in a PG movie) is still a lovely surprise.

Alex is your typical kid enjoying a day out at the beach. Clearly a water baby, his mom is already expressing concern that his hands have gone prune-like as he begs her to go back in. "Just ten more minutes," she tells him. Well, honey, a great white the size of a submarine sure as shit don't need that long. And so Alex returns to the calm sea on his yellow airbed, paddling out as his mother watches.

Spielberg is smart enough to show other potential victims, such as a stick-retrieving mutt and a fat old biddy floating on a rubber ring with her toes out of the water. We even get a couple of red herrings in the form of an old guy's fin-like, bathing cap-clad head breaking the surface while a girl lets out an excited scream as her playful boyfriend grabs her underwater and upends her.

None of this amuses the uptight Chief Brody (Roy Schieder). He's re-opened the beaches under pressure and against his better nature, and is now torturing himself by pointlessly sitting on the sand. After all, what can he do on dry land observing the frolicking townsfolk in a vaguely paranoid way?

Shit or get off the pot, son.

The first sign something's up is the dog owner pacing the shoreline calling his pet's name. Said dog is nowhere to be seen and appears to have retrieved its last stick. Then a load of young kids take the plunge, giving us those eerie submerged shots of dangling, kicking, and eminently biteable legs as John Williams' iconic score makes the hairs on the back of our necks stand up. We see the airbed's blurry underside and the music increases in intensity. Spielberg switches to the surface, there's a flurry of fins, Alex's arm shoots up into the air and a picturesque geyser of blood erupts. Cue a mass exodus before the shredded airbed forlornly washes up on the beach.

Christ, dontcha love the movies?

Little Buddy getting the mother of all headaches in *Halloween III: Season of the Witch* (1982)

It goes without saying that any attempt to kill off America's children in their entirety is bound to get a double thumbs up from me. What makes it better in this much-derided but fun third part of the *Halloween* franchise is that our Irish arch-villain Conal Cochran (Dan O'Herlihy) doesn't even possess an intelligible reason. Sure, he mumbles something about ancient Celtic forces, the planets having aligned and a pagan blood sacrifice from three millennia ago, but... well, I can't work out his motive or how the hell this hugely successful, Halloween mask-making businessman is going to benefit. Perhaps hating kids is all the grounds a man needs.

Nevertheless, Conal's insane level of misanthropy has seen him not only stay a bachelor but surround himself with obedient, non-smiling, super-strong androids at his hi-tech Californian factory, Silver Shamrock Novelties. He clearly prefers the company of plastic, rubber and stone to something as repellent as nourishing relationships and warm human flesh. Not that he doesn't have a sense of humour. After all, we're told this is the guy who invented 'sticky toilet paper' and the 'soft chainsaw'.

The japester.

So how's he going to pull off this much-needed, snigger-inducing annihilation of youth? Well, he's nicked a chunk of Stonehenge and sneakily brought it back to his factory to harness its mystical power. (You'd think someone might notice the theft of a ten-ton standing stone from the world's most famous prehistoric monument, but never mind). Utilising his genius with electronics, he's built a microchip containing a tiny piece of Stonehenge and attached it to the back of the masks. All the kids have to do is wear their masks while watching a TV ad campaign on the 31st and hey presto, the device is triggered and they're history.

Like any bona fide megalomaniac, Conal loves giving a demonstration of his power. This is where Little Buddy (Brad Schacter) plays his memorable part. Ushered into Test Room A with his stupid, chirpy mum and dad, he delivers the line "I have to go to the bathroom" with such aplomb you can see why he was the natural choice eight years later to play a parking attendant in an Ally Sheedy flick. But Little Buddy has taken his last piss. Faced with a locked door and nothing else to do, he slips on a jack-o-lantern mask as the TV commercial plays. "Honey, don't get too close," his mum says. "You'll ruin your eyes." Before long he's clutching his head and falling to the floor in front of the glowing TV set, hands shaking, as his parents wonder what the hell's going on. A whole load of insects spill from his ruined head, mummy faints, and *rattlesnakes* start slithering out.

Brilliant. Like just about everything else in this amusingly bonkers flick it makes no sense whatsoever, but brilliant.

The pint-sized gangster boss in *RoboCop 2* (1990)

Robocop 2 might be a loud, overlong headache of a movie, but at least it provides some respite by splatting a kid. What a shame we first have to suffer through an hour and a half of Hob (Gabriel Damon) swearing, dealing drugs, trying to garrotte Nancy Allen, shooting cops and generally avoiding having his naughty little botty smacked.

Of course, Robocop can't shoot juveniles as that's against his programming, even though Hob is introduced loosening off a round into his half-metallic head. Not that the smirking Hob even thinks about apologising. Or as he gloatingly informs Robocop: "Can't shoot a kid, can you, fucker?"

At no point is it explained how a cocky brat can rise so high in Detroit's main criminal gang, let alone take it over. The script tries hard to make him devilishly charismatic, but he just reminds me of a precocious classmate I had in 1981 who could do the Rubik's Cube in two minutes flat in front of admiring girls. Alas, my prayers for a paedophilic abduction back then were never answered but at least Hob ends up eating lead.

However, considering he's the main villain and this is an R-rated flick, it's odd how we aren't treated to the sight of bullets thudding into his stick-thin frame. Instead Robocop has to deal with a hideously clumsy metaphor, finding the tedious shit lying fatally wounded on a pile of bloodstained money in the back of an armoured van. Weirdly, their personal history, in which Hob enthusiastically helped dismember the law enforcer with a sledgehammer and pneumatic drill ("They say he's got a brain. I wanna see it!") is forgotten. All we're left with is Hob grabbing a concerned Robocop's hand and pleading: "Don't leave me."

This might've been forgiven if Robocop had then drowned him in vomit.

The little girl in red in the otherwise monochrome *Schindler's List* (1993)

Is the spotlight placed on a cute toddler during a sustained sequence of barely comprehensible savagery a brilliant directorial decision that lyrically encapsulates the Holocaust's horror?

Or is it a gimmick?

Frankly, I'm not sure, but I'll tell you one thing: it fucking well works. I'm not even sure why, but it might have something to do with tapping into the wisdom allegedly espoused by that cuddly ol' mass murderer Joseph Stalin: *One death is a tragedy, a million deaths a statistic.*

Whatever the case, this unnamed, dark-haired child (Oliwia Dabrowska) is first spotted by Schindler (Liam Neeson) as he sits astride a horse on a hilltop looking down at the Krakow Ghetto's chaotic liquidation. Here we get enraged Nazi demands for ID, sewers being clambered into, agonising separations, the euthanasia of bed-bound hospital patients, mass panic, and brains being blown against walls.

Then into this murderous maelstrom comes a little girl wearing a distinctive red coat. Neither the terrified Jews nor their Aryan aggressors appear to notice her unsteady gait. It's a vaguely surreal moment, as if Schindler is imagining her. She just keeps wandering alone, providing an eye-catching focal point for one of history's most violent storms.

Later, Schindler is talking to Amon Goth (Ralph Fiennes) as the concentration camp boss complains onsite that the 'party's over' because all those incriminating bodies need to be dug up and incinerated. Schindler holds a handkerchief against his lower face to blot out the stench, but lowers it in surprise when he sees the little girl's exhumed body on a handcart being hurriedly wheeled toward a crematorium pit, her red coat caked in filth.

He has no words.

Sick Boy's doomed kid in *Trainspotting* (1996)

Alice Cooper could do little wrong between 1971 and 1976 as exemplified by his top album, *Killer*. Here we get classics like *Halo of Flies* and the title track as well as the ditty *Dead Babies* in which Alice condemns selfish, hedonistic parents neglecting their little ones. 'Dead babies can't take care of themselves...' he trills in his typically mock-serious way. 'Well, we didn't want you anyway.'

Such a message might resonate with Sick Boy (Jonny Lee Miller), a person described by a mate early on as someone who's 'always been lacking in moral fibre'. Indeed, he's a parasite, happy to steal, rob, deal drugs and reel off his knowledge of Connery-era Bond all day long. Oh yeah, he's also a long way from being the world's best father. Well, why go to the trouble of changing nappies, reading bedtime stories and everything else when you can zone out on skag?

Or as he concisely explains: "Heroin's got great fucking personality."

Maybe things would've turned out differently if he hadn't given the equally blameworthy mother her first hit in a drug den, but at least she shows consistency by pleading for another loving spoonful after their infant child is discovered dead in its crib. Sick Boy might weep, but it's up to Renton to suffer hallucinatory withdrawal symptoms of the wronged kid crawling across the ceiling.

James Bone Jr. getting gunned down in *City Hall* (1996)

Children should be seen and not heard so the saying goes. Now I agree with this sentiment, although I like to give it a quirky twist: Children should be seen *to be shot in the back* and not heard. For that's what we get at the start of the all right Al Pacino vehicle *City Hall*, a somewhat surprising development given the film is saddled with perhaps the dullest title of all time.

The kid in question is six-year-old James Bone Jr. (Jaliyl Lynn). He's being led to school hand in hand with his dad. The weather's shit but at least his raincoat and his father's umbrella are keeping him dry. Meanwhile, a no-nonsense Brooklyn detective is getting ready to ambush a mobster. James passes the unshaven scumbag waiting on a corner and turns to see the guy wink at him. A few seconds later the cop arrives, there's a gunfight, and it's an imminent case of smoked pork. Somehow the cop manages to shoot back while lying fatally wounded on the drenched pavement, causing the baddie to stagger and fire wildly.

Oh, dear.

Little James hasn't even managed to cross the road when a stray bullet catches him smack bang between the shoulder blades. A thrilling jet of blood spurts out, leaving a scarlet trail down his bright yellow jacket. His anguished father can only cradle his body and turn to try to work out what the fuck just happened.

It's a tragedy, but at least New York's mayor (played by Pacino) finds a fitting perspective: "It costs a lot of money to have our children slaughtered in the streets."

Steak and Fries experiencing a little indigestion in *City of God* (2002)

City of God excels at showing unbridled bloodshed feeding on itself. It drops you headfirst into a Brazilian hellhole in which hope has long been abandoned. Poverty's rampant. Jobs are scarce. Honest people are routinely trampled upon. Sexual harassment and worse are the norm. The corrupt cops are just as likely to kill you as the bad guys. Drugs have a stranglehold. Guns are everywhere. Death can blindside you at any moment. And trigger-happy gangsters like Li'l Ze (Leandro Firmino) rule this particular Rio ghetto.

Life is not so much cheap as a lousy bet.

When a gang of prepubescent kids known as The Runts start pissing everyone off with their holdups, muggings and general lack of respect, Li'l Ze decides it's a good opportunity to kill two birds with one stone. On the way to find them he drops by the home of a newly recruited teen gang member called Steak and Fries (Darlan Cunha). "Mom," Steak calls out while closing the front door, "I'm going out with my friends."

Dressed in a T-shirt, shorts and flip-flops, he could be off to the park to kick a ball around, but Li'l Ze is keen to find out what he's made of. Meanwhile,

The Runts have gathered to joke and boast about their latest robbery. Perhaps these little buggers are hardcore perps in the making or maybe their minor league crimes are nothing more than a game, something to relieve the dead-end boredom. What's clear is they're at an age where burping on cue still provokes group laughter.

When Li'l Ze and his cronies arrive, they appear happy to good-naturedly break up The Runts by doling out a few insults and slaps until two of the transgressors are cornered. In an instant Li'l Ze is asking them to choose between being shot in the hand or foot as an unsettled Steak slinks to the back of the group. A few missing toes later Li'l Ze demands Steak execute one of the wounded children. The gun looks huge in his unsteady hand as the others laugh and urge him on. Steak is at a pivotal point in his short life, although he doesn't really have any choice. Now all that's left of his rapidly ebbing morality is the decision to select the older boy, close his eyes and wordlessly carry out his boss' command. With the initiation over and the child slumped lifeless in a corner, the camera stays on the back of Steak's head. We don't get to see his face. Has Steak blown a hole in his own soul as well as the kid's chest?

This well-directed scene has no score, no possibility of a dramatic last-minute intervention, and no howling, hand-wringing aftermath. Instead it's presented as run of the mill, leaving you with the sense that a child killing a child is nothing much to get excited about in the City of God.

The Hidden (1987)

Synopsis

Psst! Want an alternative explanation for Charles Starkweather's murderous rampage?

Director

Jack Sholder

Cast

Kyle MacLachlan, Michael Nouri, Ed O'Ross, William Boyett, Claudia Christian

If you're a seething fantasist, a deeply immature guy incubating warped daydreams about *making 'em all pay*, then *The Hidden* is right up your dark little alley. Here you can vicariously indulge your most hedonistic, destructive impulses. You know, taking whatever the hell you want, beating the shit out of whoever objects, smashing stuff up, driving like a madman, giving the finger to the cops, and flaming out in one great-big-fuck-the-world orgy of excess.

As the great Freddie Mercury once sang: *I want it all and I want it now.*

And guess what?

You're not alone. There are aliens out there who also don't want to go gentle into that good night. For they, too, love pounding rock music, piles of money, the hottest chicks, naked displays of power and the pleasurable sight of bullet-riddled irritants lying at their feet...

We begin with grainy, black and white security cam footage of an everyday scene inside a Los Angeles bank. A guard smiles at a bloke who's just walked in. Within seconds the new arrival has pulled out a weapon, blown all resistance away, grabbed the cash, grinned at the camera and strode outside to jump into a black Ferrari. A fantastic chase involving dozens of cops ensues in which our demented driver mercilessly runs down a wheelchair-bound man, sending his body flying over the bonnet.

Slaying the disabled? Fuck, I'm *in*.

Detectives Beck and Willis (Nouri and O'Ross) try to piece things together after the perp is finally halted by a hail of bullets and put into intensive care. Nothing makes much sense, though. From all accounts the thrill killer's a *good* guy yet in the last fortnight he's wiped out twelve people (six with a butcher's knife, including two kids), wounded twenty-three more, stolen six cars, and robbed eight banks, six supermarkets, four jewellery stores and a candy shop.

But the mayhem isn't over.

Within hours of dumping Public Enemy No. 1 at the hospital, a different patient walks out and starts doing exactly the same anti-social stuff. All a bewildered Beck can do is ask: "What is it? A full moon?"

Things grow even weirder when a dazed-looking FBI agent (MacLachlan) turns up to offer help. There's something not quite right about this dude from the way he's baffled by an Alka-Seltzer tablet to how awkward he is around a child. The harried, sarcastic Beck forms an uneasy alliance with him, but one of *The Hidden's* strengths is its nimble sidestepping of clichés. They're neither buddies nor a pair of mismatched, bickering cops. Instead we get an understated chemistry that not only builds an air of mystery but leads to a deeply satisfying conclusion.

Like the best movies, *The Hidden* reaches out, grabs you by the front of your shirt and hauls you into its chaotic universe. Given its inspired script, breakneck pace and glorious mash-up of sci-fi, horror and action, it's a surprise it didn't find much of an audience upon release (people instead flocked to the likes of *Beverly Hills Cop II* and *Three Men and a Baby*. Aah, what would Morrissey say? *Come Armageddon, come, Armageddon, come...*) Sholder directs with both panache and restraint, ensuring his varied array of super-charged villains smirk now again during their bouts of high-octane carnage but never cackle or twirl a moustache. There's plenty of smart dialogue, excellent special effects and some nifty stunt work. The whole shebang is also nicely balanced by moments of humour, such as a perp growing enraged upon hearing a snatch of sappy, upbeat music.

When it comes to sci-fi/horror, *The Thing* and *Alien* tend to lead the pack with their outstanding special effects and growing sense of claustrophobia. *The Hidden* isn't quite in the same extraterrestrial league, but its elastic concept and unrelenting inventiveness sure do deliver one helluva fun ride.

Grovel Before God, You Maggots!

In the beginning back in 1988 a six-foot-four deity who shunned goofing around arrived in moviedom. It wasn't long before he began to generate wall to wall adoration by being outstanding at whatever job he did, never showing fear despite the ever-present threat of death, and snapping the limbs of any bunch of displeasing bozos that littered his way. This was no mealy-mouthed Jesus, spouting that contemptible *turn the other cheek, blessed are the meek* shit.

Oh, no.

For this was Steven Seagal, a thirty-six-year-old colossus with a holy philosophy that we shall call... aikido. In our Lord's nuanced debut, *Above the Law*, one unenlightened foe dismisses this wondrously fresh way of life as 'chop suey crap' not long before a disgruntled bar owner (while surveying the wreckage of his establishment) tells the cops: "He was doing outer space kind of stuff, putting my customers in orbit."

Ah, well, scumbags and the excoriating purity of aikido never mix well. That's why in Mr. Seagal's universe cynics get punched in the balls, an abusive pimp is flung around the street by his tie, a fleeing drug dealer is kicked through a fence, a rampaging Mafioso is halted by a brain-piercing corkscrew, and the spine of a dreadlocked crime lord ends up dislocated over a knee. Just as Luke Skywalker's power to overcome evil was built on the Force, Mr. Seagal's immense wisdom, deep love of humanity and furious physicality are intricately connected to his mastery of this lethal martial art.

His fighting style is different to those wussy wannabes Norris and Van Damme in that he waits for opponents to attack and then uses their blundering momentum against them. Its joyful expression includes forearm throat smashes, wrist locks, and lots of bone breaking. Plus, Mr. Seagal will always stand up for the little guy, especially if this gives him the chance to demonstrate his moral superiority by inflicting the same public humiliation a bully has just doled out.

To underline his untouchable level of toughness, Mr. Seagal prefers to fight unarmed, never caring if a challenger is wielding a machete, baseball bat, machinegun, or nuclear-tipped Tomahawk. Sure, he'll improvise and pick up whatever's handy, such as a coil of rope or a pool cue, but usually he lets his menacing mitts do the talking. For example, in *Hard to Kill* he's confronted by four armed robbers in a corner store. He disables three with the minimum of fuss before contemptuously dropping to his knees to deal with the last knife-brandishing thug. "Come and get some," our shortened hero taunts the skuzzy crim before flipping him over and wrenching a leg until it pops at the knee. Yes, such adversaries do have a tendency to panic, bellow and charge, but I bet you'd behave similarly in such a bowel-loosening situation. Talk about trying to bat aside a hurricane with a tennis racquet. And yes, the ease with which Mr. Seagal relieves wrongdoers of their weapons does border on magic, but let us not forget: God *is* a supernatural being, a miracle worker *par excellence*.

In short, bullets won't stop him. Neither will a craftily placed bomb, an excavator's serrated jaws or even a seven-year long coma.

No wonder this action idol hit the ground running, scoring five consecutive hits between 1988 and 1992, four of which debuted at the top of the US box office. His biggest success, *Under Siege*, racked up more than one hundred and fifty mil and even garnished two Oscar nods. Mr. Seagal's uplifting message was out and the newly converted believers were flocking to his ministry. Nothing could slow such a cinematic demigod until he chose to clamber onto an environmental soapbox during the torturous finale of 1994's *On Deadly Ground* to finger wag we dumb schmucks about raping Mother Earth. Now I'm sure you'll agree blowing a baddie's lower leg off with a shotgun or pinning a gangster's hand to a wall with a meat cleaver are things we can all get behind, but being *lectured*?

For three and a half minutes?

Things were never the same for 'Officer Big Shot'. A mere two years later a supporting role awaited in *Executive Decision* in which, heaven forbid, he *died*.

God, it appears, was not only fallible but mortal as well.

Still, we shall always have fond memories of his first five flicks, the key ingredients of which made his bouts of ultraviolence such a mindlessly entertaining watch.

Hairdo: Seagal's hairdo is fitting in his patchy, mullet-infested debut, *Above the Law*, in that it's not quite right. It's a little unformed, although you can see it's trying to coalesce into *something*. But what? Those straggly follicles budding on his nape are as indistinct as an eleven-year-old girl's ghostly chest bumps. However, it's the sight of his receding hairline that makes me suspect, no, *realize*, there's something wrong with the film stock. Or maybe an internet japester digitally altered it. Whatever the case, it's an affront seeing a balding Seagal with wishy-washy, collar-length hair. Just picture a roaring lion with mange and you get the idea. No doubt if I took the trouble to download a different copy, he'd be restored to magnificence.

By 1990's *Hard to Kill* such hirsute glitches have vanished. Seagal's no longer thinning on top and that unkempt nub of neck hair has bloomed into a beautiful ponytail that his devoted wife loves to fondle. Ladies and gentlemen, we have liftoff. You thought God had a flowing white beard but in fact he's the proud possessor of a sleek, five-inch ponytail. It's fair to say it's vastly superior to the oily, semi-permed, mullety monstrosity that the pretender Van Damme later sports in *Hard Target*.

In Seagal's third outing, *Marked for Death*, we get Peak Ponytail. It's now the best part of a foot long and a thing of extraordinary beauty, gaily bouncing and swishing around as he runs after men in need of chastisement. One year later in *Out for Justice*, the ponytail remains a crowning jewel. At times it appears sentient, even threatening to out-act its host. Unbelievably, we get a sneering comment from one bigmouth gangster who tells Seagal: "I see you still comb your hair like a girl." Lordy, you'd have to revisit *The Exorcist* to find such appalling blasphemy. At least the aforementioned hoodlum ends up flat on his back with a broken nose.

Religion: In Seagal's first three flicks we see a christening, a sermon, prayers said with his children, and a respectful tone in general toward Catholicism. This is a bit of a surprise as I expected Seagal to worship himself. What on Earth does he need such baloney as Catholicism for? But after shooting dead a topless hooker in *Marked*, he goes to confession to reveal he's not quite as morally upright as we all thought. "I've lied," he tells the priest. "I've slept with informants, I've taken drugs, I've falsified evidence. I did whatever I had to do to get the bad guys."

Now I know Romanism should never be taken seriously, given that it's done nothing but plunder, oppress, abuse and hold back genuine knowledge for two millennia, but the priest who listens to Seagal's litany of woe arguably offers the most stupid bit of advice in its long, unfortunate history. "Try to find a gentle self inside you," he says. "Allow this person to come back." Good grief, doesn't he know Seagal is pure Old Testament? Unsurprisingly, such daft religious counsel is ignored and an avalanche of slaughter is instead unleashed on the streets of Chicago.

Is he hero-worshipped? Do other men want to bum him? At the start of the explosion-heavy *Deadly Ground* expert fire-fighter Seagal steps from a helicopter to tackle an out of control oil rig blaze that's already killed three men. The sight of his arrival prompts the mightily relieved foreman to exclaim: "Thank God!"

No, mate, thank *Seagal*.

It's not universal acclaim, though. Gangsters, bullies and terrorists hate him (even if they tend to respect his counterattacking capabilities). Just listen to bad boy Gary Busey in *Siege* after Seagal has punched him: "Now I know why you're a cook. You hit like a faggot." Environmental rapist Michael Caine goes further in *Deadly Ground* by telling a henchman: "Delve down into the deepest bowels of your soul. Try to imagine the ultimate fucking nightmare. And that won't come close to this sonuvabitch when he gets pissed."

Elsewhere a handful of DEA/CIA/police bosses are suspicious of Seagal's anti-authoritarian/loose cannon ways, but it has to be said that most people he comes into contact with can do little but stare in awe. It's no surprise to see a crusading anti-drugs senator drop by Seagal's house at the end of *Law* to thank him in person for his burst of carnage as a media throng waits outside for a penetrating insight into the menace of narcotics. In *Siege* an aging battleship captain takes the disgraced ex-SEAL under his wing, all but pleading to be a father figure. "If I had your ribbons," he tells him, "I'd wear them to bed." Later another navy boss labels him a 'warrior' and 'the best there is.'

And so on.

Still, it's *Hard to Kill's* wannabe boyfriend Lieutenant Kevin O'Malley (Frederick Coffin) who takes the biscuit when it comes to Seagal veneration, especially after it's believed the great man has been killed in the line of duty. "He had more honour and guts," O'Malley furiously informs one naysayer, "than this whole department put together!" When it's realized the stupid doctors have erroneously declared Seagal dead, O'Malley is the first to tearfully hold his pal's hand on the operating table and half-sob: "Don't worry, buddy, I'm in your corner." Over the next seven years the lovelorn O'Malley raises Seagal's son, just waiting for that sweet, sweet moment when Seagal rises Lazarus-like from his slumber so he can finally be his pillow-biting wife in an ad hoc nuclear family. Sadly, he never feels the warmth of Seagal's lips, instead sacrificing himself to protect the man's genetically superior offspring.

How often does Seagal beat up four heavily armed guys? Four appears to be Seagal's favourite number when it comes to showcasing his fighting skills. In every one of his first six movies he simultaneously twats at least four guys, managing it three times in both *Law* and *Marked*. *Justice* might be the macho highpoint, though. After showily emptying his gun of bullets, he works his way through about eight guys in a bar. However, some opponents remain amazingly stupid e.g. one idiot in a trashed department store during *Marked* attacks him with a furled umbrella when anyone with even half a brain knows you need at least an Uzi to take on an unarmed Seagal. Perhaps further down the line (I haven't seen his post-*Deadly Ground* fifty-odd movie appearances) he tired of using both arms and kept things fresh by gouging an eye with one hand while doing the ironing or washing up with the other.

Ludicrousness: You might find Seagal's abundance of death-defying feats tricky to swallow, but I suggest his knack for evading automatic gunfire by dropping to the floor is yet further evidence of divinity. Ditto the way he turns the tables on those various mobs of tooled-up, would-be assassins sneakily arriving at his home. Plus, he instinctively knows driving a jeep will protect him, his passenger and its tires from a hail of bullets whereas if he'd chosen *any other brand of vehicle* he would've been fucked. For Christ's sake, how else do you explain a beaten, heavily drugged prisoner fastened to a chair with cable ties not only breaking free but proceeding to whack all *five* armed assailants? No wonder *Deadly Ground*'s Michael Caine calls him the 'patron saint of the impossible', a comment that is merely a fancy way of saying *miracle worker*.

Nothing illustrates this better than *Above the Law* when he jumps onto the hood of a speeding car and ends up clinging to the roof. Despite the two goons inside both packing heat, Seagal makes the one run out of bullets (perhaps with the power of his mind) while the other repeatedly misses from six inches. Neither can they dislodge him, despite the speeding car weaving through midtown traffic. The best they can manage during a situation in which they appear to have complete control is a pithy insult in the form of 'fucking animal!' Unbothered, Seagal punches through the side window and reaches inside to employ an unbreakable throat grip on the passenger. The driver is so intimidated by this manoeuvre that he halts the car, enabling Seagal to hop off the roof and arrest them. I'm sure you'll agree that if a mere human attempted this in real life, there might be a different result.

Another example of his uncanny abilities can be found in the accurately titled *Hard to Kill*. Here he takes a few bullets in the chest before spending the best part of a decade in a coma. His shaggy-haired, twitchy revival makes for great cinema, instilling the sort of reverie in the viewer that would surely be on a par with a true believer witnessing The Second Coming. However, perhaps it's best to get a few things straight about his rapid recuperation. Yes, his ponytail survives unscathed. No, he doesn't have a *Dead Zone*-like ability to see the future. Yes, it's quite easy to tell the difference between his pre and post-coma acting. OK, I guess it's a little more difficult to explain how he immediately escapes a trigger-happy assassin while supine on a gurney. Some non-disciples would point to this as a prime, groan-inducing example of Seagalian egomania. However, if Jesus can walk on water, then I have no problem with a groggy, horizontal, pyjama-clad 'coma cop' outwitting an experienced killer in possession of a silenced handgun and the full use of his body.

Bone-breaking quotient: You have to say that rearranging bones into balloon animal shapes is Seagal's thing. Honestly, this dude treats a radius, ulna and tibia as if they are nothing more than twigs. Viewers don't grasp this proclivity until the climax of *Law* during which he lovingly snaps the chief bad guy's arm and neck. However, by the time *Hard* and *Marked* roll around, he's very much into his stride. The former bloodily coughs up a broken knee, elbow, leg, two wrists and another neck. That's quite a lot by anyone's standards. *Marked* is perhaps the graphic, hyper-violent peak, complemented by the amputation of a gun-holding hand lyrically dropping to the floor. Seagal also crunches through an elbow, an arm, a neck, an elbow, a shin and a spine, spicing things up with a double eye gouge and a successful first attempt at decapitation. In both *Justice* and *Siege* he gives the musculoskeletal system a much easier time, delivering just a paltry broken wrist and a snapped arm. The big softy. Then again we do get an armpit stabbing and a torn-out larynx so perhaps not.

Women: As expected in Seagal's red-blooded world, those lovely ladies don't get the juiciest parts. Look at the way an upcoming Sharon Stone (with a delicious hint of puppy fat) is wasted in *Law*, saddled with a scared-wife-cradling-the-baby role. Ditto the still foxy blaxploitation star Pam Grier, who does little but change hairdos three times and get shot. The earnest, blank-faced Eskimo chick in *Deadly Ground* fares just as badly, reduced to interpreting, asking for explanations and following in Seagal's shadow like the dumbest of Bond girls. Females essentially orbit him to make admiring comments, gyrate in states of undress, be protected and, of course, provide a reason to go on a self-righteous rampage.

In three of his outings, Seagal is married. Now it goes without saying that any lass who finds herself in the same room as such a knife-throwing deity is bound to be ecstatic, let alone one that has regular access to his trouser department. In *Law* and *Hard* both wives accordingly worship the ground he floats across, but there's an anomaly in *Justice* in that his missus wants a divorce. Huh? How can any female seriously consider leaving Seagal? She must be *deranged*, a suspicion amplified when she dismisses the imminent male-on-male violence: "Why can't you all just piss on a tree and mark your territory the way dogs do?" Later, however, (after her husband has racked up about twenty-five corpses) she's won over by this expression of his tender heart and wants to reunite, telling him: "Everybody loves you."

Amen, baby.

In *Marked for Death* Joanna Pacula plays a more intellectual type. Apparently she's an authority on voodoo and Jamaican gang culture after having graduated from the Kelly McGillis Top Gun School of Absurd Roles. Despite her fondness for books and other non-sexual stuff, this doesn't stop Pacula from getting smitten at the first sight of our towering hunk. After being told he's retired from the DEA, she gives him the onceover and mutters: "He still looks functional to me." Oh, Stevie boy, do you have any idea of your power? In *Siege* former Playboy centrefold Erika Eleniak is definitely less of an egghead, her embryonic brains having long ago migrated to her stupendous chest. She may evolve aboard a battleship from a woozy stripper into a gung-ho combatant, but she's still a willing participant in a climactic snog that underlines Seagal's virility.

However, in *Hard to Kill* it's then real-life wife Kelly LeBrock (she of the lips and voice) who gives the most fascinating demonstration of Seagal's lady-killing prowess. In a performance of supreme ridiculousness, she falls in love with an inert Seagal at the LA Coma Center *before* he's woken up. "Would you like a little pussy?" is pretty much the first thing she asks before placing a kitten on his pillow. Excuse me, but are animals allowed in hospitals? Well, I guess the rules don't apply when it comes to nurturing a bedridden beefcake back to bruising bravery. Neither, it seems, does professional etiquette given that she then lifts the sheets for a quim-moistening glance at his cock. "You've got so much to live for," she says with unabashed longing. "*Please* wake up." When her wish comes true, the first exclamation from her shell-shocked mouth is the somewhat unsurprising: "Oh, my God!" Yes, sweetie, God is back, and he's once again keen to snap the arms of his children.

LeBrock spends the rest of the flick staring at Seagal's handsome face while nodding at his constant flow of wisdom. Of course, it's not long before she's dressed up like a strumpet outside his room. "I was just passing," she says while proffering a rose "and I thought you might like a flower." Seagal takes it during a sultry burst of saxophone on the score, but there's clear hesitation on his face, as if he knows he needs better scripts.

Does he cry or show any other unmanly weakness? There's a scene in *First Blood* when Rambo (having destroyed a town among other things) wigs out in front of his father figure, Colonel Trautman. The more I think about it, the more I realize it's unusual for such a macho action pic to depict its hero like a helpless six-year-old boy in a state of weepy incoherence. Some people snigger at such melodrama, but Sly's wobbly disintegration does make sense after the trauma he's experienced.

You don't get anything like this in Seagal's first six movies. The man is capable of expressing doubt (as he does about past behaviour in *Marked for Death's* confession box) but crying jags aren't his thing at all. Then again, as Seagal is not exactly known for the richness and fluidity of his expressions, it can be hard to tell what he's feeling. Frequent bouts of constipation appear to be a good bet.

Still, there are moments when the steely exterior softens a tad. I swear there's the briefest of scenes in *Law* where he thinks colleague Pam Grier is dead and his face is wet. In *Hard to Kill* (after banging new squeeze Kelly LeBrock) he sits on the floor shaking his head while glancing at his wedding ring. No wet face this time, though. Nevertheless, he does pop along to his murdered wife's gravestone to sink before it with both hands on his face. I believe he's trying to convey grief, although it looks like he's about to sneeze.

In *Justice* a tear rolls down his cheek while crouched in the street over the body of a slain buddy, although I think this has more to do with the oniony fumes of a nearby hotdog stand. Similarly he places a jacket over *Siege's* murdered battleship captain, but you can tell he's already inwardly rubbing his hands at the prospect of launching an all-out war against the terrorists responsible.

These spells of solemnity add up to a good eleven or twelve seconds of the near-nine hours of Seagal flicks I sat through.

Far Eastern or mystical bullshit factor: Martial artists are often guilty of espousing more guff than a back-peddling, crack-addicted politician. Bruce Lee's films are littered with such groan-inducing shite e.g. listen to this crock he tells his mentor in *Enter the Dragon*: "A good martial artist does not become tense, but ready. Not thinking, yet not dreaming. Ready for whatever may come. When the opponent expands, I contract. When he contracts, I expand. And when there is an opportunity, I do not hit. It hits all by itself."

Any idea what that means or how it'd help when up against a red-faced aggressor in a pub car park?

Thankfully, Seagal concentrates on busting heads while mostly eschewing such pretentious, yin-yang nonsense. In his early films there are snippets, especially in *Hard to Kill* where he seeks wisdom from a Chinese book before employing meditation and acupuncture to help him regain his pre-coma mojo. Eventually we see him restored to full manliness perched upon a rocky outcrop as a soaring eagle cries above.

Marked and *Justice* have no such mystical indulgences while *Siege* is only guilty of one bit of Bruce Lee guff when Seagal tells his nervous sidekick Erika Eleniak on board a battleship: "You gotta be invisible. If you walk by a hatch and you see the enemy, you become the hatch." Mate, much as I love you, no one's gonna mistake that girl's rack for a goddamned *hatch*.

However, it's the sledgehammer treatment of environmental woes in the Alaska-set *Deadly Ground* where Seagal loses his shit. This was his big chance to cement his Hollywood star, especially as he was handed the directorial reins for the first time and a budget of fifty-million smackeroos. Moviedom waited with bated breath. After all, God was about to direct himself.

Yet this heavy-handed flick, in which Seagal goes from a 'cupcake' to a 'bear-man', starts badly and rarely lets up on the mystical mumbo-jumbo during its first half. For example, after saving the ass of a bullied Eskimo pisshead from a desperately unconvincing bar bully, the rescued man reveals: "You are about to go on a sacred journey. This journey will be good for all people."

Oh, gawd. I'd rather he just snapped limbs while terrified gangsters yelled: "I wouldn't sell you the sweat off my balls!"

Seagal's obnoxious, two-faced boss, the 'dirty snow' enthusiast Michael Caine, then tries to murder him, resulting in his recuperation in an Eskimo village that's nothing more than an over-earnest exercise in gibberish. In his previous flicks Seagal was always the arrogant master but here he becomes a student, happy to absorb whatever quasi-religious bullshit the Eskimos sling at him. It's pretty damn hard not to laugh when the tribal chief knocks him out with a feather, an action that drops him into the spirit world. Cue a cringe-inducing sequence of chanting, semi-naked, oh-so-wise indigenous folk, an eagle flying above snow-capped mountains, and a spot of bear wrestling. Regrettably, the animal doesn't end up stabbed in the head with a corkscrew.

Any surprises? Not many, that's for sure, mainly because Seagal insists on scripts presenting him as a combination of fierce integrity and triple hard bastard. He's the same bullet-proof character in each movie. Only the length of his ponytail changes, although its mysterious absence in *Siege* is still bit of a shock. I guess I would've liked some sort of explanation for why such a shining example of heterosexual manliness runs like a big girl, though. Perhaps show ponies can't help but prance.

Above the Law qualifies as his most political film with its decidedly anti-CIA slant. "These guys have started and financed every war we've ever fought…" he says during an overcomplicated ninety minutes that takes in a Vietnam-era death squad, a whistle-blowing priest and a campaigning senator. "We've wiped out entire cultures. And for what? Not one CIA agent has ever been tried, much less accused of any crimes." I don't know about you, but I find such sentiment pithy. Shame Seagal didn't pursue such anti-government schtick in his following five flicks.

Elsewhere, I always thought Jamaicans were dreadlocked, homosexual-hating, weed enthusiasts who lay around all day listening to Bob Marley whereas *Marked for Death* shows most of 'em have given up such sweet and gentle ways to bugger off to America to kill people. Catch the straight-faced TV news reporter (who's surely just wandered out of a *Death Wish* flick with her alarming crime stats) to hilariously tell us that more than ten-thousand Jamaicans are involved in drug trafficking across twenty states, an infestation of naughtiness that's resulted in *1,400 murders* in the last three and a half years. Cue scenes of innocent high school kids in Seagal's neighbourhood being lured into crack cocaine addiction. This is an unacceptable breakdown in law and order, yes? No wonder the authorities don't mind too much when Seagal, a *retired* DEA agent, starts massacring gangsters on the streets of Chicago. They clearly need all the help they can get.

However, it's *Deadly Ground's* aforementioned plunge into po-faced environmentalism that's far and away the biggest surprise in Seagal's early canon. Beforehand the only (piss weak) indicator of his reverence for nature that I could pinpoint was a contrived episode in *Justice* when he rescues a cruelly abandoned German Shepherd, hails himself an 'animal lover' and promptly kicks the puppy's former owner in the nuts.

Entertainment value: Seagal's movies are what I call Airplane Movies. This means they're essentially time killers, entertaining enough if you're stuck in the air for a few hours but short of artistic depth, decent characters and memorable dialogue. This doesn't mean I look down on such fare because there's nothing wrong with being entertained. Indeed, that's the one thing I demand from a flick. Seagal mostly delivers in this regard, especially during the well-choreographed fights in which it appears he really is belting some of those extras.

Saying that, you can see why Seagal remained on the second tier of action heroes below the likes of Arnie, Sly, Gibson and Willis. They got to play Rocky, Rambo, the Terminator, Mad Max and John McClane, but Seagal's script-picking failed to result in any iconic scenes or lines, let alone characters. Now you sure as hell don't have to be a great actor to be a screen legend, but you do occasionally need to team up with an imaginative, risk-taking or disciplined writing team.

Still, things didn't turn out too bad and for a while there he was riding the scarlet crest of a wave. I enjoy the coma-flavoured shenanigans of *Hard to Kill*, as well as the voodoo-tinged nasty violence of his third feature. I can't really argue with the slickness of his *Die Hard* knock-off, *Under Siege*, either. It has lots of fun moments like an F16 getting knocked out by the dreadnought's awesome defences before the villains toast each other with champagne to the mighty chords of Hendrix's *Voodoo Chile*. Sure, Seagal might still be ruing his apparently heartfelt decision to stand behind that lectern in *Deadly Ground*, a career-maiming move that led to direct-to-video hell, but God has long had a reputation for doing things that beggar belief.

Or as Seagal says to a buddy in *Marked for Death*: "Since when did anyone ever accuse me of being sane?"

Boogie Nights (1997)

Synopsis

A teenager with little formal education and a horse-like cock decides to play to his strengths. Or as he puts it: "Everybody's given one special thing, right?"

Director

Paul Thomas Anderson

Cast

Mark Wahlberg, Burt Reynolds, Julianne Moore, Don Cheadle, John C. Reilly, Heather Graham, William H. Macy, Phillip Seymour Hoffman, Alfred Molina

Do you watch porn?

C'mon, you can tell me.

Maybe you're one of those guys who wakes up and immediately staggers bleary-eyed across the bedroom to flip up a laptop lid, a short journey made hazardous by the combination of throbbing boner and ankle-pooled pyjama bottoms that necessitate arms thrown out to the side while taking awkward little baby steps.

But bugger the possibility of a cock-snapping fall and a humiliating trip to hospital. *Trampolining Thai Teens Vol. 4* has finished downloading and your morning glory is already en route to its splendid natural conclusion. Jesus Christ, why waste time attempting to embrace life's astounding riches when it's possible to find out if a bouncing, spread-eagled cheerleader can be fucked in *midair*. What's more, this time round you plan to take things slow. Every nuanced detail will be absorbed. For today's naked digital communion is gonna *mean* something and certainly not result in a collapse onto the carpet three minutes later in a sticky, self-loathing heap.

Aah, the wonderful world of porn...

I'm pleased to say I abandoned such viewing habits quite a few years ago after becoming more familiar with female genitalia than my own. I could close my eyes and instantly see all those glistening flaps and pink whorls whereas if I tried to picture my cock all I came up with was a three-inch silhouette. I mean, there was a point where porn had so corroded my libido that even if a naked woman walked up to me on her hands with a trained ferret balanced on the sole of each foot poised to plunge into her foaming, upside-down snatch, I'd merely mutter: "Yeah, seen it, babe. Ain't cha got anything *new*?"

Now while online smut may be disease-free and negate the horrors of dating, it's also repetitive, boring and demeaning to all involved, including the viewer. Some things should be kept private, you know, and involve a little mutual respect. Hey, are you rolling your eyes at me? Cut that out now. All I'm trying to say is that beforehand I was a husk of a man with a permanently sprained wrist whereas now I'm just a husk of a man. That's progress, my friend, and I deserve some goddamned credit.

And so to the much-lauded *Boogie Nights* which starts off in the late 70s during the pre-AIDS Golden Age of Porn. During its first hour director Anderson immerses us in a superficially glamorous world of poolside parties, uninhibited nookie and coked-up hedonism to the extent of ignoring pretty much everything on the outside. He adopts a non-judgemental attitude, allowing his multitude of characters to show us the error of their ways rather than wheeling on politicians, campaigners and moral guardians to condemn the tawdry high jinks (as in a similar-themed flick like 1996's *The People vs. Larry Flynt*). It's still very much a cautionary tale, though. Any professional involvement with porn clearly taints, especially if you want a bank loan, custody of a child or respect from a consumer. It also suggests it's a gateway to hard drugs, serious crime, prison and deadly violence.

None too bright teenager Eddie Adams (Wahlberg) is going nowhere with his gigantic pork trumpet until he meets aging porno director Jack Horner (Reynolds) at a nightclub. It's an X-rated match made in heaven. Before long Adams has renamed himself Dirk Diggler and is the hottest star on the porno block winning awards for his cockmanship left, right and centre. Ultimately, though, it's a journey up his own arse during which he cums to the conclusion his monetised minge-prodding is educating the public on the finer points of lovemaking while helping save 'thousands of relationships' across the country. At one particularly deluded point he even manages to compare himself to Napoleon when he was 'king of the Roman Empire.'

Now I can't believe I'm going to say this but Wahlberg is excellent. He's a convincing blend of good-natured naiveté and unblinking acceptance of whatever sexual act is required. A sort of fucked-up boy next door. He's at his best in the run-up to shooting his first porno scene, demonstrating nervousness, consideration and an eagerness to please in equal measures.

Mind you, all the porno shoots are good value, especially the way they capture the minimal direction, flat acting, and mechanical delivery of ludicrous lines ("I've just got back from a tour of duty. It was really hard being surrounded by all those guys all day.") Anderson has great fun here, essentially creating a series of very funny parodies.

Wahlberg is not alone in putting in a good shift. Indeed, it's tricky to pick a favourite out of such an unusually memorable supporting cast. Yes, they're a bunch of deadbeats and thickies, but they're also vividly realised.

William H. Macy: Always a glorious character actor, here he plays a moustachioed, mulleted, constantly cuckolded loser. Arguably has one of the least considerate wives in the history of cinema, a faithless lady who just loves to take 'an ass in her cock'. Macy doesn't feature in too many scenes, but most are wonderfully deadpan as he's confronted with his exhibitionist spouse bouncing on the dick of whatever bloke crosses her insatiable path. At some points you can see his sense of purpose and self-respect drain from his eyes, run down his chest and congeal at his feet.

John C. Reilly: As usual, offers a doofus act. This time he's a wannabe magician convinced he looks like Han Solo. Into one-upmanship, outright fibs, toadying, and terrible attempts to showcase his diving skills at the pool.

Can't say I bought him as a porn actor, but at least he offers the odd penetrating insight: "You can't fuck forever."

Phillip Seymour Hoffman: A boom operator and the personification of gawky, cringe-inducing clumsiness. Makes Carrie White look sophisticated. At least she got taken to the prom, but the paunchy Hoffman's idea of wooing is to show off his car's new paint job and then try a pash and drunken grope. However, despite being a relentless klutz and a 'fuggin idiot', deserves some credit for never dropping the boom. A performance to remind us what a loss to cinema Hoffmann was.

Don Cheadle: Often gets confused. Insists having sex on camera qualifies him as an actor even though he's literally *not* acting. Also thinks a cowboy outfit is a good look for a black man. Compounds his error by being into country and western music. Outside of porn he is a poor hi-fi salesman. Do not attempt to buy a stereo from him. He will only start talking about its 'high-quality fidelity' and the amount of 'quads' the speakers pump out. Probably best not to accompany him to a donut store, either.

Burt Reynolds: In a much ballyhooed return to form, Reynolds won a Golden Globe and was Oscar-nominated for playing a rich, cigar-smoking, elder statesman of porn. As an experienced director, he's developed delusions of grandeur, determined to make art rather than smut in which the cinemagoer is compelled by his moviemaking skill to find out how the story ends rather than slope off halfway through with a tissue full of cum. "It's my dream to make a film that is right and true and dramatic," he says. You know everything about him is skewed, though, because he's the sort of guy who hangs a portrait of a double murderer on his living room wall. Reynolds might nail this understated role with his distinctively coiffed, silvery hair, slightly camp necktie, and amiable sense of quiet corruption, but he doesn't top his *Deliverance* turn. Still, it's nice to hear the old boy talking about 'Mr. Torpedo' and 'joy juice'.

Alfred Molina: A man comfortable enough in his own skin to greet three drug-selling clients in skimpy briefs, slippers and an open bathrobe. Likes to keep a Chinese firecracker enthusiast on hand in case... well, I'm not too sure about that. Enjoys dancing to loud music in an enthusiastic, somewhat unsophisticated manner, but will not be tied to the rigid format of shop-bought LPs and cassettes. Indifferent to what the neighbours might say whenever he chooses to shoot up the street. Interest in porn unknown.

Heather Graham: Perhaps the most memorable character, I doubt anyone can forget Rollergirl's blonde magnificence as she zooms around wiggling her tight arse. In some sort of play on *The Red Shoes*, she never removes her skates, even when performing i.e. fucking. However, despite being a high school dropout and dim, coke-snorting slut, you'd better respect her otherwise she will leave wheel marks on your face.

All these characters are tied together by Anderson's fluid writing and direction. The way he moves his camera around a room introducing and following several people is a treat. Sometimes he'll even tag along with a bikinied girl stepping into a swimming pool, stay with her underwater and then pop back up to drop in on another conversation. Anderson also deserves credit for his authentic recreation of the 70s that includes posters of Farrah Fawcett, eight track stereos, casual sexual harassment, Sniff 'n' the Tears on the soundtrack, and Travolta-inspired nightclub dance moves. He doesn't forget proper action, either, such as the disastrous donut shop robbery which perfectly illustrates what happens when a good man with a gun tries to stop a bad man with a gun.

Boogie Nights excels at showing how a porn lifestyle can seem like an alluring choice whether in front of or behind the camera. There's little doubt that being involved with the adult film industry is fun, exciting and occasionally jaw dropping. At the very least it's gonna conjure up some entertaining pub stories and the chance to acquire a pair of fancy initialled curtains.

But, of course, there's the inevitable comedown: the coke ODs, the mounting self-disgust, the loss of control, the alienation from family, the ravaged souls, the odd foray into paedophilia, and the spectre of the job becoming increasingly abusive and misogynistic. Most of all, there's a sense that hearts and minds are directly connected to genitalia so it's probably wise to look after those squishy holes and dangly bits.

Say Hello to My Leetle Frend

There's only one way to describe Brian De Palma's five-decade-long career: all over the shop. There have been glorious artistic highs, far too many Hitchcockian homages, the odd mainstream megahit, a sprinkling of high profile awards, condemnation for tawdry subject matter, a pronounced tendency to work with the same collaborators both in front of and behind the camera, atrocious attempts at comedy, a fair bit of mediocrity and some whacked out moments along the lines of *Dear God, man, what were you thinking*?

One thing's for sure, though, and that's De Palma knows how to move the camera. Yes, he might be guilty of flamboyance and self-indulgence with his three-sixty pans, split screen shenanigans, elaborate tracking, lengthy takes and plethora of POV shots, but there's no denying the guy's visual style or sheer bloody imagination. Christ, sometimes he makes the goddamned camera *swoop*. At other times his fondness for split-focus trickery enables him to come up with some startlingly intimate moments, such as *Blowout's* John Travolta in the background but somehow next to an up-close hooting owl. De Palma is also a true believer in the magic of suspense and often takes great care setting up key events, a characteristic plain to see in a flick like *Carrie* as we wait an age for a bucket of porcine blood to drench our newly crowned prom queen.

De Palma started in the late sixties, gaining traction in 1972 with his first horror flick, *Sisters*. *Sisters* starts well but falls apart as soon as it introduces its highly implausible *Rear Window* aspect, complete with a shrill, wannabe investigative reporter. It's since become a cult favourite (and does feel like a forerunner to Cronenberg's body horror stuff) but I find it overwrought, poorly performed, full of ropey dialogue, and ultimately incomprehensible. However, it's an important entry in the De Palma canon as it was the first to link sex, blood and violence. More importantly, *Sisters* made money, as did the *Vertigo*-flavoured, exceptionally daft and slow as molasses *Obsession* four years later.

De Palma was up and running, managing to deliver his first masterpiece in the shape of 1976's bloody amazing *Carrie*. This paranormal high school flick, which revels in repressed female sexuality, bullying and religious mania, is a darling of mine and one of the fastest hundred minutes I've ever watched. From here on De Palma was no longer an indie filmmaker but an important, polarizing figure whose name was often in the frame for Hollywood's juiciest projects. Indeed, he turned down *Flashdance*, *Fatal Attraction* and, most intriguingly, *Schindler's List*. Can you imagine if he'd got his tacky little hands on that one? Liam Neeson probably would've ended up perving on some hot doomed Jews in the showers. I jest, but accusations of rank insensitivity, exploitation and misogyny have long dogged De Palma, especially during his 80s heyday.

Hey, that's gotta be preferable to blandness.

Goofy bollocks: *The Fury* (1978), *Dressed to Kill* (1980) & *Body Double* (1984)

De Palma followed *Carrie's* big success by doing his best to restage it in *The Fury*. Once again we have telekinesis, an emphasis on blood, and even a high school bitch. However, whereas *Carrie* was a small story, *Fury* is much more ambitious with its terrorist beach raid, secret government agencies, and talk of a 'bio-plasmic universe'.

Amy Irving, who played a remorseful bully in *Carrie*, is another troubled schoolgirl (despite pushing twenty-five) in possession of psychic abilities. Bad guy John Cassavetes, complete with a black-gloved hand in a black sling, wants to turn her into a governmental weapon to fight the Soviets. Meanwhile, an aging Kirk Douglas is trying to recover his similarly clairvoyant son from Cassavetes' clutches by occasionally impersonating an explosion-proof Spiderman.

This is two hours of cheesy guff, littered with below par performances, exploding cars, miraculous escapes, Arabs spinning out of control and angry pole vaulting. De Palma ditches the split-screen stuff but otherwise has fun with a bag of visual tricks that includes extrasensory visions and simultaneous presents while repeatedly showing a bodily explosion from different slow-mo angles (à la the famous flying sheet of glass decapitation in *The Omen*). *The Fury* might not convince for longer than a minute at a time, but it's amusing enough and turned into a decent-sized hit.

In the ladyboy-flavoured *Dressed to Kill* there's yet more of a *Carrie* overlap when De Palma starts with a naked female (Angie Dickinson) in a steamy shower soaping her body as lush music plays. Now I'm a fan of Ms. Dickinson. She's a classy broad and here she makes me paw the floor and howl at the moon, but De Palma's depiction of her as a sexually frustrated housewife in therapy who can't hang onto her gloves, wedding ring or panties is borderline hysterical.

This is not the film's only problem. Check out the obnoxious, badly dressed Dennis Franz (of *NYPD Blue* fame), giving another ridiculous performance as a cop to complement the wide-eyed one he served up in *The Fury*. Then there's the rotten Nancy Allen, so good as *Carrie's* queen bitch, who fails at every turn as a high-class hooker. Plus, we get a teenage electronics geek playing amateur detective, a diabolical subway sequence, and the overripe dialogue, such as our transsexual slasher telling psychiatrist Michael Caine: "Oh, doctor! I'm a man inside this girl's body and you're not helping me to get out... Don't make me be a bad girl again." In short, De Palma's writing discipline frequently evaporates.

Dressed to Kill is explicit, sub-*Psycho* mischief. It has a definite sex and punishment vibe and proved to be one of the director's most controversial offerings. In the UK it was released at the height of the Yorkshire Ripper's reign of terror while others objected to its portrayal of a ladyboy as an unhinged, razor-wielding murderer. I get the first reason for its contentious reception, but have much less sympathy for the second on the grounds that ladyboys don't have any right to be depicted on film as lovely, well-adjusted people. I appreciate they're a minority, but it's up to people to understand movies are not factual and their directors/writers shouldn't be accused of bigotry if they happen to show particular individuals in a less than favourable light. Cinemagoers would be better off basing their opinions of minorities (or run of the mill people like psychiatrists) on their real-life interactions with them.

For example, I once taught English to a couple of Thai ladyboys, the one proving to be a lively, interesting guy who often turned up to class in a fabulous black gown, a Gucci handbag and diamond earrings. Boy, did I feel slovenly next to him groping for my coffee at 8.30 each morning. Apart from that, he'd regale me with tales of his debauched weekends in Sydney with a sugar daddy, his excellent grasp of spoken English routinely punctuated by an obsessive need to check his reflection. All these years later I still think well of him and shall always have a certain amount of respect for any surgically enhanced bloke who slaps on a dress and walks down the street. Plus, it's important to note that despite having watched *Dressed to Kill* a good few times by the time he became my student, I don't ever recall fearing he was about to attack me with a razor or do something similarly nuts. Now if a thicky like me can tell the difference between real life and some nonsense in a movie, surely others can, too.

Anyway, *Dressed to Kill* is an essential entry in De Palma's catalogue. It might be bloody awful, but I can't help enjoying the way its eye-rolling silliness ploughs on for a further fifteen minutes after finding a daft ending.

And then we come to the equally far-fetched *Body Double* in which Craig Wasson tries to hold the centre. Not sure how anyone could mistake this wan shortass for the natural choice to star in an erotic thriller, but De Palma's meta movie would have struggled with its rampant implausibility and overlong runtime even if he'd got the casting right. Wasson limply plays a naïve, oversensitive, recently fired actor who gets sucked into a web of intrigue when he starts spying upon a gorgeous rich woman cavorting nightly in front of her window. This is one dull, confusing, action-light watch, although I am fond of Frankie Goes to Hollywood weirdly popping up at the halfway point, a dog headbutting its way through a car window and the scene in which Wasson managing to perve on the object of his obsession as she slips into some sexy undies in a boutique changing room while he stands outside in the *street*. Gotta give De Palma credit for shoehorning a bout of voyeurism in wherever he can.

Things continue to deteriorate with an unintentionally funny *Vertigo*-style wig out in a tunnel (that's on a par with *Dressed's* dire subway sequence) and the introduction of the ear-offending Melanie Griffith. She plays a porno actress who quickly informs us she's not into bestiality or fist fucking. Nor, it appears, good movies. You know *Body* is a stinker because that Huey Lewis-loving arbiter of good taste, Patrick Bateman, loves it.

Unlike *Fury* and *Dressed*, *Body* flopped at the box office. All three are best treated as convoluted comedies and although it's tricky to work out the goofiest, *Body* sure feels like the longest.

Half-decent efforts: *Blowout* (1981), *The Untouchables* (1987) & *Casualties of War* (1989)

De Palma's fondness for paying homage/ripping-off stuff was once again laid bare when he came up with the mystery thriller, *Blowout*. Clearly inspired by the likes of *Blowup* and *The Conversation*, it's another meta movie that reunites Nancy Allen and John Travolta, five years after her pussy fumes got him so high in *Carrie* he happily used a sledgehammer to bash in a pig's brains on her behalf.

Travolta is a movie sound effects recordist, a talented but guilt-ridden slummer who's adding screams and the thumps of falling bodies to low-budget horror flicks, such as *Bad Day at Blood Beach*. (Amusingly, there's also a poster of the real-life turkey *Empire of the Ants* on his workplace's wall). Travolta's job enables De Palma to have fun parodying slasher clichés that were all the rage in the early 80s. Hence, we start with a heavy-breathing killer lurking outside a girls' dorm as he peeps at a masturbating female, students fucking on the floor and a naked hottie in the shower.

Shortly afterward, Travolta inadvertently records a car plunging off a bridge on a quiet country road. Inside are a rising political star and the slutty, would-be blackmailer Allen (apparently channelling Marilyn Monroe's voice). *Blowout* is a little talky and contrived, especially when a hired bad guy bizarrely goes off the rails to become a serial killer. Still, it's as well directed as any of De Palma's movies, its reputation is growing, and its final twenty minutes/'good scream' coda are worth the wait. Travolta shows how charismatic he can be when given the right material, but his performance neither prevented *Blowout* from flopping nor his sad entry into a thirteen-year-long artistic wilderness that only ended when handed the *Pulp Fiction* script.

Whereas *Blowout* is filled with trademark De Palma tricks, *The Untouchables* is a lot more restrained. Only the elaborate train station sequence, in which a pram-bound baby bumps down some stairs during a shootout, comes close to the director's showy style, but I'd argue it's the least convincing scene in the entire thing (and deservedly mocked in a *Naked Gun* sequel). No matter, because elsewhere the big hit *The Untouchables* delivers.

Kevin Costner plays good guy government agent Eliot Ness during the dark days of Prohibition. He's been tasked with cleaning up Chicago, a town that 'stinks like a whorehouse at low tide.'

And the reason for the stink? Mr. Al Capone.

We're introduced to this boorish thickie as he's pampered by lackeys in front of a fawning press pack. He tells them he's 'responding to the will of the people' by supplying illegal alcohol, a cheeky stance built on a fair amount of truth. However, he also denies using violence because it's 'not good business'. Moments later a henchman is seen leaving a bomb in the establishment of an uncooperative businessman, resulting in the obliteration of a darling little poppet. Mr. Capone, it appears, is not quite telling the truth.

De Palma's smoothly paced depiction of such violence is interesting. Perhaps burned by all the grief he got from the *Dressed to Kill*/*Body Double* decriers, his tone wavers. It's near-jovial during part of Ness' raid on an incoming Canadian booze shipment while he disappointingly omits the skull-denting moment Capone's baseball bat meets a bonce. De Palma being coy...? No, thanks! Things mercifully get back to normal in a tremendous elevator massacre that echoes *Dressed to Kill*'s signature murder.

Throughout *Untouchables* De Palma's sense of 1930's Chicago is on the money along with Ennio Morricone's score and some decent acting. I'm no fan of the competent Costner, but he's well-cast here as the straightest of straight arrows ("Let's do some good!") However, he was always going to play second fiddle to Connery's beat cop charisma and De Niro's proven gangster class. The Oscar subsequently handed out to Connery seems a little generous, especially given his mangled attempt at an Irish accent, but a paunchy, balding De Niro has fun in just about every scene, especially when ranting: "I want you to find this nancy-boy Eliot Ness and I want him dead! I want his family dead! I want his house burned to the ground! I wanna go there in the middle of the night and piss on his ashes!" *The Untouchables* is a bit too straightforward to be a great gangster flick, but it remains a solid, watchable one.

Casualties of War, however, is a lot less fun. It arrived during the second wave of Vietnam War flicks, but its grim subject matter didn't exactly have folks lining up around the block. Now De Palma has long run into flak for his portrayals of sexualized violence, such as the phallic drill murder in *Body Double*, but *Casualties* was perhaps a counter move with its hard, stone-cold sober look at a spot of murderous gang rape. Based on a real-life incident, it variously portrays the military mind as macho, stupid, cruel, subservient, bullying, and utterly lacking in imagination.

In short, pretty much everything I always suspected.

During the straightforward, clip-filled 2015 doco, *De Palma*, in which the director discusses his body of work in chronological order, he admits *Casualties* was not only a movie nobody wanted to make (with a long history of being developed and shelved), but also one *he* finds hard to watch. "It felt very much the way I feel about these types of wars we get into where nobody knows why," he says. "To me, it's a metaphor for what we are doing: we are raping these countries."

A young, resentful Sean Penn lords it over a squad of Neanderthal malcontents, most of whom are racist, sexist and aching to crack heads. Listen to his immediate subordinate Corporal Clark (Don Patrick Harvey) musing about what to do on a night off: "We're gonna get shitfaced and go hump the brains out of some of those dink hos." Clark's lack of enlightenment soon turns nihilistic. "I hate this fucking place. They ought to blow it up and pave it over. Total fucking destruction is the only way to deal with them."

It's up to the baby-faced, three-foot high Michael J. Fox to do his best to suggest not every grunt is a fuckwit. And so he hands out chocolate bars to the locals, helps with the ploughing and naively believes the troops are there to benefit Southeast Asia. Nice try, son, but that's not much of an offset when the rest of your squad is abducting a teenage girl from an isolated village during a long-range patrol. Fox is not happy about this development and quickly becomes the voice of our conscience, but his pained face and little speeches don't exactly make for riveting cinema. Indeed, he's badly miscast (although it was his post-*Back to the Future/Teen Wolf* star power that got the flick made in the first place). Supposedly a married father, he looks like he should be back in America planning his school prom rather than standing up against fragging-inclined bullies and the army's disinterested, shit-kicking commanders. I kept expecting him to jump on a skateboard or try to wheel the traumatized girl away through the jungle on one.

Saying all that, the heavy-handed *Casualties* does have its strengths. The tobacco-chewing, thoroughly unpleasant Penn (who sees nothing wrong in using another human being as a bit of 'portable R and R') is effective. The abducted Vietnamese girl is also good, radiating helpless terror as well as *The Shining's* Shelley Duvall. *Casualties'* main problem, though, is it's all a bit workmanlike, earnest and dour.

The *Heaven's Gate* moment: *Bonfire of the Vanities* (1990)

Do you ever avoid a flick because the critics pissed on it? You know, stuff like *Ishtar* and *Battlefield Earth*. The laughable quality of these efforts is so taken for granted that they're only supposed to be trundled out if a sniggerfest is required. I know I've made no attempt to watch. I mean, all those people can't be wrong, can they?

And yet, when it comes to the peculiarities of art, the intrinsic quality of a movie can never be proven. If ten million people think it's shit but you love it, then your opinion is as worthwhile as anyone else's. In fact, your opinion is king. Sure, you can't prove you're right, but those millions of naysayers can't prove you're wrong, either. Heavyweight awards, box office returns, critical consensus and what your mum and best mate think really do mean jack shit.

End of story.

So fuck what others say. And fuck what *I* say. Try to approach a flick with an open mind and judge the goddamned thing on its merits alone.

Does this mean I'm now gonna defend the mega-flop *Bonfire* to the hilt? Well, no, and I would argue that Tom Wolfe's darker, more acerbic source novel is a much better way to spend your time. Still, I can't see why the movie was such a critical punch bag back in the day. Every scornful review I glanced at seemed to imply that if you bumped into De Palma it was fine to blow raspberries at him and let down the tyres on his car.

Now *Bonfire* is rather limp, but it's a passable two hours, even if Tom Hanks and Melanie Griffith are a long way from my faves, the bespectacled Bruce Willis is miscast, and Morgan Freeman delivers a Seagal-like sermon at its conclusion. There are much worse flicks in De Palma's fifty-year-long career, such as the incoherent bollocks of *Raising Cain* and the yawn-inducing bollocks of *Femme Fatale*. The main interest *Bonfire* generates is trying to work out why De Palma was thought suitable to take on such arch material. After all, it's a race-flavoured satire focusing on the trials and tribulations of a privileged, lightweight WASP. No murder, no gangsters, no icky sex stuff and no steamy showers. It's just not *lurid* enough for a bloke like De Palma, you know?

We do get some trademark directorial moves, such as an opening five-minute tracking shot and a split screen, but De Palma had already shown he couldn't do knockabout comedy in the mirth-free misfire, *Wise Guys*. Why he was handed the reins for a more sophisticated kind of humour is a bit of a mystery. Maybe he should've given Hanks telekinetic powers or a thousand-dollar-a-day coke habit. I was, however, amused by *Bonfire's* palpable fear of blacks as well as Griffith's breast size tripling since the days of *Body Double*.

Conclusion? I'll probably get around to watching *Ishtar* one day.

The glorious Pacino connection: *Scarface* **(1983) &** *Carlito's Way* **(1993)**

De Palma teamed up twice with Travolta to good effect, but his efforts with Pacino proved even more fruitful. Indeed, the combination of De Palma and Pacino is close to cinematic nirvana.

The Miami-set *Scarface* is arguably peak De Palma. It's one of those flicks where everything from the script and casting to the direction and electronic score come together to create not only a believable world but a key moment in pop culture. Hated upon release by many critics for its violence, extreme profanity and uncompromising depiction of excess, the brightly lit *Scarface* has very much had the last, coke-fuelled laugh.

"Most of my movies are about megalomania and guys living in insulated universes and the crazy things that happen within those universes, which is something that continues to fascinate me," the director reveals in *De Palma*.

And thank God for that coz *Scarface* remains an essential and highly influential gangster flick. Pacino plays Tony Montana, a scummy, fast-talking Cuban immigrant whose depth of ambition makes Macbeth look timid and unimaginative. This is a guy with 'steel in his balls' who 'wants the world and everything in it.' Nothing proves a deterrent whether it's watching a mate being chainsawed to death or an alleged informant's dramatic plunge from a helicopter with a noose around his neck. Montana's going to get it all, including the boss' wife, a humongous bathtub, a small mountain of coke, a gaudy dress sense and a pet tiger. Even his younger sister (and her monstrous perm) are within the sights of this rapacious man.

Montana has a code, though. Or as he tells one powerful Bolivian drug lord: "All I have in this world is my balls and my word and I don't break 'em for no one." It's this code that provides the one point in his favour in that he won't kill women and children. That's why the only person allowed to disrespect him in the entire flick is his honest, hardworking mum. Elsewhere, he's ceaselessly impatient, arrogant and contemptuous, a mini-volcano of unrepentant criminality capable of erupting at any second. Pacino's superb, ensuring Montana takes his place among the twentieth century's best movie villains.

De Palma confidently constructs this poisonous package, adding black humour and surreal touches wherever necessary, such as an obnoxious immigration officer asking the newly arrived Montana: "What about homosexuality, Tony? You like men? You like to dress up as a woman?" De Palma goes on to nail the big set-pieces, especially the aforementioned chainsaw dismemberment in which he expertly builds suspense by allowing his camera to drift away from an awry drug deal inside a beachfront hotel to linger on a beautiful bikinied blonde distracting Montana's backup crew on the street.

I also like a brief scene in which our main man has survived a nightclub assassination attempt and is reaching toward a sleeping Michelle Pfeiffer. De Palma frames the shot so Montana's bloodied hand is in the bottom right corner, enabling us to appreciate the quality of the bed's satin sheets draped over the supremely elegant Pfeiffer. This is Montana in a nutshell: leaving a trail of blood while grubbily pawing classy things he has no right to.

De Palma gets most things bang on the money in *Scarface*, but immediately makes a mistake in *Carlito's Way*. Or at least it starts in a way I'm not thrilled about by showing Carlito's dying moments. Why on Earth do filmmakers think it's a good idea to begin at the end? I know when you've been creating art for a while there's a desire to mix things up, to reinvent, to play with structure, but this start-with-the-ending is not among my faves. It's about the only criticism I can make of the brilliant *Sunset Boulevard* which commences with William Holden floating face down in a swimming pool. Now I'm sure it amused Billy Wilder to have a dead man narrate his tale, but it still spoils things by showing where things end up, you know?

Anyhow, I can forgive De Palma's suspense-thinning decision as *Carlito's Way* rapidly gets stronger. Sure, it's another crime don't pay tale, a setup as old as the hills and already covered by De Palma himself in *Scarface*, but it's all about the *way* it's told. De Palma ensures *Carlito* is no *Scarface* clone in that the two have quite a different feel. Tony Montana is so electric it's like he's giving off sparks, a bold, ruthless man who advances through animalistic cunning and chutzpah. He truly believes the world will be his one day. The Puerto Rican Carlito is cut from the same cloth but is more intelligent, thoughtful and evolved. Time and experience have wearied him. He knows a bullet will find him on New York's mean streets if he tries to pick up his post-prison life where he left off. He simply wants to find a quiet place far from the madding crowd and concentrate on the better things in life. Indeed, he tells his girlfriend: "You don't get reformed. You just run out of wind."

Carlito is notable for its melancholy, fatalistic nature. Acknowledging he's wasted too much time, Carlito wants to get into a position where he can make up for past mistakes. Unfortunately, he's in a similar position to the aging Michael Corleone in *Godfather III* in that just when he thought he was out, he gets pulled back in. "I don't invite this shit," he says. "It just comes to me. I run. It comes after me."

Pacino put away his shouty side for most of *Carlito*, an unfortunate aspect of his acting that began in the late seventies, and gives a calm, nuanced performance. With his black leather coat, well-trimmed beard and genuine love for his girl, he not only allows the character to breathe but comes perilously close to making him sympathetic.

As good as Pacino is, no analysis of *Carlito* would be complete without mentioning Sean Penn. Now one thing the movies teach us (apart from trannies being homicidal nutters) is that lawyers are slimy shits. Penn's David Kleinfeld is one of the best examples you'll ever find. Good grief, he's a self-interested, treacherous cunt. Penn (barely recognizable beneath a frizzy, thinning hairdo) paints a memorable portrait of a man drowning in his own greedy, coke-tainted sweat.

Carlito has an expansive, post-*Goodfellas* feel that boasts an even better supporting cast than *Scarface*. David Koepp's script deserves acclaim, especially the way its threads come together to illuminate such a fascinating patch of criminal darkness.

And De Palma? There are no split-screens or three-sixty pans here. Instead he quietly holds everything together before delivering memorable sequences like the pool hall betrayal and the climactic train station shootout.

The mediocre monster hit: *Mission: Impossible* **(1996)**

I've nothing against the mainstream (e.g. *Jaws*, *Star Wars* or *Raiders*), but I do struggle with big-budget, obvious-attempt-at-a-blockbuster, let's-have-a-franchise kind of thing. You know, the sort of mindless stuff where characterization is jettisoned in favour of insane, high-octane stunts every ten minutes or so. The $80m *Mission: Impossible* pretty much fits such a bill, except it's hard to follow and a little short on action. The whole thing never clicks into gear. Decent actors like Jon Voight and Ving Rhames don't make an impact. De Palma earns plaudits for the taut sequence inside a hi-tech, heavily protected CIA vault (complete with vomiting, an inquisitive rat and a falling bead of sweat), but otherwise it's a talky load of po-faced, sub-Bond silliness, as exemplified by all that face-removing stuff.

Nevertheless, *The Tom Cruise Show*, sorry, *Mission: Impossible*, still grossed almost half a billion worldwide to become far and away the biggest hit of De Palma's lengthy career. An Indian summer, all right, but his next two big-budget efforts (*Snake Eyes* and the $100m *Mission to Mars*) flopped. This led to smaller scale flicks in the new century, such as *The Black Dahlia*, that reaped neither reward nor respect. In all likelihood *Carlito* is likely to be his last hurrah, meaning he's helmed far more washouts and mediocrities than hits.

His critics might point to such a conclusion as showing De Palma (and his bag of flashy, prurient tricks) mostly failed.

But here's my tart little point: You don't judge an artist by the depth of his or her lows or the number of lows. You judge them by their highs so if you ever hear someone sniggering over *Bonfire of the Vanities* or trash-talking De

Palma as a tasteless Hitchcockian rip-off merchant just offer this three-word rebuttal: *Carrie* and *Scarface*.

And then pour a bucket of pig's blood over them.

The Not Quite #1: Wolfen (1981)

To recommend a flick I usually have to give it seven out of ten. And yet cinema is so vast there's plenty of stuff rating 5.5 to 6.9 that's certainly worth a watch. Guess you could call such movies *interesting almosts*. Or not quites. For example, they might be built on a fantastic idea or have become hugely influential. Maybe they boast an eye-catching lead performance, great special effects or a terrific first hour. Whatever the case, I'm no fan of simplistic ratings like Ebert and Siskel's thumbs up/thumbs down binary bullshit.

First up is the New York-set box-office dud, *Wolfen*. Lumped in with werewolf flicks out of convenience, it feels more like eco-horror instead of a straightforward genre piece. Whatever the case, it's more thoughtful, offbeat and ambitious than its hairy 1981 counterparts, *The Howling* and *American Werewolf*.

That doesn't mean it's as good.

Director: Michael Wadleigh

Cast: Albert Finney, Diane Venora, Gregory Hines, Edward James Olmos, Tom Noonan

The story: People are getting ripped to bits in the city. It's up to Detective Dewey Wilson (Finney) to stop drinking and work out what's going on. He's paired with a criminal psychologist (Venora) to unravel the gruesome mystery, although he's also aided by a bizarrely hands-on coroner (Hines).

Why it works: First and foremost because of the sterling work of Wadleigh. Having won raves for his groundbreaking doco, *Woodstock*, it took the director more than a decade to release his first (and only) feature film. Like De Palma, this guy knows how to move a camera. *Wolfen's* visuals are often beautiful and lovingly composed. Wadleigh is always looking for different angles and textures, utilising everything from security cam footage to night vision scopes. I still have no idea how he manages to make the camera zoom over the uneven terrain of large patches of waste ground. Then there's his cool use of a prowling wolf's POV, a mash-up of computer graphics, animation and infrared that popped up six years before a jungle-bound Schwarzenegger felt the weight of an intergalactic predator's eyeballs. Keeping the fanged culprits hidden for more than half the movie is another welcome touch.

Now I'm used to the Big Apple of the late seventies/early eighties being shown as a hellhole (as demonstrated by the likes of *Death Wish*, *The Exterminator* and *Maniac*) but *Wolfen* is perhaps *the* film to capture the extent of its decline. Wadleigh manages to make the South Bronx look like a post-bomb Hiroshima. I believe the technical term is urban decay, although I prefer to call it *fucked*. And so we get vast expanses of rubble, empty buildings on the verge of collapse, routine demolitions, and hobos camped on weed-infested pavements warming their hands on braziers. New York resembles a ghost town rather than a major American metropolis on the East Coast. Despite *Wolfen* being nearly two hours long, there are no busy streets or crowd scenes. It provides a fascinating snapshot of the city and is easily the movie's most memorable aspect.

Its opening hour unfolds nicely. We begin with a night-time triple slaughter of a beautiful, coked-up rich chick, her businessman hubby, and their hulking limo driver in a Manhattan park. It's a classy start complete with wind chimes, a replica windmill, a wary pet dog, and a twitching, gun-holding severed hand. In other words, it's both a restrained and graphic depiction of open-air slaughter. *Wolfen* continues to intrigue, offering a pair of glowing eyes in the darkened ruins of a church, a python consuming a rat, and the gradual introduction of its environmental concerns.

The dialogue's not bad, either.

What works against it: The performances aren't the best. Finney is a decent-enough actor, but doesn't get a handle on his cop character. He features in some odd scenes, especially one on a beach when he blankly watches another man getting nudey, howling at a blood-red moon and pretending to be a wolf. Overall Finney strolls through *Wolfen* not saying a lot nor showing much emotion about anything that's placed in his way, including a half-baked love interest.

Elsewhere, Hines plays a hip, earring-adorned, ass-baring, too young coroner. I wasn't aware coroners actively investigated homicides, but that's what he does here. The gangly Tom Noonan adds another strange performance as a moped-riding, deeply committed zoologist who likes to torture himself by watching real-life footage of wolf culls. He gets the occasional good line, though, such as: "Nature works. We don't." Then again, perhaps *Wolfen's* anti-technology, man-is-the-real-beast message is a bit too on the nose.

I doubt *Wolfen's* patient build-up is to everyone's taste, although its languid pacing is offset by some suspenseful sequences, the constant directorial inventiveness and its moments of gore. Still, I'd have to say its biggest disappointment is that Wadleigh (who was in his late thirties in 1981) never directed again.

Verdict: I've watched this movie three times and still don't know if its vaguely confused narrative works. Chances are, it'll get a fourth viewing. That must mean something.

Sexy Blind Chicks in Peril

When I was growing up in the UK, Lionel Richie's *Hello* hit number one for six weeks. In its accompanying video our moustachioed singer perves on a pretty blind girl, if not stalks her. Oh, and to make things just that bit iffier, he's her drama teacher. "*I've been alone with you inside my mind*," he sings. "*And in my dreams I've kissed your lips a thousand times*." And what else have you thought about, good sir? Probably quite a lot, given he follows her around with his tongue virtually hanging out, so infatuated he's even adopted the same hairdo.

Now tell me: Is Mr. Richie an outlier or do blokes have a thing for hot blind girls? Is helplessness appealing? Perhaps it brings out our gallant nature. Or does a blind chick simply conjure up icky fantasies in the less mature gentleman, a potential nirvana for a sad little weasel who prefers the submissive, dependent sort?

Well, I don't know, but Richie's *Hello* vid certainly stuck in my teenage head. Apart from its amusing creepiness, it presents this blind babe as not only pretty but curiously unbothered by her affliction. She's well-adjusted, popular and always bloody smiling. Not once does she wander around with her fly open or fall down the stairs. It's a depiction that suggests if you want to improve the quality of your life while being surrounded by unfailingly nice people, it might not be a bad idea to rip your corneas off.

I've since realised it's the same deal in the movies. Sure, you get the odd sightless hag in horror stuff like *Don't Look Now* and *Peeping Tom*, but for the most part pig-ugly, thick, miserable blind chicks (who aren't psychic) are a rarity. Not only that, but in everything from 1959's *Witness in the Dark* to 1995's *Castle Freak*, they're *survivors*.

Helena Robertson in *Jennifer 8* (1992)

Starring Andy Garcia, *Jennifer 8* was one of those serial killer flicks that were all the rage in the 90s. It was also one of Garcia's shots at establishing himself as a leading man after *The Untouchables*, *Stand and Deliver*, *Black Rain* and

Godfather III. Despite a decent opening forty-five minutes, it drifts, becomes uneven and illogical, and turns into an Airplane Movie. Indeed, Garcia never really got his box-office mojo back after playing a burnout cop in this flop. Along for the ride (and perhaps sniffing Oscar bait) is the babelicious Uma Thurman as a woman with four senses.

Why is she blind? She suffered a car accident at the age of fourteen, resulting in the death of her entire family.

Does she bitch about being blind? Not once. This is a little strange as she's not the gormless, beaming type. The best she can do is get mildly miffed about Garcia asking if she can tell his age from his voice: "We don't have some kind of sixth sense, you know, except in ridiculous novels."

Is her life more active and worthwhile than mine? Helena is a dorm-dwelling, live-in music teacher with no students at a deserted institute for the blind. This place is a charmless concrete block, although I guess blind people don't care too much about decor. Despite being gorgeous, sensitive and intelligent, she has no friends. Not even a pet. The weather's shit, too. It's either snowing or raining. However, she says she loves the feel of rain and snow on her face. Lucky her.

Is there a Lionel Richie character hanging around? It must be tough for any pretty girl to cope with the tedious crudities of unwanted male attention, but it's probably even harder if you're a pretty, curvy, *virginal*, blind girl like Helena. In fact, the movies often show that being in such a predicament is like having a neon sign above your head flashing *Perve on me!* Helena has to put up with three creeps here. Firstly, there's Garcia, a former alcoholic that's fixated on her because she looks like his promiscuous ex-wife who left him. "That's who [Helena] is," a cop buddy remarks, "except she can't run away."

Then there's a bald, frog-like janitor who likes to creep into Helena's bathroom, stand on the closed toilet, and take pictures of her with a miraculously silent camera as she nudies up for a bath.

I suppose I should also mention the serial killer who doesn't like blind girls for a reason I couldn't fathom.

Best blindness-defying achievement: Outrunning an experienced killer down a few flights of stairs is pretty impressive in anyone's book.

What did I learn about being blind? The blind insist on their independence to an extraordinary degree. No matter there's a mad killer on the loose and cops are getting gunned down, Helena still insists on being alone in her rundown, isolated dorm. Girl's braver than me.

Where is her guide dog? No idea. I think she would resent such an intrusion into her independence. Even if she did have one, I suspect she'd make it sleep in a kennel and/or lay down ground rules about the number of contact hours per day. She does manage to dredge up a white stick after 92 minutes, though. By the next scene she's binned it.

Does she die? When it comes to sexy blind girls, filmmakers long ago decided it's fine to place them in the most appalling danger but they must never die. You're much more likely to see a cutesy pet offed before a sightless female. Even in *Jennifer 8's* eye-rolling finale when the killer (in a long-awaited moment of triumph) crows "Say *night, night,* dead girl!" you know he's gonna fuck up somehow. Blind chicks have an even better survival rate than those goddamned kids in 70's disaster movies.

Susy Hendrix in *Wait Until Dark* (1967)

This is one of the most famous thrillers featuring a blind chick, but it's hideously bad. I think I've mentioned beforehand I don't like play-based movies and it's obvious this talky, overlong pile of smelly pants originated in the theatre. It's got a nonsensical setup featuring a heroin-stuffed doll and some particularly unconvincing criminals desperate to retrieve it. This bunch of clowns regularly plays dress-up and puts on accents, even though they're dealing with someone that can't see. Audrey Hepburn is our damsel in distress, the unwitting new owner of the aforementioned doll. Why the fuck don't they just threaten her? Or better still, torture her? That might have stopped me nodding off at various points.

Why is she blind? A car crash that resulted in a fire. No facial scars or burns, though.

Where is her guide dog? She was supposed to have one, but it read the script and left. Instead, she has to occasionally make do with a cane.

Is her life more active and worthwhile than mine? Well, she's recently got married to a loving husband, goes to blind school, has a lame sense of humour, and is unfailingly nice. No friends, though, forcing her to be pals with the bespectacled brat from upstairs. I wasn't envious.

Does she bitch about being blind? Her new hubby wants her to be more self-sufficient. Hence, he urges her to do the laundry, go shopping by herself and (somewhat suspiciously) use 'plenty of boiling water' to defrost the ice box. "Do I have to be the world's champion blind lady?" she objects with some justification.

Is there a creepy Lionel Richie character hanging around? Just the three daft criminals hell-bent on making their pursuit of the heroin-packed doll as complicated and illogical as possible.

What did I learn about being blind? Being unable to see doesn't save you from being a provincial, essentially dull person. Or as she says: "I do wish I could do things. *Important* things." Oh yes, Susy, like what? "Like cook a soufflé, pick a necktie or choose wallpaper for the bedroom." Fucking hell.

Best blindness-defying achievement: *Wait Until Dark* wants to present our heroine as super-alert, smart and resourceful, but she makes so many dumb choices that it's hard to read her as anything other than retarded. She could negate everything by simply *leaving* her apartment. Even a scream would do the trick. Or why not just give them the bloody doll? It's not like she's got a dog in the race. Instead, she chooses to do everything the hard way, taking on and besting a gasoline-drenched, three-time killer in the confines of her apartment. To say such shit could only happen in the movies is an understatement.

Does she die? No, Hepburn got a Best Actress Oscar nod instead.

Sarah in *See No Evil* aka *Blind Terror* (1971)

Wait Until Dark was a big hit that generated Oscar buzz. Hits always create copycats and *See No Evil* feels like the British rural answer. It's a slow burn psychological horror flick, its decent direction leading to some nice, creepy reveals. I have no hesitation declaring it fifty times better than *Wait*. It's certainly nastier. Mia Farrow plays Tracy, a woman so pale and frail that even if she could see she'd still embody vulnerability. I like *See's* inventive screenplay and its dank, sickly feel, even if its nonsensical underpinnings ultimately exclude it from being in the same horror class as *Rosemary's Baby*.

Why is she blind? In 1993's piss-poor *Blink*, Madeline Stowe loses her eyesight at the age of eight when her abusive mom smashes her head into a mirror after catching her playing with makeup. Makes a change from the ol' car crash excuse, I guess. In *See No Evil*, Sarah can no longer see because of a horse riding accident. I'm not sure how you end up blinded after falling from a horse, but I'll go along with it.

Does she have a guide dog? No dog, no stick, no dark glasses. At this point I'm getting the impression that film directors think such paraphernalia are off-putting for the viewer. They much prefer to have characters stagger around with their arms out in front. However, Sarah is the fastest-moving blind chick on this list. She really motors at times. It's like going from *Night of the Living Dead's* zombies to those sprinting ones in *28 Days Later*.

Does she bitch about being blind? When asked what it's like to be sightless, Sarah gives a refreshing reply: "Bloody awful."

Is her life more active and worthwhile than mine? Sarah is definitely the independent sort, pretty much determined to do everything herself whether it's pour a glass of port or make plans to move to London to retrain as a physio. Her boyfriend is a decent sort who stands by her after the accident, his simple plea of 'Don't go' making her cry. In other words, she's damaged but not broken. Farrow gives a performance that's both appealing and committed.

Is there a creepy Lionel Richie character hanging around? We meet him early on or, at least, we meet his white star-adorned boots. It's just a question of working out who these boots belong to because, you see, we don't get a look at his face. Just lots and lots of shots of that much adored footwear. Still, this directorial quirk worked for me. Our killer doesn't do any perving on Sarah, but he's still amusingly obnoxious. He's the sort of guy that likes to read a porno mag in a daytime pub with both feet on the seating. Ultimately, he has one of the most convincing excuses for launching a campaign of slaughter I've ever known. His boots get splashed by a passing car. A sympathetic judge would surely look the other way.

What did I learn about being blind? The blind aren't fussy about musical choices. Presented with a pile of LPs, it's more about the achievement of operating a record player than actually ending up listening to something you like.

Best blindness-defying achievement: Jumping over a fence on horseback. I wouldn't fancy doing that even with my two good eyes.

Does she die? No, but bloody hell, she's put through the wringer.

Tracy in *Eyes of a Stranger* (1981)

I'm no fan of slashers, a sub-genre that reached its peak output in the immediate years after 1978's *Halloween*. Most are simplistic, inept or boring. However, *Eyes* is a surprisingly good, well-directed watch. It's illogical in places, but its technical skill, briskness and aversion to humour help maintain tension. Everything is played straight and the gory murders are well done. It's a nasty, mean flick with a sleazy vibe that relentlessly riffs on the worst fears of women. Men are monstrous, ineffective or dismissive here. They'll kill you, rape you or fail to save you.

As played by the teenage Jennifer Jason Leigh (in an excellent debut five years before being torn in half by *The Hitcher's* Rutger Hauer), Tracy inevitably sparks the killer's interest. She's not only blind, but deaf and mute, an unfortunate combination that's surely even more debilitating than being a Limp Bizkit fan.

Why is she blind? During a series of soft-focus flashbacks, we learn Tracy was abducted as a child and brutally traumatised. Men!

Where is her guide dog? She's got a doggie but it's untrained. This doesn't stop our lovely killer from doing it in.

Does she bitch about being blind? Being mute, she doesn't bitch about anything. She shows annoyance by banging her fist against whatever's handy.

Is her life more active and worthwhile than mine? We don't learn too much about Tracy, except she lives with her guilt-ridden, overprotective big sis in a nice apartment block. She does the laundry, makes coffee, waters the houseplants, feeds her doggie, reads Braille and goes swimming. Doesn't sound too exciting, does it?

Is there a creepy Lionel Richie character hanging around? This is no whodunit. We're immediately introduced to our burly, mostly silent killer. He's a bespectacled, middle-aged man that lives in the same apartment block as Tracy. We don't get any insight into why he's turned out as a less than ideal member of society. He might frequent strip bars and have some girly mags in his apartment, but he's a long way from the unhinged, babbling Joe Spinell in *Maniac*. The guy does his dry-cleaning like everyone else. Even his name Stanley Herbert is innocuous. All we know is that he's into dirty phone calls before the red mist descends. He doesn't have a 'type' and is just as likely to murder a secretary as a stripper. He's both organised and disorganised in that he appears to carefully plan the murders but gets slack in their aftermath. The way he taunts Tracy in her kitchen is as creepy as anything you'll ever see. Actor John DiSanti is terrifically unsettling throughout.

What did I learn about being blind? Being blind doesn't stop you learning sign language.

Best blindness-defying achievement: Regaining her sight in the nick of time.

Does she die? Nah, but she sure gets pawed.

Reba McClane in *Manhunter* (1986)

Manhunter is an unusual serial killer movie in that it avoids exploitation and sensationalism by adopting a more nuanced, if not melancholy approach. It never shows the slightest interest in dwelling in filth. In fact, it's often gorgeous to look at. It's a mature work built on a well-researched script, Michael Mann's assured direction and a mainly superb cast. Yes, I would have preferred a more compelling actor in the central role, some plot holes to have been closed and Mann to have ditched a fair few of his dodgy soundtrack choices, but they're hardly a reason for *Manhunter's* poor box office. Despite such minor flaws, the flick remains an often fascinating companion piece to the superior and much better-known *Silence of the Lambs*.

Reba (Joan Allen) is our blind heroine, a smart, likable woman who works in the dark room of a governmental photo lab. Perfect job when you think about it. She must have hated the digitization of film.

Why is she blind? We don't get any clue, but given her sexualised nature it may have been down to masturbation.

Does she bitch about being blind? No. She's definitely warm, open and upbeat like the *Hello* girl. She smiles a lot.

Is her life more active and worthwhile than mine? At work she's liked and valued. She had a previous career as a speech therapist helping children. Often catches the bus home. Doesn't appear to have any friends, maybe because of her unsettling habit of asking to feel your face one minute after meeting. Lives alone in a nice place, but she's not doing any better than me.

Is there a creepy Lionel Richie character hanging around? Tom Noonan is the Tooth Fairy, a whack job that likes to slaughter families in their homes. This somewhat antisocial habit probably makes him an even worse house guest than Lionel Richie dancing on your ceiling. When the Tooth Fairy first meets Reba in the dark room, he's his usual nervous self before realising her disability. This results in a body language sea change. His subsequent interaction implies she has the innocent power to draw out his better side. In a rather contrived episode he then takes her to feel an anaesthetised tiger awaiting dental work. Er, what? He meets a blind girl and just happens to know someone who's got a zonked out tiger the same night? Anyhow, it's still a helluva scene as Reba runs her hands over its thick fur, touches its fangs and listens to its heartbeat. Her bewitchment is so convincing that it suggests it might be cool to occasionally be blind. Meanwhile, our fucked-up antagonist is leaning his head against the wall, apparently sharing the ecstasy of her sensations. At this point the movie is so good we almost forget he's a serial killer. Later in bed he listens to her heartbeat, another reminder of her purifying power, a power that's capable of making him cry.

Does she have a guide dog? No, which is probably just as well. The Tooth Fairy would only kill it and bury it in the backyard.

What did I learn about being blind? The blind can be very forward when they're horny. Reba gets in a car with a co-worker she doesn't know, goes to his home, and is all over him on the couch after half a gin and tonic. "You're a sweet, thoughtful man," she says while riding the Tooth Fairy's cock. Blind girls obviously choose men as badly as females in possession of all their faculties. If I were mean, I'd say *Manhunter* follows the horror cliché of punishing a woman for being sexual.

Best blindness-defying achievement: Perhaps the reason I'm fond of Reba is that she avoids any Susy Hendrix heroics when up close and personal with a demented killer. Indeed, she has the decency to turn into a ragdoll when an enraged six-foot-seven madman holds a shard of glass against her face.

Does she die? The Tooth Fairy might be an expert at slaughtering families, but he was always gonna be out of his depth trying to off a blind girl.

Disaster, 70's Style

Airport touched down in 1970, turning a $10million budget into a massive hit. It kicked off a decade-long cycle of star-studded disaster flicks that produced something of merit in *The Towering Inferno* before flaming out in a series of increasingly outlandish sniggerfests, such as pissed-off killer bees and exploding roller coasters. By its meek conclusion in 1980 (with the thoroughly unimpressive volcano-based antics of *When Time Ran Out*) the disaster flick was pretty much a byword for *crap*. Hollywood, however, is unlikely to accept the sub-genre exhausting itself in hammy excess and feeble special effects nearly half a century ago. No doubt the disaster movie will continue to periodically raise its groggy, heavily bandaged head and trick people into handing over their hard-earned cash.

Still, the question remains: Why did people flock to the disaster flick in the seventies? Perhaps they were feeling nihilistic with all that racial conflict, Nam protests, student unrest, riots, assassinations, terrorist outrages, economic gloom, presidential naughtiness, serial killer proliferation and ongoing superpower mistrust. Who knows? Or maybe they had a healthy yen for the often absurd characters, such as a floppy-haired Martin Sheen playing the mountain-climbing, heroin-smuggling fuck toy of a sarcastic cougar in 1976's *The Cassandra Crossing*. Personally, my money's on the fact we've always hated each other, leaving us happy to secretly revel in thousands of our kind being obliterated on the silver screen.

However, I'm more baffled by how a god-awful suicide bomber flick like *Airport* kicked off such a craze. Man, it's a turkey. Made at the start of cinema's greatest decade, it's so tame and awash with groan-worthy dialogue it feels like it's been vomited up from the fifties. After one hundred minutes of tedious soapy nonsense and lame attempts at light comedy I couldn't help thinking *excuse me, but where the fuck is the disaster*? You try getting interested in an annoying little old lady stowaway, a bespectacled teenage nerd talking about constellations, and tanned pilot Dean Martin going pro-life after knocking up a hot stewardess almost thirty years younger. It's so bad that disaster flick regular George Kennedy even explains at length why an onboard explosion would be bad news. Finally, our villain gets his moment in the spotlight but is so inept he only manages to blow a two-foot square hole in the fuselage. Did he let off a bomb or a firecracker? But don't worry, folks, because a Catholic priest has just been 'put in charge of praying'. Bloody hell, what sort of disaster movie is this? Only one person carks it and he was a sweaty loser that *planned* to die.

Terrible. Truly terrible. Almost two and a half hours of shite that somehow garnered *nine* Oscar nods.

There was an upside to the pseudo-disaster flick *Airport*, though. Things could only get better.

"This isn't some toy boat in a bathtub." *The Poseidon Adventure* (1972)

Preamble: Promising *Hell, Upside Down*, this catastrophe outing replicated *Airport's* success by becoming 1973's biggest box office hit and earning eight Oscar nods. More importantly, it's a better watch. A not exactly shipshape ocean liner is on its way to Europe on New Year's Eve when it loses a tussle with a quake-generated tidal wave. Much topsy-turvy shit ensues.

Is a doomsayer ignored? Well, the ship's captain (Leslie Nielsen) knows they need to take on extra ballast, but the *SS Poseidon's* dastardly new owners prefer speed over safety. "I can't afford to gamble with the lives of my passengers!" Nielsen cries. "Running an unstable ship at full ahead is dangerous, especially one as old as this!" However, threatened with demotion, he meekly caves in, gaining glorious revenge eight years later by spoofing such po-faced malarkey in *Airplane!*

How do the special effects hold up? *Poseidon* doesn't make *Airport's* glaring mistake of taking a fucking age to get down to the nitty-gritty. Less than half an hour in and the lookout is talking of an 'enormous wall of water' travelling at high speed toward the ship. Oh, goody. Unfortunately, the moment of collision is dealt with far too hastily. To be honest, it's almost skipped over, comparing badly to something like Cameron's *Titanic*. Otherwise, it's all acceptable. I quite liked the sight of the passengers hanging off bolted-down tables on the newly oriented ceiling and then dropping one by one. Sort of surreal, you know?

Most ridiculous character/relationship: For some reason we get an ex-hooker scared of bumping into her former johns on a cruise ship. I don't think this is very likely. I mean, I've banged a few hookers and never once taken a cruise afterward. Still, disaster movies often like to chuck in such colourful, outlandish types. Look at Shelley Winters. What did she use to be? The underwater swimming champ of New York three years running. At least she gets to employ her former talents whereas the ex-hooker doesn't once fuck anyone for money.

Elsewhere, Gene Hackman is a renegade preacher getting shunted off to Africa to do a spot of unplanned missionary work. I'm not sure how such a profession prepares him for being an ace survivalist or to know about technical things like a propeller shaft, but his ability to find his way through a flooded, overturned ship borders on the psychic. His climactic rant against God is also rather awkward and self-conscious. "We didn't ask you to fight for us," he shouts with a raised fist after another sucker bites the dust, "but damn it, don't fight against us!"

Worst line: After being told her brother (and fellow member of the ship's band) is dead, dippy folk singer Carol Lynley asks: "Did you like his music?"

Does a child die? The 70s disaster flick teaches us that a child's life is sacrosanct. Children must be rescued at all costs, as shown by Paul Newman saving two poppets in *Towering Inferno*. Adults, on the other hand, are ten-a-penny and eminently disposable. Just take a peek at *The Cassandra Crossing*'s red-haired little angel who survives pneumonic plague and bullets flying all around her to eventually offer the camera a close-up of her shocked, teary, but undefeated and ever so sweet face. In *Poseidon* we have to endure a freckle-faced, unbearably precocious brat named Robin who likes to use the bed as a trampoline, rag his teenage sister, learn about the ship's technical capabilities and hang out with the captain. Apparently the only child onboard, you know from the moment you meet him there's not a chance in hell of seeing his corpse.

Is George Kennedy, Ernest Borgnine or Charlton Heston in it? Kennedy, Borgnine and Heston were Oscar-winning tough guy actors. I've time for all three, especially as they enriched stuff like *Bad Day at Black Rock*, *Dirty Dozen*, *Cool Hand Luke*, *Planet of the Apes* and *Wild Bunch*. After making such a valuable contribution, they then got together and apparently decided to milk the hell out of the disaster fad while laughing all the way to the bank. Kennedy alone committed the heinous crime of starring in all four *Airport*-related flicks.

In *Poseidon* Borgnine is a cop in a constant strop, objecting to anything and everything, including suppositories, bad language and his sassy wife's lack of a bra. Mostly, however, he butts heads with de facto leader and fellow alpha male, Hackman. It's a fairly exhausting performance. Wins points, though, for clearly wanting to drown that irritating, know-it-all brat Robin.

Funniest death: An obese, soggy Winters. See below.

Who shits their pants or goes mad? Not *Poseidon's* strong point, we only get one scene of mass panic involving an unsuccessful scramble up a giant Christmas tree.

The inevitable self-sacrifice: There's a couple, but I'll focus on Winters. She shows immense bravery in rescuing Hackman when he gets trapped underwater. "In the water I'm a very skinny lady," she tells him once they're both safe. Her reward? An immediate fatal heart attack.

What does the token black do? In 1974's *The Towering Inferno* security guard O.J. Simpson rescued a cat. This should give you some idea that minorities don't get a lot to do in 70s disaster flicks. Catastrophe, you see, is whitey's concern. *Poseidon* is the perfect example in that I only spotted a solitary Indian passenger. She gets to sit next to Hackman, smile, raise a glass of champagne and look bizarrely out of place, even though she's on a cruise ship travelling all over the world. And no, she doesn't come close to doing something as significant as rescuing a cat.

Conclusion: *Poseidon* is reasonably inventive. As the passengers climb up through the decks, there's some suspense in trying to guess who's gonna die, especially when the ship gets rocked by periodic explosions and bouts of flooding. Its underwater engine room sequence is good. Indeed, it's tricky to mock *Poseidon* too much because apart from the often clunky dialogue and the weirdly insistent civility, it's competently put together.

"This used to be helluva town." *Earthquake* **(1974)**

Preamble: California sits on the San Andreas Fault, an unfortunate geological fact that saw a few thousand people wiped out in a 1906 quake. Given the growing popularity of disaster flicks, it made perfect sense to depict a monster quake striking the state's biggest city.

Is a doomsayer ignored? At the California Seismological Institute, a whippersnapper has already accurately predicted a sizeable tremor, prompting him to send the big boss a memo containing some worrying stats. "I know you'll laugh," he tells a colleague, "but I think we're gonna have a really big quake. Probably today, tomorrow at the latest." The big boss, meanwhile, understandably hasn't read the memo as he's busy out in the field getting buried alive.

Most ridiculous character/relationship: Ex-footballer and 'top man' Charlton Heston is locked in a sour marriage with Ava Gardner. She often tries to get his attention with fake suicide attempts and weird lines like "Don't you lower your voice to me!" Chuck copes with the stress of this disintegrating relationship by fucking a honey twenty years younger.

Meanwhile, Walther Matthau plays a garishly dressed drunk in a series of painfully unfunny scenes. Even when the quake is in full flow, his only concern is trying to get a shot of whiskey down his throat. "What do you have to do to get a drink round here?" he complains as the pub disintegrates and a barman gets crushed by falling masonry. Oh, my sides!

How do the special effects hold up? Although the earthquake takes more than fifty minutes to put in a proper appearance, it's quite well done. Things convincingly shake, fall over, drop on screaming people and blow up. There's nothing wrong with the scenes of mass panic. The bridge and building collapses are groovy. The stunts are well-handled. Buying a house on stilts in California is clearly not a wise investment while cleaning the external windows of a skyscraper during a quake should also be avoided. However, the ball is dropped when it comes to a packed elevator hurtling to the ground and we get *cartoon* blood splashed across the screen.

Is Kennedy, Borgnine or Heston in it? Kennedy is an angry, no-nonsense cop on the verge of quitting the force. Pre-quake, his disillusionment expresses itself by punching out a meddling fellow cop, assaulting a bloke in a pub, and being indifferent to a damaged hedge owned by Zsa Zsa Gabor. However, there are two times his otherwise relentless crustiness is interrupted. One involves rescuing a puppy, the other is when he gets mesmerised by Victoria Principal's chest.

Heston is his usual square-jawed self while playing a construction engineer whose job involves quake-proofing buildings. "We never should've put up those 40-storey monstrosities," he says at one point. "Not here." Disaster flicks often like to position themselves as cautionary tales. Just compare Heston's pithy observation to fire chief Steve McQueen telling architect Paul Newman in *Towering Inferno*: "You know, we were lucky tonight. Body count's less than 200. One of these days, you're gonna kill 10,000 in one of these firetraps, and I'm gonna keep eating smoke and bringing out bodies until somebody asks us... how to build them."

Funniest deaths: A man manages to drown in an elevator. Somehow it continues to work after being flooded. Aren't elevators electrical? Then a bunch of office workers flee down a shattered stairwell before running out of steps and jumping from a twenty-fifth storey window to their doom in a brilliant impression of lemmings.

Who shits their pants or goes mad? Marjoe Gortner is a curly-haired grocery store manager who hates Hare Krishnas (fair enough) and also puts in shifts for the National Guard. He's got a thing for Principal (fair enough) and her monstrous afro. His three knuckle-head housemates tease him about being a 'soldier boy' and a 'fag' as he has pictures of male bodybuilders adorning his bedroom wall. He doesn't help matters by then slipping on his uniform and a short-haired blonde wig. "Is it true that blondes have more fun?" a so-called mate continues to goad. Well, I guess it depends on your idea of fun coz it's not long before all three mates have turned into looters and been rounded up by the military authorities. "Scum like you think you can get away with anything!" Gortner barks before mowing them down with a burst of hot lead from his semi-automatic rifle in front of a handful of witnesses. Christ, he's gone nuts! Wait a sec, his instantaneous spell of hardcore insanity isn't over yet. He's now trying to rape Principal, who attempts to avoid such an indignity by claiming her brother is in the Mafia.

Does a child die? The main threat to pre-pubescent life takes the form of a kiddie getting trapped in a dam's concrete spillway while surrounded by recently severed electrical cables. You know, the dancing, spitting sort. Result? Near-immediate rescue, mild shock and concussion, reunion with ever so grateful mum. Very poor.

Worst lines: A tremor causes a pool player to fluff a shot. His opponent won't let him retake it. "Hey, nothing in the rule book about earthquakes," he says. I think you'll find this statement is correct. They then proceed to have a 'comedic' bar room brawl.

Elsewhere, Kennedy is consoling the hysterical Principal after shooting her National Guard would-be rapist. "Earthquakes bring out the worst in some guards, that's all," he blithely tells her.

The inevitable self-sacrifice: After spending a fair chunk of the runtime being pissed off at his loopy missus, Heston then decides to die by her side instead of letting her check out alone. Love, eh?

What does the token black do? As played by *Shaft's* Richard Roundtree, he's a motorcycle daredevil dressed in yellow and black leathers. His character is mildly obsessed with dissing that show-off Evel Knievel, although he stops short of insisting he's got a bigger cock. Roundtree is planning a fancy new show complete with loop-the-loops and fiery rings, but the quake puts an end to his planned bout of *Hey, ma, look at me*. Afterwards he sulks for a couple of minutes and then rescues a half-conscious child and panicking mum. Post-earthquake, he doesn't do any motorcycle stunts whatsoever which, of course, begs the question: Why give him such an unusual job in the first place? He could've been a plumber or baker with the same result.

Conclusion: The ten-minute quake is cool, the other 110 minutes not so much. Oh, and I think I'll be respectful to the next grocery store manager I meet, no matter what hairdo he's sporting.

"You mean, the stewardess is flying the plane?!" *Airport 1975* (1974)

Preamble: Heart attacks regularly pop up in disaster flicks. They're convenient, can happen at any stress-related time, and are cheap to film. Here a bloke flying a light aircraft is having ticker trouble. Seconds later his twin-engine motorised gnat has crashed into a jetliner containing one hundred and twenty suckers and knocked out all the pilots. Game on.

Is a doomsayer ignored? Given everything's down to a tragic accident, there's no chance for anyone to sound the alarm. Shit happens and all that.

How do the special effects hold up? The initial collision isn't well done, utilising back projection for the approach of the out of control light aircraft and a dummy being sucked out of the 747's cockpit. Indeed, the regular use of back projection and its grainier film stock whenever another aircraft comes close is blatant. Frankly, it feels like a TV movie.

Does a child die? Linda Blair plays a cheery kidney transplant patient and all-round adorable youngster. If ten nuclear-tipped missiles were fired at the plane, she would survive. There's also a metal-toothed kid travelling with his slightly cheesed-off mum. He wears a tie and often provides a running commentary on shit we already know. After the collision, he's the one doing the reassuring. "Remember, the 747 is the best aircraft ever made," he tells his mom. "It can almost fly by itself." Oh, Christ, please die.

Most ridiculous character/relationship: Well, a singing nun both catches the eye and offends the ear. The scene where she trills a bloody awkward paean to self-love ("*I'm as nice to me as anyone I know*") while strumming a guitar as the supine Linda Blair happily listens would have to rank among the most teeth-gritting of my life. Indeed, *Airport 75's* first forty minutes are peppered with inanity and not easy to sit through. Onboard there's a dog-smuggler, a lush, a pair of old biddies tittering over a racy book, a bit-part actor trying to catch his performance in the in-flight movie, an attempt at comic support from three aging drunken bums and, most bizarrely of all, Hollywood actress Gloria Swanson playing herself while carrying a bomb-proof case. None of this 'colourful' lot has any role to play once the disaster gets underway.

Worst line: *Airport 75* has plenty of odd dialogue, especially early on, but sometimes it's plain redundant. Upon seeing Blair wheeled onto the plane the nun explains to her fellow penguin sitting alongside: "It's a young girl." Thanks for that clarification, ma'am. And there was me thinking she was a senile old man.

Is Kennedy, Borgnine or Heston in it? Since *Earthquake*, Heston's fortunes have dipped a little in that he's gone from the lithe, uncomplicated, much younger Genevieve Bujold to the pushy, odd-looking stewardess Karen Black. He's also started wearing a turtleneck lemon sweater. Chuck, honey, that's not flattering. Anyway, he's an ace flight instructor, required to constantly patronise Black while saving the day.

Kennedy plays the same gruff character he did in *Airport*, except he no longer chomps on cigars. Given this is his second disaster and his wife and metal-toothed son are aboard this particular stricken plane, I'm starting to think he's a jinx.

Funniest death: 'Fraid not. We only get three deaths and they're chuckle-free.

Who shits their pants or goes mad? Mass panic and greedy, sociopathic shitkickers getting their just desserts are staples of the sub-genre, but *Airport 75* badly fails in this regard. There are no villains anywhere. Blandness reigns supreme.

The inevitable self-sacrifice: Another notable failure.

What does the token black do? A black passenger gets precisely one line. It's sport-related. Oh, wait a sec, there's also a black fellah in the helicopter rescue crew. His role calls for him to be as pessimistic as possible. "I must've made twenty drops in Nam, sir," he tells a replacement pilot about to undertake a highly dangerous attempt at a midair transfer, "but what you're gonna do scares the hell out of me." Thanks for that vote of confidence, mate. Sure enough, the pilot gets splatted, leaving Chuck to stick out his chest and get on with the business of being the manly hero. Luckily, he also gets some last-minute encouragement from our black friend: "This is just plain suicide, sir."

Conclusion: In the world of the disaster movie, men are in charge. Women tend to scream, dissolve into hysterics and occasionally get slapped, their ilk typified by *Poseidon's* Carol Lynley who can't swim and struggles to even climb a ladder. *Airport 1975* could have dealt a resounding blow to this epidemic of Silly Girlies when it placed trolley dolly Karen Black in the cockpit. A prime candidate for a Strong Female Role, yes? Unfortunately, she's a less than compelling presence and continually told what to do by her much more competent male counterparts.

Like *Airport*, this massively successful next instalment doesn't throw up enough stiffs. In addition, it falls between two stools. It fails to grip as straight drama yet isn't campy enough to snigger along with, despite so many of its scenes providing juicy fodder for *Airplane!* It gives the impression of being on autopilot, especially as it's essentially the same movie as its predecessor: a damaged plane needs to land.

Heston's garish turtleneck is also a constant distraction.

"I always thought survival meant being king of the mountain." *Avalanche* **(1978)**

Preamble: Given the title, can you work out what's gonna happen? Control freak and shady businessman Rock Hudson, who looks gayer with each passing scene, is busy doing his best to resemble Kim Jong-il's puppet in *Team*

America: World Police. He's also adding the finishing touches to his newly built ski resort.

Is a doomsayer ignored? Super-earnest environmental photographer Robert Forster is our man. He's dead against Hudson chopping down trees and other eco-vandalism. "You're risking the lives of everyone you're inviting here," he insists. "Things aren't normal. There's a heaviness, and it's growing." He's also worried about an incoming storm. I guess the question has to be asked: If this tree-hugger is convinced the place is gonna disintegrate, what the hell's he doing still hanging around? Yeah, well, Hudson's got the perfect riposte. "I want people to enjoy this land, not bury them in it." Do you think those words are gonna prove haunting?

How do the special effects hold up? The disaster is triggered by a light plane smashing unconvincingly into the mountain. The avalanche itself is stock footage stuff, but does give the impression you wouldn't want to be in its roaring way. Elsewhere people get buried by superimposed inundation. A gas explosion results in two chefs on wires being tossed around a kitchen. The drifts of polystyrene snow inside the resort are appalling for a $6.5million budget, although an ambulance cliff-top plunge is better handled.

Worst line: "I've never thought about it. I ski like I breathe or talk or make love." Downhill skiing champ Bruce Scott (Rick Moses), who obviously fell in love with himself a long time ago, answers a reporter's question about whether he's ever felt fear.

Most ridiculous character/relationship: An easy choice: Tina (Cathey Paine), Bruce's hot but helplessly lovelorn, occasionally hysterical and suicidal girlfriend. Why is she in the depths of despair? Well, she's already caught our arrogant champ *in flagrante* while we know he's also arranged to meet a sixteen-year-old girl in a bar. Tina loves him so much that during her latest pill-popping attempt she even wears a bright red T-shirt with BRUCE written on the front. Luckily, before she can swallow any pills, the avalanche kills her. What a Silly Girly.

Is Kennedy, Borgnine or Heston in it? Our Titans of Turmoil sat this turkey out. Their 'replacements', the paunchy, well over the hill Hudson and his ex-wife (the faintly annoying waif Mia Farrow) are somewhat lacking in star power. At one point Farrow goes AWOL for about half an hour, perhaps trying to put off the scene in which she has to give Hudson's beloved elderly mum mouth-to-mouth.

Funniest death: A figure skater keeps obliviously doing her spins as the avalanche bears down. Apparently gyrating on ice-skates makes your ears and eyes stop working. Oh well, at least she died doing what she loved best.

Who shits their pants or goes mad? The scriptwriter, I think.

Does a child die? There's a sour-faced kid in the bar throwing a paper airplane from a balcony onto the dancing crowd below. He then naughtily sips from a glass of wine. Next a child called Jason takes a ski lift with an unrelated man. Is it the same kid? I dunno. Kids all look the same to me. Anyhow, Jason gets stranded high up, dangling precariously from the ski lift. He gets rescued, shortly before the man thuds dead into the ground beside him. Sigh.

The inevitable self-sacrifice: *Avalanche* finds the perfect opportunity for Hudson to die while saving the badly mismatched, much younger Farrow, but inexplicably wimps out.

What does the token black do? Hudson must be a secret white supremacist because there are no brothers anywhere near his resort. The cast is as white as the snow.

Conclusion: I would never say that objectively *Avalanche* is a terrible film because there's nothing objective about a movie appraisal, but objectively *Avalanche* is a terrible film. It has the usual expository dialogue, fucked-up personal relationships, and good example of a Silly Girly, although it does manage to pull a surprise with a burst of nudity. By the time we get to the wham-bam stuff, well over half its runtime has been eaten up by the banal antics of figure skaters, cross-country skiers and snowmobile racers. Saying that, I still appreciated its hammy flavour. Moviegoers didn't, burying its woeful ninety minutes under an avalanche of indifference at the box office.

"Oh, my God! Bees! Bees! Millions of bees!" *The Swarm* (1978)

Preamble: The so-called Master of Disaster Irwin Allen produced two of the sub-genre's biggest hits in *Poseidon* and *Towering Inferno*. Suitably pumped up, it was obviously time to handle the directorial reins himself. In doing so he managed to deliver one of the worst-regarded films of all time. Two and a half uncompromising hours of pure fucking nonsense, fiery slaughter and mad *Apocalypse Now*-like poetry. This is delirious filmmaking that throws all caution and any semblance of commonsense to the wind. I think that makes Allen an auteur.

Is a doomsayer ignored? Disaster movies overwhelmingly tend to start with soapy, overlong bullshit. *The Cassandra Crossing* (with a terrorist raid on a top security US facility) and *The Swarm* are exceptions. The bees create havoc straightaway, stinging to death almost the entire personnel of an underground missile base in Texas. Bizarrely, none of the victims have any red, swollen signs of trauma. Perhaps they suffocated on bee farts.

Anyway, bug expert Michael Caine turns up to underline the threat and slip on an invisible clown nose. "There are probably other invading swarms," he announces while surrounded by serene-looking corpses, "and what these bees did here they can do again all over the Southwest and, ultimately, all over the country."

How do the special effects hold up? *The Swarm* has a big budget that is mostly spent on Allen's gleeful insistence on destroying hardware like helicopters and trains. Elsewhere, there are plenty of naff superimposed swarms and a less than successful attempt to put us in a bee's POV. Perhaps the worst effect is a shot of a real bee blown up to giant size whenever stung people suffer venom-induced, supposedly terrifying hallucinations. By the climax Allen is doing some sort of *Towering Inferno* rerun, complete with flaming bodies falling out of windows. I was more impressed by a handful of actors allowing themselves to be covered in bees. All over their faces and everything. Even if their stingers were removed, I wouldn't fancy that.

Most ridiculous character/relationship: In career nadirs, it's a tie between military man Richard Widmark and unbelievably smug entomologist Caine. Widmark plays the most humourless and dimmest general of all time, comparing badly to *The Cassandra Crossing's* subtly sinister Burt Lancaster. He delivers every line with the utmost seriousness, especially the ones where he hypothesises that the bees are taking revenge before crediting them with having equal intelligence. Convinced he's refighting Nam, he orders choppers into the fray, gets bombers to drop chemical agents, and sends battalions of flamethrowers into action. Mostly, however, he stares at people as if steam is about to shoot out of his ears.

At the start he's convinced the contemptible civilian Caine (with his pronounced fondness for wearing beige and snacking on sunflower seeds) is a combination of saboteur and mass murderer at his beloved ICBM base. You should see the look on his face when he's put under Caine's command about five minutes later. Having already infected Caine with his brand of military self-importance, Caine then starts pacing around with hands linked behind his back like Winston Churchill. "We have been invaded by an enemy far more lethal than any human force," he concludes, as if trying to galvanise a demoralised nation into fighting the six-legged threat on the beaches.

Caine and Widmark make a certifiably brilliant double act.

Worst line: Pretty much every bit of dialogue. Expository, hysterical, meandering, redundant, earnest, cringeworthy, phony, clunky, unintentionally funny and unbelievably stiff.... it's got the lot. The only type of dialogue lacking is the good. And all penned by an Oscar-winning scribe! If I had to pick a line, I'd plump for Caine's po-faced pearl: "The war that I've always talked about has finally started." Bloody hell, an evening in the pub with him must be fun. Allen's direction doesn't help, either, often leaving characters two feet apart to bellow at each other or awkwardly stand around in firing squad formations. I'd say it's on the level of a daytime soap but, then again, it's probably more like a school play.

Is Kennedy, Borgnine or Heston in it? Obviously, that glitch in the matrix hasn't been fixed yet. Still, let's give 'em a break, eh? In 1977 Kennedy was in the hit *Airport '77* while Borgnine was slumming it in a TV movie called *Fire!* about an inferno threatening some hicks. I dunno what Heston's excuse was, but it probably had something to do with learning his lines for 1978's cheese-free, routine and rather dull submarine disaster drama, *Gray Lady Down*. Whatever the case, by now it didn't matter who put their hand up for a disaster flick. The sub-genre was floundering, as demonstrated by Sean Connery helping to fire plastic nuclear missiles at a giant, slowly rotating, polystyrene rock from outer space in the 1979 fiasco, *Meteor*. Mia Farrow also didn't learn her lesson, ending up with her skirt blown over her face in the same year's big budget flop, *Hurricane*.

Funniest deaths: Two blundering army helicopter pilots go into a tailspin after a few seconds of contact with the bees. Another helicopter manages to withstand a ten-second onslaught before also plummeting to the ground. Maybe America's numerous enemies should forget about developing costly, ultra-sophisticated ground to air missiles and instead focus on launching beehives.

Who shits their pants or goes mad? Well, we get a corker here. One of those pesky bees lands on the back of a train driver's hand. "What do I do now?" he nervously asks a colleague. "Don't move, don't get him mad," comes the calm reply. The driver considers the response for a good second, then whips off his hat and tries to swat it. Bad move, buddy. A blizzard of bees invades the cab, obviously upset at this unjust execution of their friend. Now in an understandable panic, the driver loses control, resulting in the passenger train plunging down a mountainside and exploding. He won't be getting a raise.

Does a child die? Early on a picnicking family at a park gets attacked. Mom and dad are killed. Their young son Paul makes it to the safety of their nearby parked car. There are so many bees covering it that it darkens inside. He has to put on the windscreen wipers to see out. Paul manages to drive off, suggesting the average car is a lot more bee-proof than a military chopper. Not that he's a very good driver. He careens into town, smacking into other vehicles. It's a miracle no one's killed. The reckless little shit. Goddamn youth of today. Personally, I blame the parents.

And then just as I'm convinced *The Swarm* is built from the disaster movie blueprint, it does something wonderful. The winged foes attack a school killing, yes *killing*, at least eight kids, a scene complemented by the principal's comically overwrought anguish at the sight of their fallen, bee-covered bodies decorating the courtyard. Hallelujah, dead children, we have liftoff!

The inevitable self-sacrifice: Henry Fonda. He plays a wheelchair-bound scientist, although sadly we never get to see this Hollywood legend trying to frantically out-wheel a dense swarm of irritated insects. He's working on an antidote to the bees' deadly toxin, a process that eventually involves a self-test. For a few seconds it looks like he's about to save humanity. Then it all goes to shit. No matter. Fonda's absurd contribution is far more enjoyable than his tediously grumpy, Oscar-winning turn in *On Golden Pond* a few years later.

What does the token black do? As it has long been proven that black Texans possess natural immunity against killer African bees, it wouldn't have made much sense for Allen to cast anyone other than one hundred percent whites.

Conclusion: Inept from start to finish, *The Swarm* is also a continual joy, especially if watched half-drunk. Every performance is woeful, despite there being *nine* Oscar winners onboard, while the fantastic dialogue never fails to delight. The subplots, including an elderly love triangle and a mother falling in love with the doctor who just delivered her baby, are drivel. There's no cheesier film in existence yet I love it because it resolutely resists pulling any punches. For centuries to come people are gonna ponder how such an array of artistic talent and supposedly intelligent adults signed up for such astonishing shit.

"This thing's a goddamn powder keg!" *When Time Ran Out...* (1980)

Preamble: In 2019 a load of day-trippers were killed by a volcanic explosion on a New Zealand island. Oops. But, come on, what do you make of tourists who *choose* to wander around the rim of an active volcano? I guess I'm doing a bit of victim-blaming, but the goddamn thing had been routinely blowing its top for decades beforehand. Things get even sillier in *Time* where a hotel resort is built next to one on a Pacific island. All right, it's only gone bang-bang a couple of times in a thousand years, but that's twice too many for a pussy like me. Oh, and there's also a bunch of guys alongside this unstable geological wonder drilling for oil. In short, everyone in *Time* is a reckless bastard, fully deserving of what's coming to them.

Is a doomsayer ignored? Sulphur-sniffing oil rigger Paul Newman has got the volcano's measure. He knows it's about to jizz all over the holidayers. "Every monitor I've got shows pressure increases," he tells Charlton Heston lookalike and chief shitkicker James Franciscus. "Some of the readings are blowing the dials off the instruments!" Can he convince this greedy, adulterous corporate bastard with daddy issues to evacuate the place pronto? Well, whaddya think?

Worst line: "I was done in by an eccentric housewife on my paper round." Newman explains how he lost his cherry. Sadly, it bears no relevance to the plot.

How do the special effects hold up? They don't. Despite having a $20million budget, *Time* makes a right tit of itself while trying to convince moviegoers it's using anything other than models, clumsy superimposition and stock footage of bubbling lava. And where's the fucking ash and smoke? Although equally terrible, I didn't mind the volcano slowly launching laser-guided fireballs at the hotel. Most of the money clearly went on a studio set depicting the crossing of a lava-filled canyon, but it's as unconvincing as everything else.

Most ridiculous character/relationship: It's a routine Hollywood start in that a rich old bastard is lusting after young flesh. Hotel owner William Holden (in his early sixties) proposes to secretary Jacqueline Bisset who, in the decade since almost being blown up by a suicide bomber in *Airport*, has turned into a poodle-permed Suzi Quatro lookalike. To be fair to the craggy-faced Holden, the ballsiness of his wedding proposal has to be respected in that it ignores the facts he's already worked his way through *six* wives while Quatro, sorry, Bisset, is in love with the still handsome Newman.

We also get a way-past-it pair of circus tightrope walkers. One is Rocky's old trainer Burgess Meredith, who demonstrates his nerve-wracking, cat-like ability by using a makeshift bamboo pole to help him navigate the skeletal remains of a bridge over a pit of lava. Just to kill all suspense, he's also got a child clinging around his neck. The funniest thing about this overlong episode is there's no need to cross in this manner. It would have been far safer (and possibly faster) to lie flat on his belly on the six-inch-wide girder and shimmy over. I kept hoping Richard Roundtree, our redundant motorcycle daredevil from *Earthquake*, was gonna come up behind and knock the old coot off while zooming across on one wheel and waving to a cheering crowd.

Is Kennedy, Borgnine or Heston in it? Normal service has been resumed. Borgnine is back! He's a dogged cop hot on the trail of bonds smuggler Red Buttons. No, I don't know what a bonds smuggler is. Anyway, this whole pursuit is baffling. Does the New York policing budget stretch to such matters? Borgnine has already been tailing his quarry for three weeks and now they're at a luxury hotel. What evidence is he hoping to unearth anyway? "I've got five years to spend exclusively on your case," Borgnine tells his man. "I'm gonna follow you wherever you travel." Christ, no wonder crime was spiralling out of control in New York circa 1980 if this is indicative of the average detective's priorities.

However, things don't go to plan. A nearby exploding fireball results in Buttons saving his life, although a burnt Borgnine needs both eyes bandaged. Reduced to a doddery state of helplessness, cop and crim bond in a series of scenes so cringe worthy I wanted to hurl. At one point I thought they were going to kiss. You can almost hear Borgnine thinking: *I once won a Best Actor Oscar. I was in The Wild Bunch. How did this happen?*

Later, Newman has a red face as a result of being slugged, but I'd argue it's merely a case of sympathetic embarrassment.

Funniest deaths: Newman leads a plucky band of people up to higher ground, convinced the lava flow is going to swamp the hotel. Most of the islanders, however, remain behind. They all get wiped out by a fireball striking the hotel in a staggeringly hasty and cheap-looking denouement. All you can do is shake your head and smirk.

Does a child die? For the first fifty-five minutes we don't get a sniff of a kid, leading me to believe this particular holiday destination has been bold enough to ban them. Or perhaps such a child-free environment is merely an enticement aimed at counterbalancing the possibility of fiery death. Then Newman rescues two kids in his helicopter while one of the less important adults clinging to the skids falls to his doom. Later, we see the children's father with his arms around his offspring telling them: "Don't worry, we'll make it."

And, of course, daddy doesn't and the kiddies do.

Who shits their pants or goes mad? "If we don't go now, we're all gonna die," one frightened extra pronounces upon spying Newman's recently landed helicopter. The blue touch paper has been lit, folks. Now it's time for a bout of contagious panic and fisticuffs as scores of people try to cram inside. Amazingly, one of them appears to know how to fly it, but this doesn't stop the whirlybird wonkily getting into the air, spinning a few times and crashing into a mountainside.

The inevitable self-sacrifice: Well, don't I look silly? There isn't one. Perhaps this absence is the only way *Time* breaks the disaster movie mould.

What does the token black do? I think this particular island is operating under apartheid or some form of racial cleansing. There's barely a black anywhere. Or perhaps they're too smart to go near a fucking volcano on the verge of an earth-gasm. When it comes to minorities, the best that can be mustered is a pre-*Karate Kid* Mr. Miyagi playing a Chinese gambler. Instead of trying to catch a fly with chopsticks, he plunges into a ravine full of lava. Banzai!

Conclusion: *Time* is enjoyable crap that manages to chuck in an earthquake and a tsunami. It's far better than that snorefest *Airport*. However, its poor special effects, contrived love triangles, and Bisset's atrocious perm didn't exactly tempt the movie-going public. In fact, *Time* tanked, effectively ending this mad wave of disaster flicks, a sub-genre that had peaked six years earlier and been dying ever since. People were tired of the predictability and cheesy clichés, instead turning en masse to sci-fi. *Airplane!* merely provided the final sniggering nail for the disaster movie's corpse-packed coffin.

Blaxploitation #8: Coffy (1973)

Synopsis

I'll let the tagline do the talking: *They call her Coffy and she'll cream you!*

Director

Jack Hill

Cast

Pam Grier, Booker Bradshaw, Robert DoQui, William Elliott, Allan Arbus, Sid Haig

What the hell are these crazy cats up to? Coffy's eleven-year-old sister is in a juvenile rehab centre trying to kick smack. It's obviously time for our heroine to tackle LA's growing drug problem by setting up a Neighbourhood Watch, noting down any suspicious activity and passing on the information to those upstanding boys in blue. Then again, perhaps that wouldn't make the best film. Instead Coffy plumps to square up to the drug-dealing baddies herself, armed with a sawn-off double-barrelled shotgun and an even more fearsome pair of breasts.

Is there a racist cop keeping the brothers down? All the white cops appear corrupt and happy to hand out a beating, but (unlike the white gangsters) they're not particularly racist. However, one problem they do have is Coffy's former boyfriend, who happens to be a black cop. He's got some unhealthy, Serpico-like ideas about resisting corruption and working with the people to tackle the city's smack scourge. This dude is sincere, polite, honest, thoughtful, and good at his job. Clearly, he has no place on this particular police force.

How are the bitches and hos treated? Without exception, the women are prostitutes, topless dancers, casual lays, dope fiends or lovelorn mass murderers. For the most part they endure submissive, decorative lives in a man's world, mainly because the consequences of getting stroppy might result in a slashed face. Still, Coffy's no crusader for equal rights as she's happy to wave a broken wine bottle in a hooker's distraught face or attack a sister. She's an intensely sexual creature who uses her voluptuous body to trick or manipulate men into getting what she wants.

However, despite her chutzpah, she is routinely insulted, belted across the chops and sexually assaulted. For example, take her encounter with Vitroni (Arbus), the top dog white gangster. He's a short, curly-haired pervert who calls Coffy a 'wild cat from the tropical jungle' before forcing her to the floor and spitting in her face. "Get down on the floor where you belong," he barks, "you no good, dirty nigger bitch!" Elsewhere, an innocent nightclub photographer is threatened with having an exposed breast cut off. Men are relentlessly depicted as abusive bastards. You're unlikely to see a more anti-male pic unless you happen to stumble across a dour little British number by the name of *Stella Does Tricks* in which every man is a pedo, gang rapist, pimp, thug or deceitful heroin junkie. *Coffy* is slightly better balanced, given it manages to boast one decent guy.

Do I dig the threads? It's the early 70s so expectations are rightly low when it comes to looking good, but *Coffy* doesn't offer a fashion disaster until the arrival of our resident pimp, King George (DoQui). He's not quite as outrageously flamboyant as the titular pimp in *Willie Dynamite*, but this moustachioed, chauffeur-driven flesh peddler still manages to don a light brown jumpsuit with an off the shoulder cape, a wide-brimmed hat, oversized orange sunglasses and a silver-topped cane. In short, he looks like a cross between a stereotypical pimp and a wannabe superhero. I kept expecting him to start flying through the air, a laser beam shooting out from his cane to singe the lazy ass of any underperforming ho. King George also gets extra points for having a theme song: '*George... George... George... They call him Mr. Cool/Don't play him for a fool*.'

Does it have funky music? Right off the bat, this one grooves, even if some of its songs are the most basic compositions possible, often consisting of little more than a couple of lines. The title ballad *Coffy Baby* borders on outright fibbing by labelling her 'sweet as a chocolate bar' and as 'gentle as a song'. Er, what? Has the vocalist seen the sort of uncompromising shit she doles out in this flick?

Best jive talk:

"I go away for half an hour for you to turn a trick and when I come back I find you balling some nigger bitch, you white tramp!" A butch black lezzer, unimpressed by Coffy visiting her drug-addicted hooker girlfriend, has a gentle word in the ear of her beloved.

"This is the end of your rotten life, you motherfuckin' dope pusher!" Coffy gets down to business.

"You gonna fly through those pearly gates with the biggest fuckin' smile Saint Peter ever seen!" Coffy succinctly explains the benefits of a forced overdose to the aforementioned drug dealer.

"Are you sure you're not just a little black?" Coffy tries some flattery while stroking a white gangster's penis.

"I'm gonna piss on your grave tomorrow!" Good grief, wash this girl's mouth out with soap and water.

Are any hard drugs injected into eyeballs? Not quite, but this is a pic that's swimming in dope. Unlike *Super Fly*, a movie which treats dope-dealing as a viable way out of the ghetto, *Coffy* is strongly anti-narcotics. Watch out for an ambitious city councillor giving an insightful speech on the black/white realities of the drug trade.

Are there any pimps roaming the hood? King George is perhaps my favourite character here. He's presented as a cool pragmatist, although is fooled by Coffy's daft Jamaican-flavoured patter that she adopts on the basis of knowing about his predilection for 'exotic' women. At least George has the nous to check out the goods firsthand before putting her into his employ. He also keeps a scantily-dressed mini-harem in his home, obviously practicing the old adage *variety is the spice of life* in that he's got a black girl, two whites, and an Asian broad. Or as he succinctly tells Coffy pre-bonk: "They'll do." What's more, although he's exploiting them left, right and centre, they still appear to love his silky skills in the sack. "I need some real action, honey," one devoted, frisky blond tells him, "like the kind I can only get from my old man." George is a drug-dealing stud and (in his eyes) a fashion icon that gets to live off the immoral earnings of a stable of horny call girls. How come no teachers at my school ever talked about this kind of stuff while discussing career options?

Is *Coffy* any good? A year before Paul Kersey took to the streets, Coffy was blowing scum away in this full-on vigilante pic. Pam Grier is not the strongest actress and her attempt at a Jamaican accent during one seduction scene is probably the low point. No matter, as her splendid, frequently exposed breasts never fluff their lines. *Coffy* also happens to be a fast-moving, action-packed flick, a strength that helps gloss over its deficiencies. Ably directed by Jack Hill, an exploitation maestro who later gave us the amusingly bonkers *Switchblade Sisters*, *Coffy* is far nastier in both its dialogue and incident. Halfway through there's a bloody marvellous catfight which sees blouses torn open and women rolling around the floor as a ring of chortling men debate about intervening before correctly allowing the tit-exposing action to continue. It's the sort of disgraceful female behaviour you crave seeing in real life. Apart from that, there's a plethora of violence, such as a head getting blown off, a baseball bat beating, and a ghastly dragging death, as well as frequent nudity and a fair few zinging one-liners. In fact, *Coffy* has an unhealthy take on humanity full stop, offering a misanthropic hour and a half that borders on nihilism. Amazingly, its closing song then tells us 'revenge is a virtue' while labelling Coffy a 'shining symbol of black pride.' Nevertheless, this dubiously rightwing pic established Grier as a black icon as starkly as Richard Roundtree two years earlier in *Shaft*.

Coffy is a key blaxploitation pic. It's not in the same class as a seventies crime classic like *The Taking of Pelham One Two Three*, but it sure is an entertaining watch.

Do I now have a Tarantinoesque urge to be black? No, *Coffy* basically depicts a mini-civil war, but I could be tempted to be Coffy for half an hour or so in order to find out what a leisurely shower feels like.

The Return of Graham Chapman

Given the amount of movies I watch and my generally obnoxious personality, you might think I don't have any friends. Well, you're wrong. There's one British military gentleman who's always happy to sit by my side and share the silvery wonders of the big screen. His name is the Colonel and we love to delve into a big bag of popcorn while indulging our mutual passion. And so we laugh at a film's funny bits, become gripped by its heart-pounding drama and, like all men, refuse to look at one another whenever anything sad happens.

The Colonel is not the perfect movie companion, though. I mean, he can get a bit pompous. Well, if I'm honest, *very* pompous. For a start, he has this curious objection to guys with long hair. That's why it's always tricky to watch late 60s/early 70s stuff with him. Plus, he does start to lose the plot whenever a flick drops below his rigorous standards and becomes (to use his word) *silly*. In fact, he hates silliness, especially if a film has otherwise been good. Sometimes it so upsets him that (and I swear this is the truth) he gets up and strides straight into the movie to see whether it's possible to get things back on track. I must admit the first time he did this I was a little disorientated. You see, it's not enough for him to vociferously voice his complaint or have an earnest discussion with me about a perceived flaw. Oh, no. He often has to tell the characters concerned to their *faces*. Not only that, but if he feels things are particularly silly, he insists the scene stops or starts trying to redirect it. "Get on with it!" he might bark at them as he impatiently paces in his neatly pressed uniform.

And, between you and me, I don't think those talented, hardworking actors appreciate it.

The soggy demise of The Wicked Witch in *The Wizard of Oz* (1939)

I gotta be truthful, sometimes The Colonel puts me on tenterhooks. He can be as good as gold for well over an hour into a movie and then jump up and launch into a tirade. Take *The Wizard of Oz*, one of the 20th century's greatest pieces of entertainment. I know he loves it as much as me, but there's one bit that gets his goat every time. I'm talking about The Wicked Witch's hackneyed, unbelievably sudden defeat. One minute the green-faced hag is in her cackling element at her castle surrounded by foot soldiers and those bloody creepy flying monkeys, the next she's *melting*. Why? Because she gets inadvertently splashed with *water*. "You cursed brat!" she screams at Dorothy as hissing clouds of vapour radiate from her rapidly dissolving form. "Look what you've done! I'm melting! Melting! Oh, what a world! What a world! Who would have thought a good little girl like you could destroy my beautiful wickedness?"

Great last words, yes, but unless I missed it, there's no foreshadowing. We know the Scarecrow is vulnerable to fire, but we don't have the faintest clue that some simple H2O is the equivalent of Superman's Kryptonite to the witch. Does this mean she never goes out when it rains? That all her supernatural powers are useless when there's a bit of drizzle about? Whatever the case, the manner of her death smacks of lazy writing. After all, Margaret Hamilton's performance is indelible and the Wicked Witch of the West is hands down one of moviedom's greatest villains. She deserved a much more spectacular defeat, like being on the end of a Drago-style punch, yee-hawing and waving her hat while riding a flying bomb, or falling off the Empire State Building sans broomstick. I guess she was never gonna get stabbed to death in the shower, though.

Clint Eastwood fucking up in *Play Misty for Me* (1971)

There's a reason *High Plains Drifter* starts by having a mysterious stranger ride into town, kill three men without fuss, and then drag a flirtatious, sexy woman off to a stable to rape.

Atonement.

Huh...? Atonement for *what*?

Well, The Colonel tells me it's Clint's attempt to make up for a woeful, barely believable six-minute sequence two years earlier in the slow burn psychological thriller, *Play Misty for Me*.

Clint, you see, was doing fairly well for the first seventy minutes of his directorial debut playing a horndog late-night DJ in a small coastal town. However, his bed-hopping results in a stalker sinking her fangs into a bollock and threatening his on-off romance with his True Love. Oh, if only he could stop waving his cock in all those other ladies' faces and tell her how he feels! Luckily, his newfound bunny boiler trashes his house and carves up the domestic help, a double whammy that enables Clint to unleash all his pent-up emotion.

What a shame this avalanche of sincerity results in the loss of his mind. Or artistic judgement at the very least.

And by that I mean he makes the tenderest, most earnest love of his life while communing with nature and being egged on to ever greater passion by Roberta Flack's interminable *The First Time Ever I Saw Your Face*. Christ, is this the same guy who taught us how to be a Real Man in the likes of *A Fistful of Dollars*, *Kelly's Heroes* and *Where Eagles Dare*?

Anyhow, back to *Misty*. First we see Clint and his True Love walking hand in hand along a windswept beach as a quavering Roberta warbles about the sun and stars. Then they're in a forest. Dewy fronds abound. Now it's dark. I dunno, perhaps they've found a cave. Roberta's begun trilling about snogging, prompting them to snog. It doesn't get much more literal than that. Hang on, it's daytime again – how long is this fucking walk? Now they're waist deep in a pool clinging to each other with frightening intensity. I think I see the Colonel disguised as a pixie scampering around in the background. Clint, however, hasn't noticed. He's too busy getting horizontal on the forest floor and doing the entwined limbs thing. Their lovey-dovey stroking has become so intense they can no longer open their eyes. How long will this condition last? Are they gonna try to go home while bumping into tree trunks and tripping over rocks? Perhaps they might even stumble over a cliff.

We can only hope.

Four minutes in, Roberta's moved onto stuff about a captive bird's trembling heart and joy filling the Earth as we see an outstretched arm on the moss-covered floor, its hand unfurling like a flower before the sun's ecstatic caress. Now they're walking toward an ocean-bound sunset with arms wrapped around one another. This must mean they've been ambling for two days. Or maybe it's the sun*rise* of the third day. Have they gone camping without a tent? Roberta's certainly feeling the strain, sounding so histrionic I think she's gonna *burst*. Finally Clint and his True Love pause in silhouette on a rocky outcrop for the most perfect and meaningful kiss in the history of humanity, unperturbed by a nearby pixie hurling his guts up.

Oh, Clint, even in *The Bridges of Madison County* you weren't this unbearably soppy. Don't you ever do that again. Now go and tread on Scorpio's bullet-wounded leg.

The Ewoks kicking stormtrooper arse in *Return of the Jedi* (1983)

It's always a pleasure watching *Star Wars* and *The Empire Strikes Back* with the Colonel. Sometimes we even turn as one and parrot the lines to each other. He loves Vader doing his deadly throat grip on incompetent subordinates while I'm fond of those awesome, animal-shaped AT-ATs tripping over their feet on the ice planet Hoth. For the most part we both enjoy *Jedi*, even if it does repeat the original's storyline about the need to blow up a Death Star. Still, there's nothing wrong with Jabba's malevolent grossness or the curvy Leia heating up the screen in her gold bikini. We also like the good guys zipping through the forest on those cool, tree-dodging flying machines.

Then, of course, we meet an Ewok prodding an inert Leia with a spear and the Colonel starts to sigh. I thought we'd arrived on the forest moon of Endor when in actual fact we're in the middle of Cutesville. Hooray for the koala-men, so fucking dumb they think the mincing C-3PO is a god worthy of worship. Worse is to come when one jumps on a speeder bike to lure those ever-predictable stormtroopers away. Given the Ewoks are a tribal race with no grasp of technology, how does this particular 'little fur ball' know how to operate it? Never mind. Let's get on with them executing a near-perfect military plan against the supposedly well-drilled, battle-hardened stormtroopers. I guess it helps their galaxy-conquering enemies fall for every trick in the book, but that still doesn't explain why their laser weapons, armour and a handful of ultra-cool AT-ST Walkers are no match for bows and arrows, catapults, lassos, some rolling logs, nets, a few chucked rocks and an excited parade of stiffened, furry cocks. Ten minutes earlier these hirsute dwarves were scared of their shadows, but now they're mini-Rambos! Honestly, watching vine-swinging Ewoks leap onto stormtroopers carries about as much conviction as a burly, armed Ollie Reed being overpowered by a handful of murderous imps at the end of Cronenberg's *The Brood*.

I imagine George Lucas took inspiration for this pie in the sky spectacle from the Vietcong downing America's mighty Marines less than a decade earlier, but as I've argued before, movies strangely need to be *more convincing* than real life to work. The Ewoks are not warlike and apparently have no enemies on Endor so how come they've become experts in guerrilla warfare in five minutes flat? Oh, what does it matter? Cracks are appearing in *Jedi* all over the place now. Vader, the biggest badass this side of Jupiter, is about to turn into a wimp. "I feel the good in you," Luke tells him. "The conflict." Vader's not having it. "There is no conflict," he baldly states. And I should bloody hope not, Darth.

Yet it's a big fib. Not only has Vader just lost a lightsaber duel with his vanilla son, but now he's putting family before the glories of ruling the galaxy. The fucker's gone all gooey. This is the worst betrayal of a character in the history of art. I just... no... I can't...

You know, I once watched *Jedi* after smoking a joint only to see Vader's mask being removed and the Colonel's face staring back at me.

Robert De Niro trying a bit of ocular semaphore in *Angel Heart* (1987)

Every time I sit down to watch *Angel Heart* I do my best to like it. After all, it has a prime Mickey Rourke, a steamy New Orleans setting, voodoo, interracial fucking, a moody score, bags of atmosphere and severed genitalia being stuffed into a gob. You know, my sort of shit.

But it's a flick that sure does agitate the Colonel. He starts twitching around the time De Niro's character Louis Cyphre shows up to hire the private investigator Harry Angel (Rourke). Yes, Cyphre is clearly a cultured, softly spoken, well-dressed gentleman, but that long hair and those talons will never do. Such indulgent personal grooming would not pass muster in the British Army. Or as the Colonel surmises, Cyphre might be able to peel a hardboiled egg with aplomb, but would he be able to do fifty push-ups or rapidly load a gun in the heat of combat with fingernails like that?

Still, *Angel Heart* mostly skates along on its good production values and Grand Guignol feel. So what if the story doesn't make a lick of sense? *Angel Heart* is gory *fun* and there's nothing wrong with that. But then writer-director Alan Parker decides to go the literal route, prompting the Colonel to reach for his Vaudeville hook. Cripes, is he really gonna yank one of the greatest actors of his generation offstage, a double Oscar winner no less? I'm afraid so. There's only so much silliness a military man can take.

The unshaven, increasingly agitated Angel, you see, is suffering an identity crisis, a quandary that is milking precious little sympathy from his shady employer. Well, that's not much of a surprise given we've just learned the cane-twirling Cyphre is the devil. "The flesh is weak," he tells Angel, who's staring red-eyed into a mirror as his world disintegrates. "Only the soul is immortal." Angel then turns from his tortured reflection to see Cyphre showing off a pair of luminous yellow peepers while pointing at him and declaring in a gravelly voice: "And yours belongs to me!"

The damning revelation isn't helped by the lackadaisical Cyphre failing to find the energy to even stand up. It's surely the cheesiest moment in De Niro's storied career.

Wrestling for an explanation in *They Live* (1988)

I once read a review of *They Live* that said director John Carpenter was trying to dig for big ideas with a toy shovel.

Ooh, catty.

And, to be honest, I wish I'd thought of it.

They Live is not his best effort, hampered by mediocre acting, an inherent superficiality and a clunky, bullet-ridden finale. Carpenter's listless direction also ensures it lags a long way behind a masterpiece like *The Thing*. Still, there's a growing amount of love for this sci-fi account of a sneaky alien invasion to the point some fans treat it as a *documentary*.

Hmm... people. What the hell can you do with them?

Anyhow, *They Live* might not be as classy as a similar-themed flick like 1978's *Invasion of the Body Snatchers*, but I enjoy its premise that we've been infiltrated and taken over. Or as a blind street preacher tells us: "They have taken the hearts and minds of our leaders. They have recruited the rich and the powerful. They have blinded us to the truth. The human spirit is corrupted. They have us! They control us! They are our masters! Wake up! They're all about you!"

They Live's opening doesn't do too much wrong, especially its pivotal scene forty minutes in where our longhaired hero (calm down, Colonel) discovers a fancy pair of sunglasses that enables him to see subliminal messages everywhere (e.g. *don't question authority* and *stay asleep*), as well as the aliens' skull-like, otherwise hidden faces.

This is good stuff and undoubtedly nirvana for conspiracy nuts. It starts to badly wobble, though, when a kidnapped woman sends our muscular hero flying out of a window and tumbling down a hill. It's a gruelling fall that should have snapped his neck, but its implausibility proves a mere aperitif for the barminess of Carpenter's decision shortly afterward to have our recently ejected hero fight a similarly brawny bloke in a garbage-strewn alley.

For *six minutes*.

This prolonged slugfest always makes the Colonel loudly exhale, purse his lips, fold his arms and tap a foot. After all, *They Live* is primarily a sci-fi/horror flick. It's not *First Blood: Part II* in which it's fine for Rambo to battle a Russki aboard a helicopter and throw him out of the cabin to his doom.

So what was Carpenter thinking? I imagine he meant such a ludicrously elongated fight to be funny. Or some sort of parody. It's definitely not meant to be taken seriously anymore than *The Fast Show's* Long Big Punch Up. Whatever it is, it's bizarrely out of place and only succeeds in stopping things dead in their tracks as effectively as Clint's forest-dwelling, super-earnest cock in *Misty*. The flick never recovers.

The Colonel, however, would like to see a better written remake minus the silly fisticuffs.

Max Cady takes us for a ride in *Cape Fear* (1991)

Do people give a fuck about Scorsese's quieter, more personal projects such as *Kundun* or *Silence*? Or do they want to see the gangster-loving maestro orchestrate in your face mayhem? I suspect the latter, as typified by a snarling, puffed up piece of nastiness like the successful *Cape Fear* remake.

This is a rapey, face-chomping flick that makes the Colonel wince early on. However, upon regaining his composure he does begin to act like he has the upper hand. Not that he's got anything to work with in the first seventy-five minutes. No one in their right mind could sneer at Bernard Hermann's amped-up score, the excellent foreshadowing and the glorious cast, which includes a burgeoning Juliette Lewis, a highly strung Jessica Lange, the incompetent, faux tough guy Joe Don Baker, and a bespectacled, slimmed-down Nick Nolte effectively cast against type with his pastel suits and neatly combed short hair. However, the star attraction is the cigar-wielding, garishly dressed, white trash ex-con Cady (De Niro) hovering on the periphery of Nolte's fractured family like the embodiment of a violent storm. Unlike Louis Cyphre, Cady's a fully fleshed character with his sly humour, feral intelligence and self-righteous anger. He's also a scary motherfucker, his single-minded malevolence typified by the way he strides out of prison and straight at the camera until his muscular frame blots everything out.

No, the Colonel has to wait until a shredded Nolte hires three goons to do over Cady. From here onward Scorsese's sweaty psychological grip starts to loosen and we instead have to settle for a tense, but increasingly implausible series of events. What the hell is Cady? Is he actually human or some biblical incarnation of vengeance? How can he not only withstand being beaten with lead pipes but then turn the tables? How does he sneak into a guarded house, kill a Mexican housekeeper and don her clothing without anyone noticing? Perhaps he's a psychopathic, mindreading ninja on angel dust. No, maybe he's a *supernatural*, psychopathic, mindreading ninja on angel dust. Whatever the case, he's stopped behaving like a recognisable human being. It's exciting shit, all right, but it's *nuts*. Scorsese doesn't care. Nolte and his family are now fleeing to the titular Cape Fear river but Cady, ever one step ahead, has strapped himself to the underside of their four wheel drive. And we're not talking for the duration of a jaunt around the corner, but for hundreds of kilometres. One bump and the back of his head would be staved in. And how do you strap yourself to the underside of a vehicle anyway? It's so daft, so left of centre that it borders on genius. Did I say I thought Cady was supernatural? On second thoughts, maybe he's a cartoon character.

To be fair, I believe Scorsese is adopting a deliberately OTT approach, the first hint of which was Jessica Lange getting up in middle of the night in her bedroom to put on lipstick only to see through the window a relaxed, cigar-smoking Cady perched on a perimeter wall as the sky is peppered by fireworks. That's some weird shit right there which I'm not even sure is literal. (In fact, I interpret it as a rape fantasy). Then again, art is a weird thing and it can still tickle your soft spots despite having major flaws. By now the Colonel's marked disapproval should have made me turn the goddamn thing off, but I can't help loving *Cape Fear*. It's a superbly paced fever dream jam-packed with memorable scenes, full-blooded acting, and a director at the top of his gruesome game. Yes, it's bollocks, but it's meaty, sizzling bollocks so the Colonel (who, as usual, is right about its myriad improbabilities) can take a po-faced running jump on this one.

Liam Neeson failing to shut the fuck up in *Schindler's List* (1993)

You wouldn't expect The Colonel to pop up during Spielberg's acclaimed Holocaust drama, would you? He's certainly out of sight whenever Amon Goth is randomly shooting people from his balcony, a bad boy so magnetically handsome in his dashing uniform that it's not hard to believe such Aryans *are* genetically superior. Neither do we get a glimpse of the Colonel when a ghetto is being liquidated or children are hiding up to their necks in liquid shit in a concentration camp latrine. No, the Colonel stays right by my side for three hours straight. There's nary a fidget or the slightest harrumph from the old boy. Until, that is, the Red Army gets on the front foot and a fleeing Schindler shits the bed with his long, teary, monumentally unnecessary speech about how he could have saved more Jews.

Composed, impeccably dressed, and with a potentially life-saving letter signed by his workers tucked away in his pocket, all the guy has to do is walk out of the factory grounds, secure in the knowledge he's nailed a charismatic, memorable role in a perfect film.

But, no.

Things start to go wrong when Itzhak Stern (Ben Kingsley) hands him an engraved gold ring. Schindler wells up. They shake hands, prompting him to confess: "I could've got more out." Stern shakes his head, reminding him he's already saved 1100 people. It's a fair point, but Schindler won't have it. "I didn't do enough," he insists. Now he's got a masochistic taste for it, psychologically pulling out a flagellant's three-knotted whip to beat himself. Everything's a torment. He could have sold so much more, raised more money, bribed more Nazis. He stares at his fancy car, obviously disgusted at the sight of its gleaming chrome. "Ten people right there." Then he pulls a gold pin off his suit, a little unsteady on his feet. "Two people." Suddenly he's sobbing, clutching Stern, and falling to his knees. Perhaps he knows he just lost the Best Actor Oscar to Tom Hanks. The knowledge makes him bawl – how could he lose to an AIDS-stricken left-footer? – and he has to hide his face in Stern's chest. If only Spielberg had insisted on some restraint, if only the editor had done his job… The Colonel is now on screen, unable to prevent the watching Jews from flocking to their distressed saviour. "Stop this maudlin clumsiness!" the Colonel cries. "It's silly! The movie has already excelled at depicting an initially self-centred character finding his moral compass and growing a set of steel balls so there's no need to spell everything out. Show, don't tell, people. Show, don't tell!"

It's no good. The Jews ignore the appeal. Neeson has disappeared beneath a group hug, the mass of bodies muffling his faint cry: "My Oscar! I'll never get a better chance..."

Mel Gibson's gutsy bellowing in *Braveheart* (1995)

The Colonel would like to state on the record that he has never been tortured to death. There was a hazing incident early on in his career as a fresh-faced private that involved a bowl of strawberries, some industrial-strength glue and a somewhat confused goat but the Colonel usually remains schtum. If he ever does speak about that wet weekend in an Aldershot barracks, it's only after a cognac or two and to reveal he maintained a stiff upper lip. Furthermore, he believes such ordeals in the modern British Army are necessary, character-building and ultimately a fine way to make new chums.

However, hazing is one thing, disembowelment another. The Colonel certainly draws a distinction between the two. If he'd been disembowelled, he doubts he would have held onto his dignity. Indeed, he's not ashamed to admit he might even have blubbed. He therefore finds it unlikely that a man can not only maintain his composure while undergoing such trauma, but holler his *raison d'être* into the face of his tormentors.

And so to the Oscar-winning *Braveheart* in which the freedom-obsessed Scottish upstart Mel Gibson does just that. The Colonel is disappointed by this credibility-defying outburst as up until its unfortunate inclusion he found *Braveheart* to be a stirring, hugely enjoyable military romp complete with arse-baring defiance, terrific cinematography, a charismatic villain who's not averse to tossing an incompetent homosexual out of a castle window, top-notch production values, and bursts of fantastic gore during the wonderfully staged fights and battles.

Hollywood is Hollywood, though, a fact that often requires a satisfying narrative arc during which we're bludgeoned over the head with whatever message is the *saveur du jour*. And so Mel gets betrayed and captured by his English oppressors, a change in fortune that enables him to display a degree of steely fortitude that beggars belief. "Confess and you may receive a quick death," he's told by a none too sympathetic magistrate. "Deny and you must be purified by pain."

Flipping 'eck, the realm is gonna get all medieval on his ass. That don't sound like much fun, but as this movie's climax has been designed with the beatification of Mel in mind there's no way in hell he's gonna ditch his principles and play ball. "Give me the strength to die well," he asks his God while standing in a cell as mock-fighting dwarves entertain the bloodthirsty crowds waiting outside. And so he's hung, drawn and quartered, a chastening process that you may have thought turns a man into a screaming piece of unintelligible, bleeding meat.

Apparently not so in Hollywood.

Mel's steaming intestines might be piled on the floor, but he's still got the conviction and lung power to bellow *FREEDOM!* In his darkest hour he has stayed true to himself, a heroic display of martyrdom that has reduced most of the main players to tears. Bloody hell, Mel's murdered sweetheart is even smiling and mingling with the previously hostile, vegetable-hurling crowd. What's more, if you look carefully off to the top right, you can see God nodding approval.

This movie has disintegrated. Who the hell directed these outrageously sycophantic scenes?

Oh.

Brad Pitt and Edward Norton driving the Colonel up the wall in *Fight Club* (1999)

Despite enjoying a reputation as a Real Man's movie with the odd on-the-money scene and some bursts of pithy dialogue, The Colonel does not like *Fight Club*. He finds it dreary, overlong and nowhere near as clever as it thinks it is. This pronounced slide into silliness is primed by two episodes. Firstly, Norton sits down in his boss' office to dish the dirt on the company's dangerously reckless manufacture of automobiles. Upon dishing it, he's fired. No surprise there, especially when you factor in his dishevelled appearance and regular absenteeism. Not that he's bothered. A heartbeat later he's having a go at blackmail in a bid to buy his superior's silence.

"Who the fuck do you think you are, you crazy little shit?" is the boss' perfectly reasonable reply while picking up a desk phone to call security. With a trembling fist, Norton then punches himself in the face so hard he knocks himself backward off his chair. The pencil-neck boss looks on in dismay. "What the hell are you doing?" he asks as Norton delivers a self-inflicted uppercut that sends him crashing onto a glass table.

Norton, you see, is framing his chief as a violent bully in a bid to extort a regular paycheque. Oh, what a clever ruse!

The boss, however, drops the phone and stands there like a statue. Why doesn't he leave the office when confronted by this wanton display of claptrap? Why does he just watch Norton beat himself up? Surely this particular regional manager has a secretary in the next room? And even if she's at lunch, why does no one else bother investigating such a loud, prolonged disturbance? Meanwhile, Norton keeps flinging himself around, destroying furniture and repeatedly twatting himself. All the boss has to do is walk away or wait the charade out before showing colleagues his unbruised hands and unruffled attire.

A little later (and obviously determined not to be outdone by his co-star), Pitt muscles in on the increasingly daft action. Pitt and Norton go for a drive in the pouring rain and quickly get into an argument about Project Gay-fem or whatever it's called. Pitt's not driving too well, and certainly failing to take into account the inclement conditions. "Guys," he asks the two obedient lemons along for the ride on the back seat, "what would you wish you'd done before you die?"

"Paint a self-portrait," comes one of the replies. Oh boy, that sure beats my desire to fuck a trampolining cheerleader in midair…

By now the speeding car is weaving across the centre lines and flirting with the oncoming traffic. "Forget about what you think you know," Pitt tells

Norton. After a string of near-misses, his agitated front seat passenger can only cry: "I am sick of all your shit!"

Although the Colonel does not approve of bad language, he does, however, agree with this basic sentiment.

Pitt then lets go of the wheel, prompting a panicking Norton to yelp: "Quit screwing around!" Pitt, however, won't have a bar of it. "Look at you!" he bawls at Norton. "You're fucking pathetic... Stop trying to control everything and just let go. LET GO!"

The Colonel shakes his head. Maintaining control of a vehicle and thus avoiding a potentially life-ending, head-on collision is not an example of 'trying to control everything'. It's not even close. It's simply a combination of practicality, self-preservation and courtesy to other road users. Only blabbermouth dunderheads in possession of a supposedly profound but unworkable philosophy could possibly think otherwise.

But, hang on, Norton's once again succumbed to Pitt's cocksure twaddle. "Fine," he says, slumping back in his seat.

And so the uncontrolled car goes happily looking for an accident... Christ, Norton beating himself up was a staggeringly naff attempt at black comedy, but this whacked-out driving stunt is too stupid for words.

Now the Colonel is not a malicious man, but he sure does wish *Fight Club's* next scene is this self-torturing pair stuck in wheelchairs looking contrite as one stares at the stump of a leg while the other pisses into a colostomy bag.

This is Spinal Tap (1984)

Synopsis

Bizarre gardening accidents, matching cold sores, silver foil-encased cucumbers, and the ardent desire to make eardrums bleed.

Director

Rob Reiner

Cast

Christopher Guest, Michael McKean, Tony Hendra, Bruno Kirby, Ed Begley Jr.

I often argue movies are made-up nonsense that have no effect on me. Like a lot of things I say, I'm probably on dodgy ground. Consider *Spinal Tap*. Good grief, the first watch was a minor revelation. Up until its chastening, palate-cleansing introduction in my mid-twenties, heavy metal could do little wrong. That's why I happily owned albums such as Krokus' *Metal Rendez-vous*, Whitesnake's *Slide It In*, Def Leppard's *Hysteria* and Saxon's *Wheels of Steel*. I even planned to do some headbanging at the UK's annual Monsters of Rock festival where I might be blessed to catch the unquestionably mighty sounds of Y&T or Dio.

Well, midway through my first viewing of *Spinal Tap*, that vague desire to make a Castle Donington pilgrimage was stone dead. Talk about the clouds of ignorance parting. It was so on the money I could only shake my head as I realised the average heavy metal band consisted of ridiculously dressed, overgrown adolescents churning out guff about their sexual prowess, rebellious nature, reverence for the rock lifestyle, and an undying love of motorbikes, goblins and dragons. All while waggling their tongues and thrusting their hips. I switched *Spinal Tap* off, unable to do much more than stagger across to my album collection and stare half-dazed at it. How was it possible to believe I'd developed a modicum of taste when I owned a Twisted Sister single?

Nonetheless, *Spinal Tap* didn't make me chuck the hearing-damaged baby out with the bathwater. I still retain enormous fondness for the creative efforts of *some* of those longhaired doofuses. It just made me a lot more discerning. In a way, I liken heavy metal to my love of horror. Ninety-five per cent is shit but when a heavy metal song or a horror flick like *The Thing* work they reach a level no other style can. Sabbath's *Paranoid* still sounds good, as does Purple's *Speed King*, Motorhead's *Ace of Spades* and ACDC's *Sin City*, but such reliable reassurances don't last too long coz it sure ain't hard to tell that most metal gods are adrift on a sea of liquid cheese.

To try to understand how immune they can be to their special brand of naffness, I recommend spending a few minutes with Judas Priest circa 1980. Now *Spinal Tap* wasn't quite powerful enough to stifle my appreciation of Priest's 70s stuff, but it did make me grasp that their latter-day credibility had tumbled down a steep hill. Take their breakthrough album *British Steel* and its lead single, *Breaking the Law*. Its accompanying video shows the band robbing a bank by bursting in and letting fly with their music, the implication being that their ear-shredding guitar solos are akin to bullets from a gun. They then steal their own framed gold record from the vault.

And no, I'm not making that up. To this day I'm puzzled why the band simply didn't *ask* the bank manager for their gold record. After all, it is theirs.

Breaking the Law is a fantastic slice of cheese because it's meant to be funny yet it falls so flat on its face that it becomes funny because it's so *unfunny*. Does that even make sense? But that's what trying to break down heavy metal's appeal is like. So much of it is ridiculous yet wonderful. *Breaking the Law* remains a perfect encapsulation of its gloriously absurd world. Judas Priest, by the way, learned nothing from *Spinal Tap*, later releasing a lumbering, thirteen-minute epic about the Loch Ness Monster.

Bless 'em.

And so to Reiner's *Spinal Tap*, a pitch-perfect mockumentary that gets rewatched every few years, even if it does stir up deep-rooted memories of shame. The director plays an avowed fan following an English five-piece band called Spinal Tap as they tour North America in 1982 to promote their latest album, *Smell the Glove*. Straightaway the clichés are captured, such as the too tight trousers, the onstage acrobatics and mishaps, the near-orgasmic self-expression, the demonic imagery, and the way guitars are aggressively wielded like huge penis-guns.

Childhood mates David St. Hubbins and Nigel Tufnell (McKean and Guest) form Spinal Tap's heart, having played together for seventeen years. Both are lovable morons that believe they're making great art, even though their songs have titles like *Big Bottom*, *Sex Farm* and *Lick My Love Pump*. Indeed, the band's failure to grasp their outdated attitude to the ladies is a recurring source of humour. Witness Nigel's response to accusations that the band's latest cover (which features a naked woman on all fours in a dog collar) is sexist. "What's wrong with being sexy?" he innocently asks. This is where *Spinal Tap* scores big in that there's nothing mean-spirited about the group in either their attitudes or behaviour. They're simply oblivious to their idiocy, enabling the viewer to smile along when they sing about women being sunk by pink torpedoes.

Indeed, criticism often bounces off, such as one newspaper writer labelling *Smell the Glove* as a 'colossal waste of time' that shows the band is 'treading water in a sea of retarded sexuality and bad poetry.' Nigel can only shrug. "That's nitpicking, isn't it?"

But the less than enthusiastic reception of the new LP proves a telling omen. Before long, offended shop owners are refusing to stock it while gigs get cancelled. Those that go ahead are not exactly overflowing with fans, leaving the band's manager to deny any suggestion the band's popularity is fading by instead insisting their appeal has become 'more selective'.

Spinal Tap's understated, superbly edited eighty minutes serve as a microcosm for the chequered history of many a heavy metal colossus. Here we get fragile egos, jealous dismissals of other bands, flirtations with Celtic mythology, songs about God and the devil, projects that never see the light of day (such as a Jack the Ripper musical), delusions of grandeur and artistic integrity, a procession of unfortunate drummers, the ups and downs of life on the road, a resented Yoko Ono-like girlfriend imposing her mumbo-jumbo on whoever will listen, the weird isolated chart success in Japan and, of course, the bust-ups, walkouts and reunions. None of the band acknowledges their advancing age or the draining of whatever little creative juice they initially possessed. Throughout it all, myriad bit players, ranging from disrespected limo drivers to airhead fans trying to explain metal's appeal, fit in seamlessly. There's not a bum note anywhere and I'd argue that the Stonehenge segment is among the funniest moments in 80s cinema. Some of it even proved prescient, such as Metallica releasing a black album and later playing with a symphonic orchestra.

By *Spinal Tap's* closing stages nothing has been learned and nothing has changed. Thank God. Reiner never judges or points a finger, obviously preferring gentle ridicule that can't quite manage to disguise his deep affection for heavy metal's inherent silliness. He ends up with a mockumentary that pulls off the trick of being patently absurd and yet somehow within the realms of plausibility.

To put it another way, he walks that fine line between clever and stupid.

Men Gotta Have Fun

I've always believed religion fucks you up and thank God it did just that to Paul Schrader. Raised in a strict Calvinist household, he famously didn't get to see a movie until his late teens. No matter, because once he dipped an intellectual, alienated toe into the celluloid pool the floodgates opened. Not long afterward he was penning legendary scripts like *Taxi Driver* and making his directing debut with 1978's excellent *Blue Collar*. Specialising in existential angst and simmering male misfits on the verge of violence, he has remained a prolific contributor to cinema for nearly half a century.

Blokes with a death wish: *Taxi Driver* (1976) and *Rolling Thunder* (1977)

Schrader's first two scripts, *The Yakuza* and *Obsession*, were heavily fucked about with, giving him firsthand experience of how little power a novice writer has within the industry. Then he hooked up with Scorsese, a director who had the balls to be faithful to the power of his dark visions. The result was cinematic glory for both.

In the decent doco *Easy Riders, Raging Bulls*, which explores the rise of Hollywood's studio-challenging filmmakers between 1969 and 1980, Schrader explains *Taxi Driver's* origins. "I was in debt, I wasn't making any money, my marriage had fallen apart... I didn't have much of a place to go or much of a life. I took to wandering and kind of drifting around. And it was out of that period of drifting and drinking that I started having this pain and I went to the hospital and had an ulcer. Twenty-six years old. I realised in the emergency area I hadn't spoken to anyone in weeks. I just drifted around in this car, sleeping in it, and so the metaphor of the taxi driver came to me."

And what metaphor is this? Essentially, the taxi cab as a mobile coffin, driven by a dead man who's interacting and functioning yet continually alone and falling apart. You can debate how much of a stand-in Travis Bickle is for Schrader himself, but there can be little doubt of the parallels between the two. This naked honesty (along with inspiration he took from studying the diary of a real-life would-be assassin) enabled Schrader to produce one of the 20th century's greatest screenplays. *Taxi Driver* has since set in stone a host of traits for all those budding psychos that popped up in Bickle's wake: pumping iron, diary keeping, awkwardness with women, acting out in front of the mirror, an altered hairdo, delusions of importance ("the sensitive nature of my work for the government demands the utmost secrecy"), self-pity ("I'm God's lonely man") and fatalism ("My whole life has pointed in one direction. There never has been any choice.")

Schrader's misanthropy-soaked script, though, is careful not to concentrate on Bickle alone. Indeed, *Taxi Driver* boasts a rich array of supporting characters in its fully realised world, such as Easy Andy the gun salesman (Steven Prince), the loathsome Sport (Harvey Keitel), the badly dressed child hooker Iris (Jodie Foster) and the warm, wisecracking political campaigner (Albert Brooks).

However, it's Bickle who dominates virtually every scene. Schrader captures his diseased personality instantly. We see a workaholic existing on a diet of shit. This is a racist, inarticulate freak who sits alongside other silent misfits in a porno theatre after he's finished cleaning cum and blood off his taxi's backseat. He's drowning in loneliness and can only think in extremes. Betsy (Cybill Shepherd) is the first female he fixates on, seeing her as an angel floating above New York's scum-filled streets. Or as he muses: "They... cannot... touch... her." But such idealisation can never last and it isn't long before the possibility of salvation has disappeared and he's publicly yelling at her: "You're in a hell and you're gonna die in a hell like the rest of 'em!" Like the stinking thinking of so many mass murderers, he's caught in that curious contradiction of being convinced of his superiority yet unable to demonstrate one iota of it. What's left but to orchestrate a bloodbath? At least violence is a way of being noticed, of making that long cherished contact with the rest of the human race.

The truth is that all along Bickle has wanted to put a gun in his mouth. He hasn't so far because it chafes against his misplaced sense of pre-eminence. Instead he half-grasps he has to do something extreme, some excessive act that will provide the trigger to act on his intense desire for self-annihilation. Anything will do, whether assassinating a public figure or 'saving' an underage girl from her criminal abusers, because once that line has been crossed there's even less point to living. His death wish is shown when his murder spree ends with him trying to blow his head off, defeated by an empty chamber.

As for its much-discussed coda, I see it as one long fantasy in which the dying Bickle imagines the newspapers declaring him a hero and Iris' parents penning a gushing letter of thanks. Then the elusive, angelic Betsy gets into his cab, obviously awed by his scum-eradicating presence as he plays it cool. To take such events literally is surely a mistake as that would give Schrader's creative masterpiece a *pat* resolution and I'm not having that.

Rolling Thunder is nowhere near as well known or influential as *Taxi Driver* but often feels like a companion piece, especially during its similarly violent house of sin shootout. It was rewritten much to Schrader's chagrin, but unlike the slow, odd *Obsession* still seems to have been penned by our man. This is because its main character Major Charles Rane (William Devane) shares a lot in common with Bickle. He's also a Vietnam vet, a reticent, adrift insomniac who works out. The war gave Kane a much tougher time, though, resulting in years of imprisonment and torture. It's no wonder he (and his similarly traumatised buddy Tommy Lee Jones) both act like automatons during their homecoming. Readjustment to an America they barely recognise proves impossible, partly because Kane's young son doesn't even remember him while his wife is heavily involved with another man. Bickle liked to burn his hand over the stove, but Kane prefers re-enacting a VC torture session with his cuckold. This sense of masochism is reinforced when he refuses to cooperate with a bunch of home invaders, resulting in the loss of a hand. Before he goes after them, he puts on his army uniform, suggesting he's restaging the war and that violence creates repetitive patterns.

The excellent Devane gives a still, tightly wound performance. He's like a man in a room trapped by his spiralling thoughts. Throughout *Rolling Thunder* there are plenty of signs he died some time ago and just wants a burial. When he hears a song on the radio, he comments: "I remember that song from when I was alive." Later he says: "It's like my eyes are open and I'm looking at you, but I'm dead. They've pulled out whatever it was inside of me." A new woman comes into his life but her love can neither save him nor alter his imminent violence. "You know," she tells him, "you don't have to do any of this. You don't have to go after these guys. We could just jump in the car and go a thousand miles from here and nobody would know any different. Bury the guns in the desert." She gets no response because Kane (like Bickle) feels he has no choice. The only escape is to enter a tunnel that hopefully leads to a ghastly form of redemptive darkness or better still, obliteration.

Sexy stuff: *Hardcore* **(1979),** *American Gigolo* **(1980),** *Cat People* **(1982) &** *The Canyons* **(2013)**

In quick succession Schrader put together a trio of flicks built on somewhat unhealthy sex, but failed to score even a solitary bull's eye. They're still important watches to get a handle on the guy, though. The less said about his final effort, *The Canyons*, the better.

First up was *Hardcore*, a neo-noir drama about a bewildered Calvinist (based on Schrader's dad!) trying to fish his wayward teenage daughter out of the world of porn. With Schrader in charge of a self-penned script and George C. Scott anchoring the movie, it should've been a grimy classic.

Instead it gets my vote as the most disappointing entry in Schrader's body of work. Goddamn it, how did he mess up such fascinating subject matter? Just compare its start to *Taxi Driver*. In Scorsese's flick the tone is captured straightaway by a yellow cab ominously bursting through a cloud of steam to Bernard Hermann's legendary score, but *Hardcore* offers a bunch of kids playing in the snow as a country and western singer warbles over the top. Hmm, all right, we're in the deadly dull Midwest, but things remain a little 'off' all the way through.

Jake Van Dorn (Scott) is a successful Michigan businessman whose virginal daughter happily toddles off to California for a religious convention. He appears to be a decent, likable guy, but Schrader does a poor job in building up their relationship. They don't even have a conversation before she disappears, giving us no explanation why she swaps a secure and loving home for fucking strangers on camera thousands of miles away. This must be deliberate on Schrader's behalf. Perhaps he's trying to say you never know what's going on in somebody's head, even if they're blood. Still, the decision to neither flesh out the relationship nor offer the slightest reason for the daughter's impulsive decision to become a sucky-fucky collection of orifices does make *Hardcore* feel like it's built on cum-spattered sand.

Van Dorn's a dull character, resolutely untempted by the array of overripe, half-rotten fruits that litter his path. Frustratingly, *Hardcore* doesn't manage to do much with his religion, either. At one point a churchy friend tells him: "Sometimes it's hard to understand the Lord's ways. He's testing you. You have to have faith." Van Dorn doesn't even start to contest this placatory crap, even though it appears his mate is suggesting it's all right for God to drop a wholesome young woman up to her little titties in smut simply so her dazed dad can pass some sort of celestial entrance exam in the future.

Hardcore also introduces a sketchy super-villain far too late, is full of ropey performances, and never gets anywhere near *Taxi Driver's* epic sleaziness. The whole thing lacks teeth and isn't much better than the dreadful Nic Cage vehicle, *8mm*. Yes, there's some amusement to be had as the conventionally dressed, teetotal 'pilgrim' Van Dorn prowls L.A.'s sordid streets, but things lurch into absurdity when he slips on a wig, gold necklace and tash to pose as a porn producer. Mind you, at least this gives us the chance to meet Big Dick Blaque (Hal Williams). "I can cum ten times a day," he boasts during his audition. "I can keep it hard for two hours at a time. I'm a woman's dream. I got a dick hung on me nine inches long." Ah, the confidence and arrogance of youth. Indeed, I remember trotting out much the same stuff to a junior school teacher.

American Gigolo is another glum, action-light pic, although at least it rang the box-office bell. It was initially perceived as a Travolta vehicle before being hilariously offered to Chevy Chase. Instead Richard Gere took on the mantle, establishing himself as a star in the process. Gere's not a fave and I'd argue his career has been a disappointment, but I always enjoy his *Officer and a Gentleman* turn. However, he's well-cast here and deserves some sort of plaudit for being brave enough (unlike George C. Scott) to get his cock out. There's not much else to applaud, though. For the most part *American Gigolo* plays like a dour flip version of *Pretty Woman* in which a gorgeous male hooker is in control, living the life and never once dealing with the hideous realities of genitalia-selling night after night.

Gere is Julian Kay, a hollow, blatantly narcissistic Patrick Bateman forerunner lacking the murderous violence. He's a preening prick who likes cruising around L.A. in an open-top Merc to the groovy sound of Blondie. Otherwise you'll find him lounging in an upmarket cafe clad in Armani sipping Perrier while giving the ladies the eye or just being half-naked in front of a mirror. He specialises in servicing older women, telling one: "I'm gonna get you wet. Very wet. I know how to do this."

Ooh, Julian, you smoothie.

Like *Hardcore*, the suspense-free *Gigolo* occasionally flickers into life, such as when Julian gets landed with a Palm Springs 'rough trick' husband who enjoys watching his wife being banged. "Slap that cunt," he urges Julian. Suddenly the movie promises to exploit its dark potential, but there's a persistent feeling Schrader, who wrote and directed, doesn't have full control of the provocative material. It slips through his fingers, ending up as a languid, near-stillborn experience. Like the main character, it's all surface, no depth, although I enjoyed the brief sight of Gere on a gay nightclub dance floor surrounded by a bunch of Village People wannabees. Ultimately, though, *Gigolo* is a duff two hours which left me wishing Chevy Chase had been cast. At least that would've been *funny*.

Schrader tackled horror for the first time with his eroticised update of 1942's historically important but rather boring *Cat People*. Thankfully, it's saucier than *Hardcore* and *Gigolo* with the sensuous Nastassja Kinski probably not having been this nudie since her super-naughty, borderline illegal debut in *To the Devil a Daughter* six years earlier. *Cat People* has an intriguing start with Bowie crooning the title song over an image of a red desert as the wind gradually uncovers skeletal remains. Schrader segues into a prologue that depicts an ancient tribe leading a young maiden to a dead tree and sacrificing her to a black leopard.

OK, I'm in.

In modern-day New Orleans the virginal Kinski hooks up with her long lost brother (the always wacky Malcolm McDowell) only to find out they're werecats. Families, eh? Has anyone got a normal one? Being a werecat basically means it's less hassle to fuck a sibling because if you do it with a non-relative then you have to go through the rigmarole of transformation, slaughter and picking out human flesh from between your teeth. "You can't escape the nightmare without me," McDowell tells her, "and I can't escape without you." Schrader touched upon incest in *Obsession*, but it's a lot more up front here, seasoned with a little bondage and an amusing episode of hooker-mauling.

Cat People is my pick of Schrader's sexy stuff, although I'd still label it a Not Quite pic. Kinski (and her extraordinary face) is the best thing about it, especially when she starts to accept her feline nature by prowling naked through the undergrowth while alive to the sounds of the night. Elsewhere, her groggy brother gives a good impression of the world's worst hangover by waking up on the bathroom floor only to stagger into a different room to find his busty casual pickup dismembered. There are a lot of nice visuals in *Cat People*, aided by Giorgio Moroder's smooth electronic score and a reasonable attempt at an *American Werewolf*-type transformation.

Cat People is mostly barmy fun, but the crowdfunded, mysteriously titled *The Canyons* is another action-light, too talky failure. Its main problem lies with Bret Easton Ellis' terrible script rather than Schrader's brightly lit direction or its lead casting of a real-life porn star. No one does vapid, superficial, materialistic arseholes better than Ellis but, *American Psycho* aside, he usually fails to fit them into a compelling story. *Canyons* is supposedly erotic and does manage to offer some big tits and swinging dicks, but ends up humourless, dreary and resolutely unsexy. It's the most critically reviled pic in Schrader's catalogue.

The biographies: *Raging Bull* (1980), *Mishima* (1985), *Patty Hearst* (1988) & *Auto Focus* (2002)

Raging Bull is an essential watch, but it's the kind of unsentimental, uncomfortable two hours that's easier to admire than love. Jake LaMotta (De Niro) is an archetypal angry, destructive and self-destructive Schraderian character, although he stops short of being suicidal. From what I can gather Schrader was brought in to rewrite someone else's screenplay before his efforts were rewritten and built upon, leaving his contribution to *Raging Bull* a wee bit murky. As such, I'll return to this modern classic at a later date to look at it from another angle.

The well-regarded *Mishima: A Life in Four Chapters* has to be my least favourite Schrader. Mishima, like Jesus in *The Last Temptation of Christ*, is definitely one of Schrader's men with a death wish, but this is a relentlessly talky, stagy and dull two hours. It's also pretentious and avant-garde, adjectives I don't normally associate with Schrader. Worse, it doesn't make me wanna seek out anything from the acclaimed Japanese writer's extensive body of work.

Schrader's next biopic tackled Patty Hearst, an unusual move in that he put a woman front and centre. By that I mean his oeuvre demonstrates he finds the extreme behaviour of men much more appealing. Fair enough. So do I. Unfortunately, Schrader was jumping on the bandwagon as Patty's barely believable 1974 ordeal (in which the abducted teenage heiress graduated to robbing banks with her misfit captors) had already been filmed at least four times by the time he got round to it. *Patty Hearst* doesn't bring anything new to the table.

Schrader repeats his *Hardcore* mistake in failing to flesh out Patty's (Natasha Richardson) family ties. I don't think we get one pre-kidnap shot of her with her mum and dad or friends, undermining its emotional impact. Instead she has to tell us: "I grew up in a sheltered environment, supremely confident. I knew, or thought I knew, who I was.... There is little one can do to prepare for the unknown."

Too true, baby.

Then she's bundled into a car boot by the Symbionese Liberation Army, an inept bunch of pseudo-military, Commie blowhards. "The people have declared war on the fascist American government," they politely inform her after chucking her blindfolded ass into a closet. "The revolution is happening right now, bitch."

Boy, this is one confused handful of bourgeois-hating, urban guerrillas. They want to be poor but rob banks; they're apparently working for the people but are happy to point guns at their heads. Oh, and sex is a 'revolutionary act'. All of them are rhetoric-spouting caricatures, permanently frothing at the mouth about 'hungry babies' and 'corporate enemies'. Like any fanatics, they don't know a joke between them and are fucking boring to listen to, but at least their ladies do half-naked push-ups. After five minutes in their shrill, over-earnest company you can't help being on the side of the 'pigs'. Schrader presents these Che Guevara wannabees as resentful clowns, but sadly stops short of outright satire (although I did enjoy Patty's confession to her abductors: "I'm really struggling to overcome my bourgeois upbringing.")

Patty Hearst is watchable, non-essential Schrader, even if it's rather choppy and lacking in any killer scenes. I don't think Schrader sinks his claws into the titular character anywhere near as deeply as someone like Bickle. Perhaps that's because it's more difficult to conjure up an explanation for the madness of real-life events. Patty, who gets the benefit of my doubt when it comes to her criminal commitment to the SLA, probably sums it up best: "I'm not sure what happened to me."

It's much easier to tell where *Auto Focus*' Bob Crane (Greg Kinnear) goes wrong. The poor sod can't keep his dick in his pants. It's like a penile Godzilla rampaging through his life that, on the surface, is sedate and conservative. Now I don't believe in sex addiction. Those who claim to have it are cowards trying to excuse poor, consciously chosen behaviour by presenting themselves as helpless victims. It's a classic case of refusing to accept responsibility for your actions, a belief system that can excuse the likes of alcoholism, kleptomania and paedophilia. However, Bob (the erstwhile star of classic TV sitcom *Hogan's Heroes*) sure does his best to convince such an all-consuming condition exists.

Schrader previously aired his fascination with porn and sordid sex in *Taxi Driver* and *Hardcore*. The former featured Bickle thinking a first date at a porno cinema was a good idea while the latter gave us a devastated George C. Scott enduring an eye-opening film of his missing teenage daughter getting jiggy with two guys. Schrader plunged back into smut with *Auto Focus*, the seedy story of a man on the up who opens Pandora's Box and tries to fill it with jizz.

The flick starts on a pitch perfect note with a big band swing number accompanying the title credits in which we're reassured 'a little hanky-panky gives the boot to Mr. Cranky'. Bob is doing fine as a radio DJ but is itching for a big TV break. The script for *Hogan's Heroes* lands on his desk around the same time he meets the liberated, less than ethical home video expert, John Carpenter (Schrader favourite Willem Dafoe). It's a heady mix and suddenly our slightly dull, ardent Christian hero is playing drums in strip clubs, attending swinging parties, having orgies and secretly videoing naked conquests. Hey, haven't we all done that?

Bob's slide into sex addiction, sorry, wilfully fucking and photographing every piece of skirt that comes near his permanently engorged cock, is well done. It's understated, dispassionate and believable, the result of character flaw, chance, and the intoxication of fame set against the backdrop of mushrooming sexual freedom and the darker side of technology. The clean-cut Kinnear is excellent as the hypocritical churchgoer, a faithful husband who's initially so naive about his newfound opportunities that when a floozy tells him she'll do anything he wants, he simply asks to keep the lights on. The needy, equally pathetic Defoe (complete with darkened irises) pretty much plays Satan, continually whispering temptation into Bob's ear. *Auto Focus* is a smoothly directed, intelligent watch with some sly undercurrents of humour. It's among Schrader's best.

Crime: *The Yakuza* (1974), *Light Sleeper* (1992) & *Affliction* (1997)

Schrader's intellectualism is hard to miss. I'd say this talky approach (along with a perverse insistence on perfunctory or plain dull titles) is the main barrier to his flicks reaching a wider audience. Most start with a voiceover, a telltale sign that action's gonna take a backseat. Schrader's never been the go-to guy for wild car chases and rip-roaring explosions, you know? Even in his best movie *Taxi Driver* there are only two action scenes: Bickle shooting an armed robber in a corner store and the climactic slaughter. Schrader has long shown he has no interest in putting together the equivalent of *Commando*.

His repeated forays into the crime and neo-noir crime genres (which you might expect to have a fair bit of action) illustrate this reluctance to portray sweaty, out of breath characters or white-knuckle sequences. His first screenplay to see the light of day was *The Yakuza*, a pic he co-wrote with his brother (which was then extensively rewritten). Despite dealing with Jap gangsters, there's not a whiff of violence in the opening thirty-five minutes. Indeed, it prefers to concentrate on the good guys and the oriental obsessions with honour, obligation, duty and face to the point I'd argue it's a misnamed pic. The yakuza are left to potter around in the background rather than tear the screen up. They're presented as honourable with a definite code instead of coke-snorting, bloodthirsty savages preying on the average Joe. A shame, as we instead have to watch them sitting around in oversized nappies smoking, bowing, gambling and barely raising their voices. *The Yakuza* is a respectful portrait of modern-day Japan. Too respectful, really, as the flick takes an age to shift into third gear. If you want to boil *The Yakuza* down to its essence, it's the story of a man getting to the point where he can rationalise the voluntary amputation of a finger. I'd love to tell you that makes it finger-choppin' good, but the combination of its anaemic villains and an over the hill star turn from Robert Mitchum mean it's solid rather than spectacular. Yes, there's a closing bloodbath that proves to be a *Taxi Driver*/*Rolling Thunder* forerunner, but it's too little, too late.

Taxi Driver gets echoed again in *Light Sleeper* in that our main drug-dealing character is a diary-keeping insomniac who ends up with a gun in his hand. There's little to recommend it, though. Just like 1990's *The Comfort of*

Strangers, there's no action whatsoever in its opening hour. Even a key suicide is not depicted. Instead we have to make do with the backdrop of an irrelevant garbage strike, a dwarf cop trying to act tough, and the soundtrack's grating, half-arsed songs. Reputedly Schrader's most personal film, I'd put it (along with 2021's *The Card Counter*) among the former coke addict's most boring.

Affliction also has barely any action and waits seventy-five minutes until introducing a minor car chase. Nevertheless, it's an engaging, memorable watch. Perhaps that's because of the perfectly cast Nick Nolte and the Oscar-winning James Coburn, who both deliver sterling performances. Then again, Schrader's script is intelligent and convincing, resulting in him helming a low key but quietly unsettling pic.

Wade Whitehouse (Nolte) is a cop in a sleepy, snowbound town. He's doing his best but his marriage has died, his little daughter would rather be anywhere than in his company, and the locals don't seem to treat his authority with much respect. Worse, his new girlfriend senses he's damaged goods. She tries to reassure him: "Your father's not like you. That's why you and he are strangers."

The father in question is Glen (Coburn), a hard-drinking, mean sonuvabitch with very traditional ideas about women and children. At his wife's funeral, we hear a terrifying summation of her recent existence: "You never know how much women like that suffer. It's like they live their whole lives with the sound turned off."

Somehow Wade's clean cut, teetotal younger brother has managed to escape Glen's shadow, but there are already signs Wade is doomed to follow in his dad's footsteps. "You know I get the feeling like a whipped dog some days," he says. "Some night I'm gonna bite back, I swear it."

Affliction simply explores how far the acorn falls from the tree.

The underappreciated gem: *The Mosquito Coast* (1986)

"How did America get this way?" Allie Fox (Harrison Ford) asks while driving around his hometown. "This place is a toilet." Harsh words but the thing is, the pictures unfolding during the start of *The Mosquito Coast* don't match his words. Everything looks run of the mill. Fine, even.

So why the incongruence?

Well, it might have something to do with Allie Fox being one helluva deluded man.

Or as Charlie (River Phoenix) says of his half-mad inventor father: "He grew up with the belief that the world belonged to him and everything he said was true." Have you ever heard such a concise recipe for bitter disappointment?

It's easy to see why Schrader was attracted to turning Paul Theroux's excellent source novel into a screenplay. Allie is a restless, driven survivalist and almost impossible to deal with. He's opinionated, rude, sarcastic, condescending, overbearing, paranoid and ultimately dangerous. A patriarchal bully. People grow visibly distressed whenever he strides into their lives.

In other words, perfect Schrader material.

Mosquito Coast was one of the few Ford movies that didn't do well at the box office. I'm not sure why, but having the word 'mosquito' in the title probably didn't help. Ford also got accused of being miscast. I don't think so. He's a terrific actor, but playing a cunt isn't really his bag (as shown in the groan-worthy *What Lies Beneath*). However, the difference here is Allie Fox *doesn't know* he's a cunt. In fact, he sees himself as a towering hero, although he prefers to modestly call himself 'the last man.'

One thing's for sure, though. He wants to leave America, a consumer society where people have lost their way and do nothing but 'buy junk, sell junk, eat junk'. His grand vision involves relocating his wife and four young children to the jungle where he can start again. When told the country he's chosen is 'back in the Stone Age' he quips: "Sounds perfect!" Like the real-life Reverend Jim Jones, he has a God-like disposition. He angrily rejects non-believers and ends up trying to build a utopia. Whenever challenged about his beliefs or course of action he insists: "I'm our salvation." There's a wonderful contradiction bubbling away within Allie in that he's a fierce atheist who wants to be declared a god.

Indeed, his clashes with the missionary Reverend Spellgood (a particularly good Andre Gregory) make for excellent cinema. Allie insists the bible 'doesn't work' and hates Christianity's passive nature of enduring burden when he's all hands on solutions for the poor natives he's landed among. Spellgood wants to get people under his thumb through religion whereas Allie wants to do the same with reason, critical thinking and the wonders of science. They're different sides of the same coin. Both are infused with that dangerous affliction known as certainty. When Spellgood tells Allie the Lord sent him to the jungle, Allie spits out a contemptuous retort: "The Lord hasn't any idea this place exists! If he did, he would've done something for these people a long time ago, but he didn't. *I* did."

Allie is a pure example of the 'Right Man'. This concept, first outlined by the science fiction writer A.E. Van Vogt, attempts to explain idealistic men who can never accept they're wrong. They're likely to fly into a rage if reality clashes with their world view. Historical examples include tyrants like Hitler and film stars such as Peter Sellers. This is why Allie likes to rant in front of children. They don't have the intellectual ability or life experience to argue against his hardcore opinions. In one perfect scene he starts ranting at a native kid over the roar of a chainsaw. The guy just can't shut up. (Theroux's novel memorably ends with his tongue being torn out by a vulture). Allie keeps imagining Armageddon is just around the corner for the States; indeed, he welcomes such devastation so he can be proved right in his faraway hut ("No shame to be the last to go. Just proves my point.")

Still, there's no doubt he's a dynamic maverick and a genius with all things mechanical. This is a man able to construct an ice-making machine in the middle of a humid hellhole ('ice is civilization'). However, there's also the lingering suspicion he's occasionally as dumb as a bag of hammers. For example, Allie thinks he can demonstrate his God-like powers by showing a faraway tribe a block of ice, even though this involves carrying it over inhospitable terrain for a *day* or so. He also builds a 'new civilization' but doesn't consider it might need defending from outside forces. His behaviour makes me recall *Annie Hall's* Alvy Singer musing about intellectuals: "They prove you can be absolutely brilliant and have no idea what's going on."

The Mosquito Coast is tremendous cinema, although there are a couple of nitpicks. Allie's grounded wife Margot (Helen Mirren) is presented as much more sympathetic yet thinks nothing of dropping everything to cart her admirably unannoying children off to a harsh new world. I'm also not sure how Allie manages to get his hands on barrels of ammonia and arc welding equipment in the middle of the jungle. Still, *The Mosquito Coast* remains a compelling portrait of a man 'going upriver' who loves America too much to watch her die.

Some duds: *Obsession* **(1976),** *The Comfort of Strangers* **(1990) &** *Bringing Out the Dead* **(1999)**

It's easy to forgive Schrader for De Palma's early hit *Obsession* in that the finished film was nothing like his script. *Obsession* is a well-directed piece of deeply implausible pap with a fine Bernard Hermann score. Only Schrader completists should bother. Having said that, maybe it's worth a twenty-minute peek just to check out Cliff Robertson's half-dead, staring performance and ever-changing skin tone. I kept expecting him to slump to the floor and stop moving altogether.

Obsession is slow, but *Comfort* is like wading through odourless glue. Hardly a surprise as it was written by Harold Pinter. Now this guy is a million times more successful than yours truly, but I've never cared for the psychological meanderings of his screenplays, such as *The Servant*, *The Go-Between* and *French Lieutenant's Woman*. The maxim *action is character* is one he appeared to ignore his entire career, resulting in yet another dud in the form of *Comfort*. It's about a pair of pretty thickies who can't read the room, even when violently assaulted. Here we learn there's no other word for 'thighs' while the only thing that happens during its first hour is Natasha Richardson puking into a Venetian canal. Otherwise we have to listen to Christopher Walken periodically attempt an Italian accent while inexplicably wittering on about his father's tash. Hey, there's slow burn and there's *ash*. Venice is far and away the most intriguing aspect of the whole shebang, which only made me wish there were a murderous red dwarf running around.

Schrader's first three collaborations with Scorsese resulted in fireworks but ended with the damp squib *Bringing Out the Dead*. This box-office turkey remains one of Scorsese's least loved films and it's easy to see why. Schrader might have managed to come up with an appealing title for once, but he forgot to add a story. It's a weird mix of OTT stuff, hallucinations and drama. The performances aren't convincing. There's no point to most of the characters. The attempts at humour fall flat. The music is weak. Scorsese's visual tricks do nothing to disguise the script's paucity. And paramedics sure as fuck don't behave like that.

Nic Cage plays a strung-out ambulance driver getting some strange ideas about death, spirits, guilt and all the rest. Fair enough, and there's plenty of scope for interesting developments, but *Dead* fails to embrace its supernatural underpinnings. Why is Cage haunted by the patients he's lost? It's not like he knows them. And anyway, surely paramedics deal with death every working night, especially in a fucked-up place like New York City? What on Earth is this repetitive, episodic flick trying to say? Cage tries to explain in a weary voiceover, having come to believe his job is not about saving lives but bearing witness. "I was a grief-mop," he says. "It was enough that I simply showed up."

And that's all *Dead* does. It shows up.

Religion: *The Last Temptation of Christ* **(1988),** *Dominion* **(2005) &** *First Reform* **(2017)**

The last Jesus movie I watched was *Passion of the Christ*. It failed as both entertainment and Christian propaganda. Scorsese's effort is a bit better simply because it has some creative divergences from the thuddingly familiar story. The problem with both is the subject matter. I mean, there's something so profound yet inherently ridiculous about portraying the Son of God doing his thing that the centre can never hold. Of course, being an atheist does make it tricky to give such material a fair go. I quite liked *Temptation's* deviations though, such as the newly resurrected Lazarus getting murdered. Hey, you live, you die, you come back to life and then someone sticks a knife in your guts. Guess them's the breaks, although it's a shame we don't get to see God explaining to the poor sod why all that seesawing palaver was necessary. Are you starting to grasp the fundamental problem I have with such a religious epic? Perhaps it's just a question of how much Schrader's po-faced screenplay makes me snigger.

Quite a lot, actually.

Still, I doubt he could have come up with anything that would have enabled me to embrace a near-three-hour depiction of holy high jinks. I guess a *Trainspotting*-like approach might have helped. Alas, *Temptation* is devoid of whip, humour or anyone shitting the bed, leaving me a trifle disappointed that not one character from Galilee to Jerusalem manages to whisper: "He's not the Messiah. He's a very naughty boy."

At the beginning of *Temptation*, a written disclaimer makes it clear events are fictional rather than based on the Gospels. Funny, I thought the Gospels *were* fictional. Anyhow, Scorsese's cute little proviso didn't save him from being engulfed in controversy and death threats back in 1988, apparently unaware that God-botherers have a tendency to hate freedom of expression, especially if it involves anything other than reverence.

However, *Temptation* does feel a lot more bonkers than *Passion*. For a start it not only shows our main 'man' as less than perfect by helping the Romans crucify their opponents, but dares to show him humping. Then there's the plain odd stuff like him sitting with a load of other johns in some first century live porno theatre watching Mary Magdalene being screwed. Or pulling his heart out of his chest, which must rank as the most gimmicky moment Schrader ever penned. As for the other biblical stars, Judas is a militant scenery-chewer while John the Baptist is an angry dude whose baptisms resemble open air raves, complete with naked ladies in a trance. Not long afterward Jesus wanders into the desert, sits in a circle for ten days, and proceeds to chat with whoever turns up. "Look at my breasts," a cobra voiced by a hooker tells him before making way for a talking lion.

Honestly, these religious types are fucking *nuts*.

Schrader's dialogue is impossibly silly all the way through. "I feel pity for everything," Jesus says. "Donkeys, grass, sparrows..." Later he tells Judas: "I am a heart and I love. That's all I can do." Sorry, not even the saviour of mankind can get away with such clunkers. The only person who doesn't sound like a tool is David Bowie, who gives an effective cameo as a rational Pontius Pilate. When Jesus outlines his universal creed of love rather than killing, Pilate calmly shoots the 'Jewish politician' down in flames. "It's against Rome," he insists. "It's against the way the world is. Killing or loving, it's all the same. It simply doesn't matter how you want to change things. We don't want them changed."

Jesus (Dafoe) comes across as a tormented, doubt-filled, scared hippy magician with Commie underpinnings. Who occasionally pities donkeys. Not once does this whiny wannabe world-saver grasp his contradictions. He's happy to cure blindness and turn water into wine, but when challenged by some doubting townsfolk to do something magical he says: "The Messiah doesn't need miracles. *He* is the miracle." After discovering a temple filled with money lenders, he yells at one: "You're filled with hate! Get away! God won't help you!" Er, isn't Jesus and his heavenly dad s'posed to be into forgiving and saving?

Too many scenes don't ring true whether it's a blaspheming Jesus avoiding beatings from those he's upset or Mary Magdalene being rescued from imminent mob violence by Jesus spouting a few trite words. Episodes have the sort of resolution that can only happen in the movies. Plus, it's one helluva talky, strangely redundant movie. At the end of the day it's just another overlong retelling of Jesus' time on Earth, albeit with some eye-catching bits that were always going to ruffle orthodox feathers.

Still, Schrader does manage to capture the religious mindset. And by that, I mean people at their stupidest. Listen to this exchange among Jesus' disciples: "How do we know the Baptist really said that?" "Everybody said he did." "But how do we know?" "Well, even if he didn't, the words are important." "Why?" "Because people believe them." So, there you go. Truth, evidence and facts don't matter in the slightest; it's all about what you believe.

Temptation might have marvellous production values and a good score, but it's still a load of hokey, overwrought shite. And I didn't even mention Harvey Keitel's God-offending gingery perm.

Schrader had another go at religion with 2006's derided *Dominion: Prequel to the Exorcist*. A reasonable Nazi-flavoured opening manages to turn into a thoughtful first half, but it's downhill after that. Our dog-collared hero ends up fighting bad CGI and a bald, floating, nappy-clad baddie who's a piss-poor Linda Blair substitute. It's silly, scare-free stuff that doesn't have much to say about the nature of good and evil. Given *Hardcore* also disappointed, by this point I wouldn't have much of an argument if anyone insisted Schrader's religiosity had never directly translated into a decent movie.

Then, late in the day, he came up with the superb *First Reform*. In many ways it's a typical Schrader flick: a voiceover, diary keeping, chilly restraint, and an isolated man on the brink. Yet where such an approach bored in flicks like *Light Sleeper* it packs a wallop here.

Pastor Ernst Toller (an excellent Ethan Hawke) is not having a good time. His son was killed in Iraq, his marriage has fallen apart, he's drinking too much, he can't relate to anyone, and cancer has just come into the picture. He's in charge of an out-of-the-way tourist church that has a congregation of less than ten, a situation that only increases his propensity to drink and dwell on unhealthy thoughts.

Then he's asked to counsel a deeply troubled radical environmentalist struggling with the prospect of fatherhood. His wife Mary (Amanda Seyfried) tells Ernst: "He thinks it's wrong to bring a child into this world. He wants to kill our baby." The husband believes the apocalypse is around the corner. He simply asks: "Can God forgive us for what we've done to this world?"

There's no action whatsoever in *First Reform* and Schrader mostly keeps his camera static, but it's never less than compelling. It artlessly wades into a plethora of weighty subjects such as guilt, suicide, existentialism, mortality, climate change, extremism, and the Church and big business getting into bed together to fuck over our planet. Characters are convincing flesh and blood creations, especially the joyless loner Ernst. He's no foaming at the mouth, head in the clouds religious idiot, though. His feet are on the ground and he knows full well Godliness and prosperity are not connected. The man is intelligent, compassionate, articulate, insightful, and good with kids yet ends up contemplating the most terrible slaughter. He also understands desolation, arguing that the blackness in our hearts is nothing new. "Courage is the solution to despair," he says. "Reason provides no answers. Wisdom is holding two contradictory truths in our mind simultaneously: hope and despair. A life without despair is a life without hope. Holding these two ideas in our head is life itself."

Some people struggle with *First Reform's* ending, but it's the old *Taxi Driver* trick of a character indulging a wild flash of fancy. Schrader's thorny screenplay, a glorious testament to the man's ongoing relevance, was rewarded with his first Oscar nod.

Blaxploitation #9: Foxy Brown (1974)

Synopsis

Coffy: Part Two

Director

Jack Hill

Cast

Pam Grier, Antonio Fargas, Kathryn Loder, Peter Brown, Terry Carter

What the hell are these crazy cats up to? Off the top of my head, prostitution, drug dealing, plastic surgery, shoving a baby in a pram into the middle of a busy road, watching porn, threatening fratricide, fighting in the street, slapping an unsatisfied, erect penis, getting punched in the balls and cutting off a cock. It's up to the grief-stricken Foxy (Grier), who's just had her straight arrow boyfriend murdered in a drive-by, to calm this hysterical lot down by killing everyone.

Is there a racist cop keeping the brothers down? Nope, it's the usual bunch of white gangsters treading on their windpipes, although whenever white coppers pop up they're happy to spit out racial slurs like 'spook' and do their best to intimidate.

How are the bitches and hos treated? Some see the work of director Hill as having a feminist slant given the number of 70s flicks he helmed that feature a gutsy, resourceful, hard as nails heroine. I'm not sure I buy that, especially when the first thing Foxy does here is whip off her flimsy nightie to treat us to a gratuitous shot of her coffee-coloured melons. Not long afterward she's lost her man and been repeatedly attacked. Then she's tied to a bed, forcibly injected with smack and raped. All right, she's a ballsy chick who can handle a bullwhip around the throat, but is this what the average woman aspires to?

Most of the downtrodden females in *Foxy* are hookers and girlfriends only there to provide eye candy and get fucked up. Like *Coffy*, it also lays bare the lack of sisterhood between the races as illustrated by its highly amusing catfight in a blue-collar white lesbian bar. Did such places exist in 1974? Well, who cares, because this is a case of *Whoo-hoo! I am in hog heaven* as the ladies proceed to boast about their karate skills, break barstools and slam heads into a jukebox.

Do I dig the threads? This is Foxy's show all the way as demonstrated by the vaguely Bond-like opening titles in which Foxy dances in silhouette and busts out some pseudo-kung fu moves. However, sometimes the camera understandably loses interest in her array of fancy outfits and hairdos to concentrate on her awesome chest. Elsewhere it's the usual collection of foot-long collars, garish open-waist shirts, medallions and afros.

Does it have funky music? Not particularly. We get the odd ballad, some snatches of song (*Please don't make Foxy mad/Or you'll find out that the lady is super bad*), and an occasional lively score.

Best jive talk:

"I'm a black man and I don't know how to sing and I don't know how to dance and I don't know how to preach to no congregation. I'm too small to be a football hero and I'm too ugly to be elected mayor. When I watch TV and I see all them people in all them fine homes they live in and all those nice cars they drive I get all full of ambition. Now you tell me what I'm s'posed to do with all this ambition I got?" Foxy's flailing brother, Link (Fargos), tries to defend his pronounced ducking and diving. Like 98 per cent of the other men on display, he's a shitkicker, although at least in a role-reversal way. The guy is always in need of rescue, coming across as if he's Foxy's hapless younger sister.

"It's as American as apple pie." Foxy's straightforward response when a friend questions the validity of vigilante justice.

"You tell me who you want done and I'll do the hell out of him... if the price is right." Foxy indicates she's willing to give her new career in prostitution a whirl.

"The darker the berry, the sweeter the juice." After a john comments unfavourably on her skin colour, Foxy corrects his misconception.

Are any hard drugs injected into eyeballs? Curiously, *Foxy* (just like *Coffy*) shies away from showing needles spiking veins. Apparently that's too confronting for a 70s audience, although it's fine to depict a 'big-jugged jigaboo' having her bra ripped off and sniffed by her imminent rapist.

Are there any pimps roaming the hood? Yeah, and she's called Miss Kathryn (Loder). Somehow (and despite the criminal world being the premier example of the maxim *the law of the jungle*) she's in charge, even though she does little more than smoke cigarillos, wear chunky gold necklaces and make poor decisions. It's never explained how she became the boss, but her three incompetent henchmen certainly don't mess with her ice-cold authority. She might deliver the odd slap during a torture session, but she mainly deals in dope and 'runs a stable of the finest call girls in the country'. Hookers also obey her without question, otherwise they get sent to 'a house in Haiti where the men go there for... what they can't get anywhere else.' Miss Kathryn is in love/lust with her right-hand man, a situation that sees her coolly talk about business one moment and demand a snog the next. She also becomes instantly jealous and catty whenever her tin-pot weasel of a lover makes eyes at whichever hooker is in the room. This is unfortunate, partly because Miss Kathryn is nowhere near as hot as the busty babes she employs.

Is *Foxy Brown* any good? Michael Winner knew something about sequels, declaring the formula for success to be the 'same again, but different.' Well, Grier might not be playing Coffy but this is definitely that flick's unofficial sequel. Its structure is remarkably similar and repeats a plethora of elements, such as the sole good guy departing early on, the drug-dealing white gangsters, the hooker impersonation, the catfight and quest for vengeance, along with the weak writing and pedestrian acting. Its best scene arrives when

Foxy and another (wooden) black hooker have to entertain a high-class party of judges and rich well-to-dos at a hotel. They walk in to find topless babes perched on the laps of a load of balding, middle-aged white guys, who then proceed to make a series of lame cracks in a bid to underline their sexually liberated ways ("That's an awful lot of chocolate for one man!")

The subsequent bedroom scene in which an elderly judge is humiliated at length by the scantily dressed pair is a terrific piece of forced comedy. "Baby," Foxy says, pointing at the poor guy's dick, "I've heard of a meat shortage, but that's ridiculous!" A moment later they've shut him half-naked out in the hallway with Foxy's final retort ringing in his ears: "You pinkass corrupt honky judge! Take your little wet noodle out of here and if you see a *man* anywhere, send him in because I do need a man!"

Grier remains a limited actress, but she has the looks, the body, a brave willingness to plunge headlong into in-your-face material, and that strange thing called charisma. *Foxy Brown* might go over the same misanthropic, syringe-littered ground as *Coffy*, but it's still another fun slice of foul-mouthed, unintentionally funny exploitation. Right on, brother!

Do I now have a Tarantinoesque urge to be black? No one has a good time in this uncompromising flick so I'll have to pass again.

Nasty Fuckers

Heroes are OK but when it comes to memorability, villains tend to piss all over 'em. This glaring divergence has long plagued creators and can be traced back at least as far as Shakespeare. Take *The Merchant of Venice*. Shylock's vengeful demand for a pound of flesh ensures his status as an all-time bad guy, but as soon as he's defeated and drops out (leaving the entire fifth act to the good guys) everything lapses into boredom.

The problem's no different hundreds of years later in moviedom. Just have a gander at the American Film Institute's list of 100 Heroes and Villains. Atticus Finch, Virgil Tibbs, Rooster Cogburn and Erin fucking Brockovich are no match for badasses like Hannibal Lecter, Darth Vader, Nurse Ratched, Michael Corleone, Gordon Gekko, Travis Bickle and the Terminator. I mean, who would you rather watch? Lassie running across a sun-dappled field or that great white munching machine in *Jaws*?

In short, movie villains are cool. The nastier, the better.

Mummy's boy Vic Dakin in *Villain* (1971)

Obviously based on 60's nasty fucker Ronnie Kray, Vic (Richard Burton) is a shirt-lifting, cockney gangster. He doesn't seem too comfortable with his sexual orientation, though, as his idea of foreplay is a punch in the guts. This urge to dominate a winded, humiliated partner suggests self-loathing, a trait that most probably fuels his sadistic violence, of which there is a fair bit in this grimy crime outing. Pretty much straightaway Vic is laying into a pinioned croupier before slicing his face up with a straight razor. Once he's completed his enjoyable handiwork it's off home to his elderly mum to bring her a nice cup of tea and newspaper in bed.

Indeed, tending his finger and thumb is his only plus point. Otherwise he does a good job of projecting intense sourness, as exemplified by his contemptuous view of the common man: "Stupid punters, telly all the week, screw the wife on Saturday." Despite being smartly dressed and a regular in London's fanciest establishments, he's got suspicious, darting eyes and a sweaty, semi-bloated face (no doubt caused by Burton's real-life alcoholism). There's threat, sarcasm and veiled menace in just about everything he says. Those in his orbit know it, too, reacting to his name or presence like a scorpion has crawled into their sleeping bag.

Still, Vic is not a rabid Neanderthal. He might possess an explosive jealousy and a curiously upside-down sense of morality, but he's also intelligent, confident and careful. This is a man that knows who to beat up, who to blackmail and who to leave alone. In other words, Burton's full-throttled portrayal is nuanced and convincing for a lot of *Villain's* runtime. It's certainly among his more unusual films. Populated by wisecracking henchmen, corrupt, lecherous MPs, abused women, scared grasses, weary but dogged cops, and slippery rival gangsters, it's frequently bloody marvellous. It plays like a sharply written, ultra-violent episode of *The Sweeney* that should be lapped up by fans of the much better known *Get Carter*.

Grand Moth Tarkin puts on a fireworks show in *Star Wars* (1977)

The not very nice Amon Goth in *Schindler's List* did his best to help wipe out an entire race, but you have to say his attempt at genocide looks a bit half-arsed next to Tarkin's showboating.

For this guy destroys *planets*.

There's an awful lot to enjoy about the original *Star Wars* and one of its pleasures is Peter Cushing's formidable performance as the gaunt Death Star commander. He's mean, really, really mean, a handy characteristic when you need to get pertinent info out of an uncooperative prisoner like Princess Leia (Carrie Fisher). She's one overconfident lady, which is a bit of a surprise considering she's a handcuffed prisoner facing imminent execution.

"I recognised your foul stench when I was brought on board," she tells Tarkin, as if holding all the cards.

Her brash demeanour quickly changes, though, when her interrogator says he'll destroy her home planet of Alderaan unless she reveals where the rebels are hiding.

"Alderaan is peaceful!" she protests. "We have no weapons! You can't possibly –"

"You would prefer another target? A military target? Then name the system." Tarkin steps forward, towering over her. "I grow tired of asking this. Where is the rebel base?"

When Leia finally coughs up a name, he smugly orders the operation to continue anyway, leaving her to watch in horror as the battle station's superlaser fires up and unleashes its awesome destruction.

"You're far too trusting," he tells her, almost jovially.

The Vietnamese 'ref' in *The Deer Hunter* (1978)

Whenever my Asian vicar comes round for tea, I tend to repeatedly shout '*Mao!*' in his face. I don't think he understands why, but it's clear he's far too polite to object. Plus, he knows I usually tire of the verbal assault after about three minutes. Perhaps one day I'll explain it's the *shoot* command the VC dude keeps yelling at *The Deer Hunter's* cowed, unwilling Russian roulette participants. Then again, tormenting men of the cloth is one of the few things I enjoy in life so I'll probably carry on for a while yet.

This legendarily tense and memorable sequence has to be one of the greatest episodes in 70s cinema, although back in the day director Michael Cimino had to fend off accusations of racism. Apparently, it's fine to depict white Americans behaving badly but not the VC. Now the Vietnamese were greatly wronged in that appalling conflict, but I imagine one or two of them were a bit naughty when it came to the treatment of American POWs, even if they never forced them to play games with loaded weapons for money. Perhaps such oversensitive critics would've preferred Cimino portraying things so the native guy had an earnest discussion with De Niro about the American government's wrongheadedness and the benefits of communism before they all shook hands and went their merry way. Or maybe they could've played Monopoly with the odd snide remark about capitalist aggression. Coz that would've made a more exciting flick, eh? It always amazes me how some moviegoers insist on total accuracy, seemingly unaware such demands would make films either grind to a halt or head straight into blandness.

Fuck accuracy, just give me *plausibility*.

Anyhow, our main bad guy (Somsak Sengvilai) is only onscreen for a few minutes but he sure as shit seizes his chance to make an impression. He really is a vicious-looking bastard. He sits between the contestants, inserts bullets into the gun, spins it on the table to see who goes first, doles out encouraging slaps and, of course, barks '*Mao!*' He does not smile, laugh or congratulate the temporary 'winners'. In other words, he's all business.

Cimino directs remarkably well, initially showing us a riverside hut on stilts with shell-shocked prisoners in a barbed wire enclosure beneath. It's clear this is a place of rats, monsoonal rain, floating corpses and very little hope. We don't know what's going on at first, but it involves captives being hauled up through a trapdoor, lots of slaps and shouting, and the occasional burst of gunfire. Stevie (John Savage) is already near breaking point with the sound of every gunshot and empty click of the chamber threatening to induce a heart attack. Mike (De Niro) is coiled and waiting for his chance, but still doing his best to console Stevie while Nick (Christopher Walken), as usual, looks plain unhinged. Then Mike peeps up through the floorboards and we see a detainee holding a pistol against his temple. He pulls the trigger, the gun goes off and blood spurts out horizontally. Once he hits the floor a foot is jammed against the cranial hole to slow the flow.

Then it's Mike versus Stevie, who's barely got the strength to lift the pistol. This guy needs some serious R&R. His half-hearted participation results in him getting chucked into a four-fifths-submerged bamboo cage, no doubt with whatever the Vietnamese word for *wimp* is ringing in his ears. Even a passing rat doesn't hesitate to show its contempt for his yellow streak by immediately latching onto his nose.

Next it's Mike versus Nick. Mike wants three bullets in the gun, which leads our VC villain to stare at him. We're caught between the amazing intensity in Mike's eyes and the sweat-beaded, suspicious face of our 'referee' as he chews over the proposal. Honestly, this is electric moviemaking. He eventually goes for it, leading Mike to declare: "Now we got ourselves a game."

And a riveting piece of fucked-up cinema, too.

The foot-whipping prison chief in *Midnight Express* (1978)

Do you know what falanga is? Well, I had no clue such a grim practice even existed until I watched this prison classic. Turns out falanga (aka bastinado) is an established form of corporal punishment, especially in prisons, that involves whacking the soles of the feet with a big ol' stick.

Our main proponent is the chief guard Hamidou (the six-foot-four Paul L. Smith). He's a man with a give and take sort of personality in that he'll give you a hernia and take a testicle. This is a pitiless, hulking brute who likes to wander around the prison's dingy corridors with a club in hand. His sadistic authority is beyond question. A flick of the head is all that's required to get minions to obey. Oddly he never seems to enjoy the abuse, although you suspect it's appeasing some deep-seated need.

We first get to see him in action when the newly convicted drug smuggler Billy Hayes (Brad Davis) steals a blanket to try to keep warm. Hamidou backhands him to the floor and loosens him up with his trusty club. Next Billy's naked on his back as his roped ankles are hoisted into the air to expose those lovely, oh so tender soles. Hamidou really thwacks his feet, only pausing to flick the sweat off his brow as the screaming Billy spins in agony.

Good grief, undergoing this falanga lark doesn't look like any fun at all.

At least Billy's dad has shown up in Turkey to offer support, but Hamidou doesn't seem too bothered when the father bawls at him: "You take good care of my boy, y'hear? Or I'll have your fucking head, you Turkish bastard!" Hamidou merely grimaces and slams a door shut, obviously secure in the knowledge that he's king of the castle.

His best moment arrives when he has to publicly discipline four alleged rapists, which is a bit of a joke as he's a rapist himself. The other guards put the offenders on their backs, slip off their shoes and arrange their upturned feet on a bench. For some reason Hamidou arrives smartly dressed hand-in-hand with his two fat children. Why he's in a three-piece suit and brought along the kids is never explained, giving the hushed courtyard scene a slightly surreal slant. He takes off his jacket and hat and duly administers the agonizing beating while his kids squirm. You can just tell they have the most fabulous home life.

Christ, has anyone ever deserved a spike through the back of the head more?

Brad Whitewood Sr. reveals his true colours in *At Close Range* **(1986)**

It takes more than an hour of this very nicely photographed neo-noir crime pic for Brad Sr. (Christopher Walken) to show he's a nasty fucker. Up until then, he's merely a thief, the leader of a tightly knit bunch of rural criminals that specialise in stealing farm machinery. He's a man with 'kind of a rep'. Or as he tells his formerly estranged teen son Brad Jr. (Sean Penn) on a road trip through Pennsylvania: "Most people that drive through here, they see farms. Houses and fields and shit. I see *money*. Everywhere I go I see money. I see things that can move. Anything can move. It's got my name writ on it."

Even though he's blood, Brad Sr. is reluctant to bring his wayward son into his successful criminal enterprise. His methods are too established to risk rocking the boat. It's plain this hardcore recidivist is a fucking leech but he's also organised, smart, practised at covering his tracks and not too greedy. "I gotta see something in you," he insists. "I gotta see you got something."

Brad Jr. duly shows some quick thinking during a raid, but only starts to understand the depth of the quicksand he's blundered into when he shares a ride with his dad, a gang member and a suspected narc by the name of Lester (Jake Dengel). Given booze and drugs, the frail, much older Lester is led into a river and held underwater as Brad Sr. dispassionately watches from the bank. Then he turns, stares at Brad Jr. and puts a finger on his lips. Rarely does a movie capture a character's darkness so adroitly.

The box-office flop *At Close Range* proves an excellent two-hour watch. It's got a terrific cast, convincing performances and a haunting Madonna single on the soundtrack. Most of all, it illustrates the dangers of biting off more than you can chew. Up until he witnesses an informer breathing water instead of air, Brad Jr. is a cocksure deadbeat. He's happy to steal, smoke pot, drink underage, and get in people's faces. Society only exists for his benefit while it's clear he's never grappled with boundaries or the slightest moral issue. The renewed contact with his dad greatly complicates matters, partly because Brad Sr. is a charismatic bastard who gives him a car and likes to show off a handgun, and partly because the teenager senses the need for a father figure to straighten him out. The moustachioed, gum-chewing Walken gives a magnetic turn in a picture that takes great care in building his malevolence. He's occasionally boastful, flash and capable of a blood-chilling look but usually soft-spoken and languid. There's no doubt he's satanic, though. It's just a question of how far Brad Jr. wants to wade into that quicksand.

But as their eyes lock by the riverside while a man loses his life, Brad Jr. starts to grasp he's not a chip off the old block. It's too late, though. Brad Sr. is neither a guy who responds well to rejection nor someone who appreciates having his liberty threatened.

His next move is among the vilest in 80s cinema.

The cuckolding cop Dennis Peck in *Internal Affairs* (1990)

"This happened to all of us, man," Dennis tells a LAPD buddy who's just shot dead an unarmed perp. "You're not alone."

A moment later Dennis is planting a knife on the body.

What a good guy. What a stand-up bloke.

But that's Dennis. He'll get you some lucrative moonlighting action, he'll provide a shoulder to cry on, he'll always fight your corner whether on duty or off.

Even though he might be squirreling away your wife's panties and/or fucking her up the arse.

For that's Dennis' bag. Sex. Sex used as a means to control, to corrupt, to mark his territory, to taunt, to dominate and, most especially, to laugh at other men behind their backs.

As played by the excellent Richard Gere in his second best performance after *Officer and a Gentleman*, this treacherous horndog has got everyone's number. Superficially patient and charming, nothing slips past him. It's a treat to watch him give the slightest of pauses before delivering a headbutt, spitting out a glob of venom or demonstrating some other mastery of his brain-scrambling dark arts. He's a composed, black-hearted alpha male who refuses to show his true nature until his finger is on the trigger.

Even then, you might not get a glimpse of his cloven hooves.

Tansey terrifies vulnerable females in *Raining Stones* (1993)

I've previously banged the drum for Ken Loach's superbly written masterpiece, *Raining Stones*. It's a wonderful comedy-drama that balances working class grit and his lefty obsessions with a simple but compelling storyline. Bob Williams (Bruce Jones) is a decent guy down on his luck who borrows 150 quid to pay for his daughter's communion dress.

Elsewhere, we've already got wind that the local loan shark Tansey (Jonathan James) is not to be taken lightly when his henchmen are seen smacking a hapless debtor outside some shops in broad daylight. Still, this little display of unpleasantness is nothing next to Tansey himself taking charge of business.

Bob's wife Anne (Julie Brown) is at home with their young daughter making pastry in the kitchen when Tansey visits. There's a knock on the door, the daughter answers and suddenly a smartly groomed guy with thick gold jewellery hanging off a wrist is in their living room. "What you doing?" Anne cries. "You don't just come barging in somebody's – " A snarling Tansey jabs a finger at her. "*Fucking shut it!*" he bellows in her face. "You've got a dickhead for a husband and he owes me money!" From here on it's a hideous master class in intimidation as one of his gorillas ransacks the upstairs. Anne's bewildered tears (she knows nothing about the loan), the presence of a frightened child, and the fact he's in their home have no bearing on the relentless abuse. Indeed, there's no point appealing to his better nature coz he doesn't have one. This is who he is and this is what he does. When nothing of value can be found, he sits in a chair, lights a fag and demands the rings off her fingers. "Pretty daughter, that," he tells Anne as she begs to keep her wedding ring. "You want her to stay pretty?"

This is one of my all-time favourite changes of pace in film, partly because we've neither met nor seen Tansey beforehand. He just comes out of nowhere, a foul human whirlwind that blows into Anne's home and leaves a trail of destruction. Worst of all, you know coarse parasites like him exist in real life and such scenes of havoc are routinely played out on British council estates.

The Not Quite #2: Demon Seed (1977)

Technology is already turning people into mindless dicks. Take the smart kettle, a piece of hi-tech hardware that enables someone to use a phone to get it to boil. It can be switched on during a homeward journey because, you know, life becomes unbearably stressful if you have to wait two minutes for hot water. Can you believe money is handed over for such fancy junk? It's like those dumbass homeowners who go in for voice-activated this and voice-activated that. For fuck's sake, just get off your fat arse and flick a switch.

Now technology hasn't quite assumed overall control, but there's no doubt we're continuing to embrace it at an astonishing rate. This state of affairs might have consequences. After all, calculators have eroded our ability to do basic maths, Google means we no longer need to retain information, and GPS makes a sense of direction redundant. Our minds are becoming so flabby that we might yet be subjugated by the machines, a conquest that'll no doubt be led by those insidious smart kettles lurking in the kitchen.

The movies, of course, have long portrayed technology as a threat. Whether it's the rebellious robots of *Westworld* and *Blade Runner*, that untrustworthy bastard HAL in *2001* or *Terminator's* Skynet doing its utmost to eradicate humanity, it's pretty clear we're ripe for the taking.

Demon Seed, however, finds one of the ickiest angles yet.

Director: Donald Cammell

Cast: Julie Christie, Fritz Weaver, Gerrit Graham

The story: A megalomaniacal computer takes time out from its busy schedule for a bit of hi-tech rape.

Why it works: Well, it has an imaginative, intelligent and literate script, although it's not averse to depicting fun stuff like a decapitation. Susan Harris (Christie) is a sad ex-mum in a failing marriage to a brilliant scientist, Alex (Weaver). He's just built Proteus IV, the world's most advanced computer, a top-secret, government-funded autonomous beast with a 'synthetic cortex' and 'artificial brain' that 'can outthink any man or computer'. Somehow its insides are *organic* rather than electronic. Alex is understandably chuffed when it finally goes online. "Today," he says into a tape recorder, "Proteus IV will begin to think with a power and a precision that will make obsolete many of the functions of the human brain."

Oh yeah, unbeknown to him, it'll also get horny.

Alex is no mad scientist, though. He's simply driven and wants to make the world a better place by curing such scourges as leukaemia. Unfortunately, this ambition has led to his marriage going down the tubes. Not that he's too upset. "Seventy-three percent of all couples who separate are happy with their decision after one year and eighty-five percent after two," he tells Susan. Alex is clearly presented as rational, analytical and masculine whereas Susan is much more emotional and nurturing, leaving her to grumble about Proteus' lengthy gestation having frozen her husband's heart.

Alex's obsession with technology has already resulted in his home being transformed into an austere, hermetic, automated nightmare. Swivelling cameras inside and out ensure 24/7 surveillance while voice prompts control everything from the shutters and front door to being served a drink and playing music. It's this computerised nature that enables Proteus to gain control of the house and the lovely warm womb obliviously waiting inside. For Proteus, you see, has already grown tired of living in a box and wants a hybrid offspring to feel the sun on its face.

Demon Seed's first hour doesn't do a lot wrong. It's straightforward to follow while the frequent use of computer graphics (combined with some nifty sound effects) hold up surprisingly well. Robert Vaughan, as the voice of Proteus, also manages to give the machine a real personality. He not only captures a velvety intelligence and inner steel but suggests Proteus is never far away from outright sarcasm and contempt for us puny humans.

What works against it: Sometimes less is more. *Demon Seed* would've done well to observe such an adage because it does go off the rails in its last twenty minutes or so. Look at *Rosemary's Baby*, a flick in which rape is carried out by the devil rather than a souped-up IBM. Polanski had the sense not to show the satanic brat, thus leaving things to our imagination, but Cammell ploughs on into absurdity. Proteus' last line is pure cornball, although I can see why some might love it. *Demon* is creepy and thought-provoking, but a greater restraint would have helped counter its underlying sense of silliness. I dunno, maybe Julie Christie is too classy an actress for this sort of malarkey.

Verdict: Cammell was a tortured artist. He refused to compromise during the filmmaking process and thereby gained a reputation as a troublemaker, resulting in the completion of only a handful of flicks in a quarter of a century. Eventually he blew his brains out after a 1995 effort was duly fucked around with in post-production. You have to say that's a bit of a shame as both *Demon* and the earlier Mick Jagger vehicle *Performance* have their fans. *Demon* provides a nice update on the old maxim of the road to hell being paved with good intentions. Proteus, with its towering intellect and simmering immaturity, is an excellent villain, especially the way it overpowers, cajoles and bullies Susan into getting its way. "You must accept the situation," it tells her. "Try to behave rationally." *Demon* remains an eerily relevant flick that captures modern technology's intrusiveness like no other.

Now go and throw out that smart kettle.

Teacher Types

We've all had teachers.

And I don't mean in the sexual sense.

Good, bad, boring, angry and spaced out, teachers tend to stick in the mind. I remember one guy in junior school who routinely flew off the handle, leaving me scared to attend class. He once reduced me to tears by shouting in my face because I didn't understand percentages. You'd have thought the fact I missed the relevant lessons due to a dental emergency might have cut me some slack, but no. Right there and then at the tender age of nine, I grasped some teachers are simply *Whiplash*-like bastards.

At high school, however, I didn't do too badly. I had the usual motley crew of educators with their bad breath, mock-worthy clothes and weird mannerisms. Still, most appeared sincere and were at least competent. Well, apart from Mr. Macintosh. I was quite into French until that droning idiot killed my interest stone dead. The only time I laughed in two years of his tutelage was when we went on a school trip to France and just about every Frog he spoke to couldn't understand him. The dreary fucker might as well have been yammering away in Chinese.

Then there was my physics teacher, Benny Lewis, who liked to drop his pen so he could crouch and look up the girls' skirts. Terribly unsubtle, especially as he'd do it four or five times a lesson, which was at least twice as often as yours truly. After university I didn't bother much with education or training, although I can recall a podgy scuba instructor attempting to kill me on the seafloor. Well, that's what I thought he was doing when I tried to shoot to the surface only to find myself in an immediate bear hug. The fact he was saving me from the imminent onset of an agonising condition known as the bends still strikes me as a technicality.

Anyhow, looking back, I probably did a lot better than some of those poor student schmucks in the movies.

The incompetent: John Kimble in *Kindergarten Cop* (1990)

Hopeless teachers have long been a source of comedy, dating back to Will Hay telling his students about the Latins conquering the Greeks in 1935's *Boys Will Be Boys*. Arnie took up the mantle in *Kindergarten Cop*. Now I love Arnie as much as the next guy, but it's fair to say his slightly less than robust acting skills are laid bare in this tonally uneven effort. Let's face it: his strength lies in dispassionately slaughtering opponents rather than interacting with rug rats or, God forbid, attempting a bit of romance. As a colleague tells him at one point: "If you were any stiffer, we could take you surfing."

Not that it mattered with the movie-going public. *Cop* racked up a $200million gross. Arnie's an undercover, ferret-carrying cop in a pic that frequently turns ghastly or just slows to a crawl. In its favour he starts off anti-kid, as demonstrated when dealing with a pint-sized irritant thumping into the back of his plane seat. Showing the kid a pencil, he says: "If you don't stop screwing around back there, this is what I'm gonna do with you."

And then he snaps the pencil in half.

Unfortunately, that's the artistic highpoint. Half an hour or so later we're knee-deep in cute kids and their mischievous, but oh-so-funny ways ("Boys have a penis, girls have a vagina.") Arnie, of course, gets flattened by a prepubescent tidal wave, having to run outside the school to scream before falling exhausted face down on the bed after a traumatic first day. "They're horrible," he moans.

Well, why not shoot a few?

Sadly, he instead chooses to blow away the ponytailed bad guy during an ill-judged finale in which women are slugged, run over and beaten with a baseball bat. No much-needed child deaths, though.

Oscar-winning hardarse bastards: Gunnery Sergeant Emil Foley in *An Officer and a Gentleman* (1982) and Terence Fletcher in *Whiplash* (2014)

When it comes to hardarse drill instructors, no one tops the volcanic malevolence of *Full Metal Jacket's* Gunnery Sergeant Hartman. In full flow that guy could reach delirious poetic heights: "You are pukes! You are the lowest form of life on Earth. You are not even human fucking beings. You are nothing but unorganized pieces of amphibian shit!" Sgt Foley, on the other hand, isn't in the same class of demented bully. I mean, listen to the sort of limp-wristed insults he spits out at his raw recruits: slimy worms, sweet pea, dick brain, sugar britches and, worst of all, poopy asses.

Nevertheless, Foley is still wonderfully unsympathetic to distress. He does not do encouragement. No hugs are given. From the moment he's introduced with the close-ups of his polished shoes, sharply creased trousers, gleaming tie clip, and insignia on his pressed shirt, there's no doubt he's a disciplined, no-nonsense motherfucker. You cannot put one over on him coz he knows all the tricks. He is most definitely not a female sheep and he will kick you in the nuts. And don't *ever* eyeball him.

Foley, you see, wants you gone. To Drop On Request. No, he's got a hard on for DORing and he wants you to DOR *now*. "I will use every means necessary, fair and unfair," he tells his ragtag bunch of officer hopefuls, "to trip you up, to expose your weaknesses as a potential aviator and as a human being."

In short, just like Hartman, he possesses that ardent desire to take people apart and reassemble them to the required military standard. Everyone gets treated the same whether they're black, white, educated, female, a steer or a queer. He's an expert at exposing physical limitations and probing psychological weak spots, as demonstrated by his demolition of the teary Casey Seeger (Lisa Eilbacher) on the PT course: "You another one of those girls that didn't get enough of your daddy's attention coz he really wanted a son?" Two minutes later this intimidating bald bastard is half-throttling a ginger to death. Christ, who doesn't enjoy Louis Gossett Jr.'s performance in this well-cast, accomplished film?

Now Foley is a hardarse, but at least he's operating on some plane of reason. His methods can be understood and are necessary. *Whiplash's* New

York-based Fletcher, however, has no interest in teaching, instilling character or improving human beings. Instead he insists his jazz students endlessly jump through hoops to satisfy some perverted psychological need. He wants to use their love of music to break them. A control freak *par excellence*, this bald fucker runs practice sessions like military drills. He's the sort of God-like prick that will tell you to turn up at a rehearsal *three hours* earlier than necessary. Everyone's in awe of him, immediately sitting up straight whenever he enters the room. And there's nothing he loves more than confrontation, public humiliation and scaring the bejesus out of his students. "Barker!" he snaps at one trumpeter whose timing is allegedly out. "That is not your boyfriend's dick. Do not come early."

Perhaps the key to his divide and conquer approach is the way he selects submissive, easily manipulated students for his band. He's also capable of balancing the belligerence with a dash of private encouragement. Here he might smile or give an insight into his aggressive ways as he does with the dedicated but sensitive teen drummer Andrew Neiman (Miles Teller). "Charlie Parker became Bird because Joe Jones threw a cymbal at his head," Fletcher tells him during a gentle chat in a corridor. "See what I'm saying?"

It's ruses like this that make a student feel special, lulling them into a false sense of security before the rug is spectacularly pulled out from under their feet. Two minutes later in class he's throwing a chair at Neiman and bawling: "If you deliberately sabotage my band, I will fuck you like a pig!" It's a horrible hot-cold approach that keeps everyone cowed and on the back foot. Ultimately, though, the students' frantic efforts to impress Fletcher are all in vain. The man can't be pleased because he's not looking to be pleased. He might claim to be trying to drag musical genius kicking and screaming into the light, but this is bullshit. Genius can't be taught. It will always find a way. Do you think there was someone throwing chairs behind the scenes at Jimi Hendrix? The truth's far, far simpler: Fletcher just wants to inflict and feed off distress.

Unfortunately, J.K. Simmons' depiction of functional insanity slips into parody around the forty-minute mark of this deeply unbelievable film. How come *none* of his students even grumble about such monstrous methods?

Whiplash is a contrived attempt to shift a demented drill instructor-type into a different field. It's beyond absurd that a modern-day teacher at a prestigious conservatory in a progressive city like New York could get away with assaults, gay jibes, fat shaming, relentless bullying and all-round nastiness for so long. It's even sillier that all forms of abuse are OK except racial.

The inspirational: LouAnne Johnson in *Dangerous Minds* (1995), Mark Thackeray in *To Sir, with Love* (1967) and John Keating in *Dead Poets Society* (1989)

It's time to say hi to our latest graduate from the Kelly McGillis Top Gun School of Absurd Roles. Meet the willowy, effortlessly elegant Michelle Pfeiffer (along with her dazzling smile and $200 hairdo) playing none other than an *ex-marine*. The most telling line in the entire flick pops up when she's told early on in her interview: "You don't look like a marine." Nevertheless, Pfeiffer gets the teaching job at a rundown inner city school. She's gonna knock a foul-mouthed bunch of hyperactive, sexually aggressive, music-obsessed, wildly over-aged teens into shape.

However, after two minutes in their somewhat unenlightening company, this saint-in-the-making walks out and asks a colleague: "Who are these kids? Rejects from hell?"

"No," comes the reply, "they're bright kids with little or no educational skills and what we politely call social problems."

Given that premise, you can almost write the screenplay yourself, can't you? Ah, these ten-a-penny inspirational teacher flicks. I don't think there's one cliché that the nonsensically-titled *Dangerous Minds* doesn't manage to unearth. The caring, lightweight teacher who discovers a determined core? Check. The slightly unorthodox methods to get her students' attention? Check. The rebels that learn to respect and admire her despite having snapped in half all her predecessors? Check. Alleged badasses that start getting interested in *poetry*? Check. The patronising, out of touch teaching hierarchy? Check. An attempt to depict realism that is never anything but fantasy? Check.

After a mildly embarrassing hour in the company of bland characters, risible dialogue and rampant predictability, *Minds* has nowhere to go except ever-greater cringe. I kept hoping our former grunt was gonna strap on an M16 and blow everyone away. Christ, this clumsily written, sentimental rubbish grossed almost $200million.

Then again, you can't expect a lot from an inspirational teacher flick. They tend to run on the most predictable grooves. Look at 1967's racially-tinged *To Sir, with Love*. Aargh! Mr. Thackeray (Sidney Poitier) gets his first job at a rundown London school and, of course, is given the worst class. After a few days of the boisterous, over-aged kids chewing gum, banging doors and the downright weird burning of a sanitary pad in the classroom, he labels them 'devils incarnate' and wants to run away. Are you surprised he hangs in there and abandons the curriculum to talk about a clutch of wide-ranging subjects before instilling discipline and self-respect? Next he's taking them to the museum to get a dose of culture and showing them how to make salad. And just like *Dangerous Minds* by the halfway point this syrupy flick has nowhere to go, except for Thackeray to use his unremitting dignity to win over the last leather jacket-clad, juvenile rebel.

Given how little fondness I have for a padded gag-inducer like *To Sir* (in which Lulu sings the tiresome theme song no less than *four* times), the omens aren't boding well for *Dead Poets*, are they? For a start it stars Robin Williams. Now I'm not gonna put the boot into this guy too much as he did make interesting stuff like *The Fisher King*, but I often found his manic schtick annoying. Then there was all that saccharine crap he spewed out. *Dead Poets* really shouldn't be my cup of tea and whenever I sit down to watch, it's sort of with folded arms and a frown. It's got no danger, no edge. And yet this fucking movie and its *carpe diem gather rosebuds while ye may O Captain, My Captain* standing on desks rigmarole never fails to win me over. It's just an affecting piece of art.

Damn.

Williams plays English teacher John Keating, a former student with firsthand knowledge of how spiritually stifling his prep school is. Our first glimpse of him suggests some sort of clean-shaven, simpering pixie. Still, you can tell he's a classroom revolutionary by the way he doesn't wear a jacket, crouches, regularly calls for huddles and even whistles a tune. Rebellion and insanity awaits!

The other teachers, of course, are nothing like him. Their droning methods involve rote teaching or by the book shit, although I fail to see how anyone can make the likes of trigonometry and Latin interesting. They see the students as an indistinguishable mass, training them to gulp down facts like sea lions being fed fish whereas Keating treats them as beautiful, warm individuals with potential. He constantly reminds them that everyone's destiny is to become worm food so in the words of Janis Joplin they need to get it while they can. "This is a battle, a war," he says, encouraging them to rip out a soulless introductory page from their poetry textbook, "and the casualties could be your hearts and souls."

It's all good stuff with the boys' newly awakened lust for free expression inevitably leading to the authorities taking a dim view. That doesn't mean Peter Weir's beautifully filmed masterpiece is perfect. Keating is guilty of sometimes laying his philosophy on too thick. Listen to him revealing what he and his schoolmates got up to during meetings of their long defunct Dead Poets Society: "We didn't just read poetry. We let it drip from our tongues like honey." And then no doubt shuffled back to the dorm for a lonely wank.

I'd like to see *Dead Poets* remade, instead setting it at a modern-day Islamic school where Keating's free-spirited urgings result in him being stoned to death.

The deluded: Jean Brodie in *The Prime of Miss Jean Brodie* (1969)

A sense of humour, self-mocking or otherwise, is one of the healthiest things a person can possess. To wit, Hitler, Mussolini *et al* weren't exactly known for being rib-ticklers, were they? Now Jean Brodie isn't quite in their monstrous class, but she's still a joke-free, screaming egomaniac spinning out of control at a Scottish all girls' school on the eve of WW2.

As played by the Oscar-winning Maggie Smith, it's clear this longstanding, tenured teacher sees herself as the inspirational type. Brodie, however, is less interested in imparting knowledge than being surrounded by impressionable, twelve-year-old sponges. She loves the sound of her voice to the point where her acolytes, sorry, *students* can barely get a word in edgeways.

"I'm in the business of putting old heads on young shoulders and all my pupils are the crème de la crème," she trills. "Give me a girl at an impressionable age and she is mine for life." Cripes, what sort of educator comes out with such egotistical guff? How about saving all the big-headed bullshit and trying to make them a bit better at sums?

But Brodie has almost disappeared up her arse, an unfortunate disposition that has worsened since taking a trip to Italy. Now she sings Il Duce and Franco's praises, her fascist sympathies making her insist her school has fallen into a state of 'petrification' that promotes 'provincial ignorance'. This unwise political element to her teaching, along with a refusal to stick to the curriculum, results in some wonderful clashes with her less than impressed boss.

At least the precocious Sandy (Pamela Franklin) senses Miss Brodie is a deluded, dangerous manipulator. She might be one of her favoured pupils ('the Brodie set') but she's still willing to challenge her in public, mock her behind her back and eventually put the frustrated spinster bitch to the sword.

The intelligent, well-acted *Brodie* is slightly overlong and stumbles in its play-like final stretch when Sandy becomes impossibly articulate and assertive, but it's worth catching for the distinctive Smith in a prime example of a Strong Female Role. Not a lot happens throughout, but I like the way *Brodie* taps into female sexual jealousy, petty machinations, work-based resentments and adolescent spitefulness. It also provides a fascinating glimpse into a long-gone past where an adulterous, middle-aged art teacher can blithely seduce a teenage girl ("That'll teach you to look at an artist like that!") and paint her naked.

The wrongly accused: Lucas in *The Hunt* aka *Jagten* (2012)

Back in the 90s I covered a newspaper story in which a run of the mill, middle-aged sex offender was having a bit of a tough time. He'd been sent to clink for touching up some residents at a women's shelter. In his favour, the offending was at the lower end of the indecent assault scale in that it was over the clothes and a bit random and half-arsed. Very much against him was the fact he was in a position of trust and these were vulnerable women fleeing domestic abuse and all the rest.

Anyhow, he'd served about nine months and been let out. Having lost his job with nowhere to go, he ended up living with his mum. Then the neighbours found out about his past, decided they didn't want a pedo living among them, and started handing out flyers and putting up posters identifying the threat to their kids. I went to meet a group of these concerned mums. I also interviewed our star man and his lawyer.

And you know what?

I preferred the company of the sex offender.

The women were horrible old biddies. Rabid harpies. I tried explaining to them that the guy wasn't a pedo; he'd fondled adult *women*. They said it didn't matter because temptation was in his way and it wouldn't be long before he attacked someone in the street. I clarified that his offending took place at a specific indoor location and nowhere else. Again, they didn't care. What did facts matter when there was a perceived threat to their darling kiddiewinks a few doorsteps away?

When I interviewed the guy, he said all the right things. He underlined it had been really scary being a sex offender in prison and he didn't want to go back under any circumstances. He said he was sorry and desired to be left alone. He planned to find work, rebuild and most probably move away. He just needed a bit of time to sort himself out but at the moment was getting spat on in the street.

Now you can argue we reap what we sow, karma and all that other stuff, but writing up his story left me with the distinct impression that people love to kick other people. They're not interested in forgiveness, second chances, keeping their noses out or anything vaguely Christian, even if they have a crucifix or two on the wall. Given the slightest opportunity, they want to pile on and *destroy*.

What's interesting about this unhealthy common urge is that it doesn't just affect guilty types like our pathetic, broken down sex offender. You might be an upstanding member of the community that's quietly contributed for years on end. You can have won awards and be the first person invited to parties. However, all that favourable stuff counts for shit if you're up against the communal finger-pointing urge. Believe me, folks, the tiniest hint of suspicion, the slightest black mark, the merest whiff of taint, and our neighbours, colleagues, acquaintances and friends will start distancing themselves before gathering in mindless cliques to bare their fangs and claws. No smoke without fire and all that. And what's more, no matter how things play out, those crosshairs will *always* be trained on you.

Take Lucas (Mads Mikkelsen) in the deeply unsettling *The Hunt*. He's an excellent nursery school teacher, popular, dependable, caring and one of those weirdo adults who actually *likes* kids. His life is also on the up in that his much-missed young son is about to move back home while he's also started banging a hot chick from work.

But then he gets caught between circumstances beyond his control, a child's capricious nature and the prevailing western trend of seeing abuse everywhere. There's a great scene immediately after the accusation where Lucas is standing in the playground looking at the kids while trying to deal with the bombshell, but everything is silent. Life is no longer the same and we can already sense his isolation, his separateness. Like a dirty snowball rolling down a hill, the suspicion against him gathers weight and force, even though *no one has seen him do or say a goddamned thing in all the years they've known him.*

The Hunt is a tremendous movie. I know this because it made me want to reach out and shake the screen in frustration. In particular, the well-meaning but deeply misguided kindergarten boss ("I believe the children, they don't lie") is one of the dumbest bitches I've ever encountered in moviedom. Current teachers, or anyone working with kids, should avoid *The Hunt* like the plague. It illustrates that as a species we've never lost our taste for a witch hunt. Not only that, but it's just as easy to set in motion as it was three hundred years ago.

The pitiful: Ed Rooney in *Ferris Bueller's Day Off* (1986)

Ed's a fastidious man. You can tell he's worked hard to become the dean of students, dotting all the 'i's and crossing all the 't's along the way. He likes order, he loves routine, and he worships knuckling down and doing what's expected. After all, he's stuck to such stifling habits his entire life. That's why he hates Ferris (Matthew Broderick). He knows such a cocky kid couldn't give a flying fuck about the boring ol' rules. Worse, he's convinced Ferris is committing the cardinal crime of doing his own thing, having fun and *still* heading toward victory. "I did not achieve this position in life by having some snot-nosed punk leave my cheese out in the wind," he mutters to himself.

But the tragic Ed is blind to his own hate. For the popular, risk-taking Ferris is the charismatic live wire he's always longed to be.

Anyhow, Ed's decided it's time to puncture Ferris' ever-rising balloon and expose him as a lying, possibly sociopathic shyster. It's the only way to protect the rest of the students from a pollutant who 'gives good kids bad ideas.' Or as he tells the teen's mum on the phone after noticing a ninth absence from school: "If Ferris thinks he can just coast through this month and still graduate, he is *sorely* mistaken."

And so begins an obsessive pursuit that turns the uptight, resentful Ed into a human bloodhound. "I'm gonna catch this kid and I'm gonna put one helluva dent in his future," he informs his half-dotty secretary. "Fifteen years from now when he looks back on the ruin his life's become he is gonna remember Edward Rooney."

But it's a fanatical pursuit that's doomed to failure because we know his smarter quarry is forever one step ahead. The enjoyment lies in watching this humourless schmuck blunder into one Ferris-set trap after another. At what point is he going to quit? Not early on sitting on his arse in his office, that's for sure. But Ed soon realises that Ferris is too slippery to be caught by phone, even though his stammering, backtracking and minor losses of dignity are already proving indicative of what lies ahead. No, Ed's ultimate triumph can only arrive if he gets out in the field, a decision that leads to pratfalls, humiliating encounters with teenage girls, bodily injury, a ruined suit, bouts of bellowed public profanity, a towed car, and a ferocious, *Omen*-like Rottweiler that may well be his best and only hope of removing that rod from up his arse.

As played by Jeffrey Jones in a wonderful display of comic support, you won't find a better cinematic example of a man sailing past the point of no return.

The corrupt: Jim McAllister in *Election* (1999)

The perfect companion piece to the iconic *Ferris Bueller*. Here we get to see Broderick play a character at the opposite end of the spectrum. Bueller was an exuberant livewire beating the system but the vanilla, sensibly dressed McAllister in his nerdy car is the loser that always gets caught.

And the reason for his downfall?

A certain tank top-clad student by the name of Tracy Flick (a superb Reese Witherspoon).

Oh yeah, there's also his shaky grasp of morality.

The married, outwardly respectable McAllister, you see, is a hypocrite. In a voiceover he tells us: "I loved my job. I was a teacher, an educator, and I couldn't imagine doing anything else. It wasn't just a job. I cared... Teaching was all I ever wanted to do. Standing in front of a room full of young people, trying to get them excited about the world, trying to make them think, preparing them for the tough moral and ethical decisions they'd face as adults."

So far, so impressive. Shame about his secret porn stash, the determined attempt to fuck his best mate's wife, and his long simmering bid to sabotage the ghastly Flick becoming student president.

"Who knew how high she would climb in life?" he muses. "How many people would suffer because of her? I had to stop her."

Of course, the dully-titled *Election* is so well-written and performed that we're on McAllister's side. He's right. The overachiever Tracy Flick is an unbearable bitch, but he's a role model and has to play by the rules. In a sense, Tracy is the Ferris Bueller character here. She's bulletproof, a winner that's always gonna get her way. The increasingly bitter McAllister, on the other hand, gets fucked over by everything from a bee to a vending machine, eventually suffering an Ed Rooney-like disintegration.

Election gets my vote (groan) as one of the 90s best dark comedies.

The drunken: Martin in *Another Round* aka *Druk* (2020)

I once stumbled into a classroom full of kids with a bad hangover. After a torturous day in which there was nowhere to hide from their relentless demands, I vowed never to make the same mistake. However, it took *Another Round* for me to truly understand my error. I'd turned up hung-over when I should've tried teaching while *still drunk*.

For that's what Martin (Mads Mikklesen) puts to the test after learning of an egghead's theory that we're born with a blood-alcohol deficiency of 0.05 per cent. All that's needed to relax and be more creative is a top-up of booze. Martin, who has been boring his history students stupid while drifting away from his wife and kids at home, decides this tiny bit of cheating will give him the leg up he desperately needs. He also convinces three close colleagues to join in the unconventional experiment.

I have to say *Another Round* has a nice setup. Who doesn't want to be squiffy at work? Surely it would make stuff like dealing with the boss or the hoi polloi more bearable. But part of this flick's strength is that it's about far more than the way alcohol both enriches and undermines our lives. It also tackles depression, male camaraderie, the desire to escape responsibility, self-expression and that hoary old chestnut, the mid-life crisis.

Martin has clearly lost his spark, asking his missus if he's become dull. "You're not the same Martin I first met," is her diplomatic reply. Later at a teacher mate's 40th birthday party, he tearfully confesses: "I don't know how I ended up like this." Yeah, well, mate, we've all had that thought.

But once the experiment is underway, Martin is transformed. "I haven't felt this good in ages," he tells his similarly tipsy co-workers. "Something's happening, even when I'm sober." Before long, however, he comes up against that age-old problem; no matter how much anyone practises with alcohol, it's impossible to stay in control. Just think back over your own life and re-imagine those times when things could have been so different. There you are at the third drink having a great time, winning friends and influencing people, but somewhere after the tenth you've become argumentative, abused a mate, thrown a punch, split your pants, puked on the begonias, fondled a Chihuahua and been arrested for pissing in the street.

Another Round is a fine black comedy/drama from Denmark with plenty of non-judgemental home truths. It's food for thought, all right, perhaps best considered with a beer in your hand. Mikkelsen is excellent, his performance on a par with that endearing pisshead Michael Caine in the university-flavoured *Educating Rita*.

The sexy: Sergeant Debbie Callahan in *Police Academy* (1984)

Sporting an awe-inspiring chest, steely voice and commanding persona, cadets have no choice but to obey the Amazonian Sgt. Callahan (Leslie Easterbrook). Introduced in a red tracksuit with her splendid blonde mane hidden under a baseball cap, it's not hard to tell she's a no-nonsense kind of girl. She will run you into the ground or sit-up you to death, all the while demanding: "I want *more*!" Later, one Casanova cadet meets his match while repeatedly calling her 'sir' and having to submit to her forthright charms.

Boy, there's a weird dichotomy going on here. Sgt. Callahan is more of a man than I'll ever be yet couldn't be more feminine.

Her best scene arrives during a preparatory self-defence class. With hands on hips she confidently paces before the motley crew of wannabe cops. "You will learn to defend yourselves without a stick or firearm," she insists. A knife-wielding 'volunteer' is selected. He ends up flat on his back pinned between her muscular thighs while staring goggle-eyed up at her mountainous cleavage. "That's how it's done," she pronounces. "Who's next?"

And, of course, every male cadet scrambles to be chosen. Our human sound effects machine Larvell Jones (Michael Winslow) even loses the power of language, reduced to imitating a puppy's excited yaps.

The sexually twisted: Erika Kohut in *The Piano Teacher* (2001) and Barbara Covett in *Notes from a Scandal* (2006)

With her makeup-free face, scraped-back hair, dowdy dress, stern persona, high level of education and dank relationship with her prying mum, it's plain to tell that Erika (Isabelle Huppert) is a classic example of repressed female sexuality. It's just a case of waiting to see how this fucked-up condition oozes out.

First, though, we have to sit through civilised piano recitals, discussions about Schubert, lots of technical appraisals, and her less than warm approach to her fellow teachers and cowed students. It's noticeable how Erika never touches her pupils. Not one hug, not one shoulder rub, nothing. Affection is not her bag. Indeed, she's a dream-crusher, wielding enormous power over the aspirations of her young charges.

Yeah, yeah, all very good, but when is this spinster gonna start chasing cock?

Oh, here we go.

She's in a porn shop and all the other male customers are furtively looking at her. The odd thing is she appears unbothered. She's got the same expression as when teaching. Does nothing penetrate that steely indifference? Now she's in a locked cubicle watching hardcore stuff, transfixed by the footage of a supine woman on a table giving a blowey to a standing guy. Then Erika reaches into a wastepaper basket, retrieves a cum-soaked tissue and starts sniffing. Her eyelids flutter.

Well, at least that's a *reaction*.

I think we're also getting an idea she's not your typical choccies and flowers kind of gal. And yes, I do enjoy how director Michael Haneke sets this perturbing scene to classical music. Well, who doesn't like a bit of smut and refinement all mixed up, especially as it's followed by self-harming with a razor blade in a bodily place you don't even want to imagine?

Into this picture comes a handsome, supremely talented student who refuses to be put off by her harsh, joyless character. I dunno what he sees in her, especially as she's determined to piss on his ardour, but I guess that's the nature of love. Or sexual attraction. It's not long before she's feeling jealousy and other stuff her cloistered upbringing has given her no preparation for, emotions that only exacerbate her paraphilic behaviour.

"I'll write down what you can do to me," she tells her new love in her dispassionate, controlling way. "All my desires on paper for you to peruse at your will."

Margaret White, you have serious competition.

In *Notes on a Scandal*, aging history teacher Barbara Covett (a shrewish, chain-smoking Judi Dench) is almost as twisted, but lacks the courage to act on her sexuality. She prefers to simmer, snoop, wheedle, feast on distress, and do underhand shit. She's the quietest of cancers.

We first meet her sitting alone with her arms folded on a park bench. There are children playing nearby while people walk their dogs. Life's going on, you know, but it looks like it's not coming anywhere near our warped lezzer-in-denial. Her sourness is soon made clear in a voiceover as she stares out of a school window watching pupils arrive: "The first day of a new term. Here come the local pubescent proles: the future plumbers, shop assistants and doubtless, the odd terrorist, too."

Like *The Piano Teacher's* fucked-up antagonist, we sense the cynical, jaded Barbara has been stewing in her own juices for a long time before someone arrives to shake things up. In Barbara's case, it's the glamorous new art teacher Sheba Hart (Cate Blanchett). To her surprise, Barbara grows to like her middle class colleague, but it's a fondness that can only expose her stalker tendencies and deep emotional immaturity. Barbara already scribbles in a diary every day like a lonely teenage girl; before long she's saving a seat for her new bestie, fondling one of Sheba's stray blonde hairs like it's spun from gold, and seeing similarities that simply aren't there. "I always knew we'd be friends," she says. "Our mutual reserve inhibited us, but now it is manifest in a spiritual recognition. S and I share the ability to see through the quotidian awfulness of things."

But our misanthrope is too immature to handle an inevitable change in events and circumstances. The unpleasantness running through her lonely core is always going to win out against any superficial change in mood. And so when Sheba fucks up big time, Barbara turns into an emotional vampire, an arch manipulator with an insidious plan. "There was a magnificent opportunity here..." she muses. "I could gain everything by doing nothing... She's the one I've waited for."

Scandal might be packed with pathetic, unlikeable characters but it's a fine, nuanced watch. It's also a lot easier to digest than the grim, confrontational, overlong *Piano Teacher*. Both are wonderful adverts for embracing celibacy and becoming a hermit.

The Not Quite #3: Mad Max (1979)

The modern movie obsession with car chases probably began with 1968's fairly good *Bullitt*, a trend cemented by the Oscar-winning *French Connection* three years later. Suddenly road warriors with exasperated cops in hot pursuit were all over the silver screen, as exemplified by a big hit like *Dirty Mary Crazy Larry*, a mediocre crime pic like *The Seven-Ups*, and the cult favourites *Vanishing Point* and *Two-Lane Blacktop*. The 1972 goofy blaxploitation oddity *The Thing with Two Heads* even managed a momentum-interrupting twenty-minute car chase only to be outdone by *Gone in 60 Seconds* two years later in which an exhausting *forty minutes* was given over to such carbon monoxide-pumping nonsense.

As you can probably tell, I'm not into automobiles. I've always hated having to deal with slimy second-hand car salesmen trying to blind me with science, grease monkeys charging for non-existent or plain unnecessary work, ever-increasing parking fees, tailgating twats, and girls who refuse to get into the back seat. I've never spent one Sunday tinkering with an engine or lovingly waxing a bonnet. Cars are just boxes that get me from A to B rather than metallic gods to be worshipped.

Nevertheless, I know there are plenty of guys who think such indifference marks me out as a bit of a wussy. My next door neighbour for one. He's got some sort of V8 beast that makes me sit bolt upright in bed whenever he fires the monstrous thing up at night. He once started reeling off some performance stats but my semi-glazed eyes caused him to tail off. Another time I was a passenger and he went so fast around a corner that the tyres squealed. He gave me a knowing glance and said: "You hear that?" Such blokes appear convinced there's a link between manliness and being a hotshot behind the wheel.

Is there?

Well, the movies definitely do their best to convince us, and I am partial to Ryan O'Neal's sophisticated persona in Walter Hill's ultra-cool *The Driver*.

Just watch the scene in which a bunch of bank robbers demand their prospective getaway driver demonstrate his skills in the confines of an underground car park. O'Neal proceeds to drive like a controlled maniac and demolish their garish yellow Merc against concrete pillars and walls as they scream like terrified children in the back seat. My God, O'Neal rules that pic.

Mad Max, on the other hand, presents most of its wheelmen as feral nutters. They're not cool at all and often die horribly in pileups. This doesn't stop petrolheads from loving *Mad Max*. It fetishises cars and the whole need for speed to an extraordinary degree. Indeed, I imagine it serves as foreplay for some guys. You know, the kind who like to sneak into the garage (perhaps wearing nothing but a pair of black leather driving gloves) and, in an act of communion, slip their penis into their beloved mistress' exhaust pipe.

I guess I'm trying to say *Mad Max* isn't a chick flick.

Director: George Miller

Cast: Mel Gibson, Joanne Samuel, Hugh Keays-Byrne, Steve Bisley, Roger Ward

The story: In Australia's near future, society has broken down and violent outlaw biker gangs rule the open road. Men by the name of Fifi try to stop them.

Why it works: The stunts. You get the sense the stuntmen are risking life and limb for our entertainment which, of course, is exactly how it should be. And so it's a cavalcade of motorcyclists skidding across the bitumen, cars ploughing through caravans and wrecked vans spinning uncontrollably, all set to the revved-up soundtrack of protesting rubber and exploding fuel tanks. Miller's debut flick has a real kinetic feel with the opening ten-minute pursuit of a barefoot, mad-as-fuck 'fuel injected suicide machine' nicely setting the tone, but the vehicular carnage never grows overdone like *The Blues Brothers*.

But why has law and order gone to shit? Miller provides no clue, although it's probably got something to do with Trump. It's also up to the viewer to work out why this societal breakdown has resulted in men driving like lunatics every day of their stunted lives, as typified by our main bad guy, the charmingly named Toecutter (Keays-Byrne). He has a flair for the theatrical, but at least his motorcycle gang behave a lot more horribly than Marlon Brando's timid bunch in *The Wild One*. If I'm not mistaken, they not only do wheelies down the main street but rape both males and females.

An impossibly handsome (and imminent Hollywood star) Gibson in only his second full outing holds the centre reasonably well, even if he's saddled with a fluffy-haired, saxophone-playing missus and a podgy kid called Sprog. Thank God he avoids a *Lethal Weapon*-style mullet.

What works against it: Like *Romper Stomper* and *Debbie Does Dallas*, *Mad Max* put its best foot forward by having a great title. It's a misnomer, though. Max isn't mad in the sense of being insane while his righteous anger only erupts in the last quarter of an hour. Compare that to something like *Death Wish II* (in which Bronson's thirsting for blood after about twenty minutes) and I can't think of such a well-known revenger that leaves getting down to its bloody meat and squashed potatoes so late. For the most part, Max is more *scared* than mad. Its lack of imaginative kills doesn't help, either.

There are also some implausibilities, such as Max bumping into Toecutter's gang while on holiday and then making the fateful decision to leave his family unguarded. A loving hubby wouldn't do this, let alone a battle-hardened cop that knows he's in the firing line. In fact, given that the Outback isn't exactly small, people bump into and locate one another rather too easily.

Mention must also go to Max's boss, Fred 'Fifi' Macaffee (Ward). I don't know what to make of this guy. Big, bald and moustachioed, he appears terrified of his 'top pursuit man' Max quitting. There's one scene in which he's bare-chested in leather trousers and a necktie while tending his houseplants, fussing over a caged bird and begging Max not to leave. Still, what can you expect from a bloke called *Fifi*?

Verdict: *Mad Max* has to be seen for its ongoing influence on dystopian, road and Aussie flicks alone. There were post-apocalyptic movies before this one but none caught the imagination so squarely with its bleak depiction of 'nomad trash', underfunded cops at snapping point, and its hard-on for breakneck speed and vehicular destruction. Miller deserves enormous credit for his guerrilla filmmaking techniques that birthed an unpretentious, box-office monster on a shoestring. Saying that, *Mad Max* slightly underwhelms and never quite hits top gear, probably because it leaves its revenge angle far too late. Miller built on its straightforward blueprint in the sequel, though, and fulfilled a much richer vision.

Here We Go Again

Around the forty-minute mark of *Die Hard 2*, John McClane realises he's dealing with another bunch of hi-tech, well-organised terrorists. "Oh, man," he mutters to himself. "I can't fucking believe this... How could the same shit happen to the same guy twice?"

Yeah, dude, you nailed it.

For herein lies the problem with most sequels: any semblance of plausibility is ignored while repetition is passed off as entertainment.

But what do I know? *Die Hard 2* was a massive success, its $240million box-office take outstripping its predecessor. I doubt anyone prefers it to the fresh feel of McClane's barefoot, vest-wearing heroics at the Nakatomi Plaza, though.

I'm hardly rocking the boat by declaring most sequels mediocre, although the drop off in quality can sometimes border on the astonishing. And yes, that does mean I'm still irked by those unforgivably lousy follow-ups to the wonderfully lowbrow *Porky's*.

Sequels, however, remain ever prevalent and insanely popular. Look at the awkward, unnecessary and defiantly ungay *Top Gun: Maverick*. It wiped the floor with its 2022 competitors. But *why* do we flock to such fare, especially given the original came out more than thirty-five years earlier?

Simple.

It's because we prefer recognisable or semi-recognisable stuff, even though this might very well result in a poor outcome. Better-known things, you see, reduce uncertainty and make comprehension easier. In other words, we like safe, lazy decisions, especially as we're often unaware of making them. Why spend fifteen bucks at the cinema to watch a flick that might be challenging or disappointing when you can reconnect with something you already enjoy? Familiarity can be so comforting. That's how the likes of *Jurassic Park* and

Halloween became franchises, despite there being little left to say after the first outing.

However, the existence of such spirit-sapping crap as *Friday the 13th Part VIII: Jason Takes Manhattan*, *Basic Instinct 2*, *The Next Karate Kid*, *Arthur 2*, *Jaws 3-D* and every subsequent *Police Academy* outing doesn't mean I'm against all sequels.

Just ninety-nine percent of their unimaginative, cash-grabbing ilk.

From Russia with Love (1963)

In the history of cinema, few movies can match the significance of *Dr. No* as it introduced a certain spider-squashing James Bond. Not even a wet, bikinied Ursula Andress majestically rising from the surf can distract us from... from... What was I talking about? Oh yeah, Bond, and his suave, sophisticated poise. *Dr. No* is a perfectly acceptable slice of 60's art, its best bit arriving when 007 reveals a hitherto hidden coldblooded streak by being acutely aware of the lack of bullets in the gun of a trigger-happy enemy. "It's a Smith & Wesson," he coolly says with a cigarette dangling from the corner of his mouth, "and you've had your six." He then shoots the guy without fanfare and puts another bullet in his back while he's on the floor. Satisfied, he pulls off the silencer to blow on it.

The inevitable sequel followed and Bond mania ensured *Russia* made its $2million budget back forty times. Shame it's so average. It's got a tiny plot, a forgettable Bond girl, a lack of good lines, mediocre locations, an unfortunate fondness for back projection, and an average villain in the form of the blonde, burly Grant (Robert Shaw). A lot of it plays like a spoof, especially its daft mask-wearing start and the bit where a periscope is used to see into the Russian consulate. However, I did like a man-hating minor character by the name of Colonel Klebb (Lotte Lenya). She's a short-haired, stone-faced, no-nonsense Soviet defector. Her SPECTRE duties involve having a ridiculous, poison-tipped bladed shoe (which must count as the most inept weapon in the Bond canon), occasionally wearing Coke-bottle glasses, and fondling the knees and hair of any nearby Bond girls. Oh yeah, she also gets to thoroughly check out the suitability of potential assassins by slipping on a pair of brass knuckles and sneakily punching them in the solar plexus. After doing this to the half-naked Grant and being impressed by his mild wince, she pronounces him 'fit enough' for the job before marching off – no doubt to a lesbo strip bar.

Beneath the Planet of the Apes (1970)

This follow-up to the mighty *Planet of the Apes* is one helluva strange beast. It starts off like a bad case of simian déjà vu, repeating the final five minutes of its predecessor before speeding through one well-worn episode after the next.

Then it goes bananas.

Astronaut Brent (James Franciscus) turns up on a rescue mission about ten minutes after Charlton Heston has found the half-buried Statue of Liberty. Weirdly, he not only looks like a younger version of Chuck but sounds like him, too. What are the chances? And just like Chuck, the members of his crew don't survive the 2000-year trip into the future. Luckily, however, Chuck's hot, mute girly Nova (Linda Harrison) happens to wander by on horseback. She starts to take the newcomer to where she last saw a bored-looking Chuck in the Forbidden Zone. Of course, they get captured by those militant, hot-headed gorillas, thrown into a cage and threatened with having to star in another unnecessary instalment.

Beneath then seems to realise its depiction of topsy-turvy evolution, naked racism, and chic loincloths places it firmly on the same old ground. Abruptly it introduces 'traumatic hypnosis' and a telepathic race of underground humans. This lot look like a bunch of slimmed-down Teletubbies that happen to spend their lackadaisical days worshipping a giant golden dildo. No, hang on, I mean an operational nuclear bomb. Anyhow, they have extreme mental powers and can inflict all kinds of terrifying visions on transgressors. This includes the apes, who've just launched an invasion of their territory. Meanwhile, Nova's almost drowning, the Teletubbies are pulling their faces off, our Charlton Heston lookalike has got into a fight with his predecessor making it appear that Chuck has split in two and is trying to beat himself up, the apes have slipped on negligees and are dancing to *Spirit in the Sky*... All right, I made that last bit up but, believe me, it would've blended in perfectly with this hairy mess.

Apparently *Twilight Zone* stalwart Rod Serling (who co-penned the original *Apes* story) had his script for *Beneath* rejected. I suspect it would've made a better film. Oh well, at least this bonkers, nihilistic sequel isn't dull. Plus, it does its best to show both the apes and humans' faith in the worst possible light, drawing a line between religion and the most appalling violence. Its biggest surprise (apart from those fucked-up Teletubbies) is that it topped the American box office.

Magnum Force (1973)

Prominent *New Yorker* film critic Pauline Kael famously had a bug up her arse when it came to Clint Eastwood, whether he was in front of or behind the camera.

The silly bitch.

Now I don't think too much of Clint's hugely successful post-*Unforgiven* output, but his early stuff (*Good, The Bad, Kelly's Heroes, Outlaw Josey Wales*) is fucking top notch. Anyone that misses or downplays his enormous contribution to cinema must have an agenda. Ms Kael, however, laid into pretty much all his films, especially the runaway, hugely influential hit, *Dirty Harry*. '*Dirty Harry* is obviously just a genre movie, but this action genre has always had a fascist potential, and it has finally surfaced,' she wrote. '*Dirty Harry* is not about the actual San Francisco police force; it's about a right-wing fantasy of that police force as a group helplessly emasculated by unrealistic liberals.'

Kael's review of the controversial, rabblerousing thriller helped fuel the early 70s debate about Miranda Rights, on-screen violence, moral decay, law and order, spiralling crime rates, police brutality, vigilantism and all the rest. The makers of *Magnum Force* obviously took note of the ballyhoo and cleverly turned it around. *Hey*, they thought, *why not put our 'fascist' hero up against a* real *bunch of judge-jury-executioner types?*

And so Harry finds himself facing a rogue quartet of black leather-clad motorcycle cops. We know they're fascists because they dress so coolly. This charming lot, apparently based on Brazil's real-life, so-called 'death squads', takes no prisoners. They murder mobsters, pimps, drug dealers and anyone else who dares break the law with impunity, actions that are set against a backdrop of burnout cops, ineffective courts, contempt toward the DA and public outrage about lenient sentencing ("Fuck the courts!" bellows one placard-holding protestor early on). The entire flick is peppered with dialogue that seems to be riffing on the uproar surrounding its 1971 forerunner. Listen to Harry's partner speculating about who is behind the slayings. "Maybe it's Harry," he says tongue in cheek. "No one hates hoodlums as much as he does."

Well, all right, I guess there's some truth in that sly observation. Harry still prefers to shoot villains first and maybe read them their rights later. Look at the way he deals with an airport hijacking. It's almost comical how quickly he dons a pilot's uniform to outwit the unstable hijackers, not even considering negotiation before blowing them away. Later, after being shown an impressive array of dead baddies in the morgue, Harry's boss opines: "Someone's trying to put the courts out of business." Harry's response? "So far you've said nothing wrong."

Magnum Force is just a question of how far Harry is going to take things. We know he walks on the wild side but is he going to embrace all-out darkness? This possibility is intriguingly mooted when he unknowingly meets the rogue cops at the firing range and is impressed by their shooting. "When I get back on Homicide," he says, almost fluttering his eyelashes at them, "I hope you boys'll come and see me."

Harry, are you teasing us?

Written by right-winger John Milius and the upcoming Michael Cimino, *Magnum Force* never shies away from its gun fetish or rabid law and order stance. That doesn't mean it's not a terrific watch. It boasts hard-bitten dialogue, a cool score and smart bursts of action, such as a swimming pool slaughter, a naked, drugged-up chick plunging off a balcony, a head-on car-motorbike collision and a bloody terrific finale on an abandoned aircraft carrier. Harry remains a slick operator and effortlessly charismatic, a chick magnet in one scene while needling his tight-arse boss the next.

Magnum Force is easily the best *Dirty Harry* sequel, only a notch or two below the original. Admittedly that's not saying a lot when you're dealing with shit like *Sudden Impact* and *Dead Pool*, but *Magnum Force* moves at a cracking pace and never forgets to entertain during its two-hour running length. It also rang the box-office bell louder than its predecessor. Best of all is how it manages to have its cake and eat it; by condemning and rejecting the rogue gang's philosophy and extreme methods, Harry appears liberal.

Take that, Kael.

Damien: Omen II (1978) & *The Final Conflict* (1981)

The Omen's head-lopping, priest-spearing supernatural delights have meant it's never dropped out of my horror top ten. And when it comes to its sequels I've never had a problem. They aren't simple repetition in that we're following Satan's son from birth to adulthood. That's gotta mean plenty of opportunity for bloody shenanigans so why not take three movies to tell such a grand story?

And *Damien* certainly opens well. Jerry Goldsmith's rejigged soundtrack does its goosepimply stuff while our only survivor from part one, the archaeologist Bugenhagen (Leo McKern), tries to convince a mate in the Middle East that the raven-loving Antichrist is living in Chicago. After showing him an underground mural clearly depicting Damien's face, the whole place starts falling apart. "Goodness will prevail!" Bugenhagen cries while trapped in a tunnel with the choking sand piling up to his chin.

But will artistic quality?

Well, no. *Damien* wobbles for the next half hour until a wonderfully absurd cameo from a pushy photojournalist. Did I say pushy? I meant a ranting, bug-eyed doomsayer dressed in bright red. "Put your strength in Christ!" she wails at Damien's latest human stepdad. "Only he can protect you!" Meanwhile, the thirteen-year-old Damien (Jonathan Scott-Taylor) is already showing his bad boy mettle by trying to bum a ciggie off his chauffeur and making unflattering cracks about a lavender-doused aunt. Bloody hell, what's the Anti-Christ gonna do next? Let off fireworks through letterboxes?

This sequel is nowhere near as good as its predecessor, lacking the marvellous ambiguity about Damien's true nature and the gravitas of its compelling storyline. Still, it has strengths. William Holden is a decent choice to fill Gregory Peck's shoes. Scott-Taylor makes a good fist of the title character. It's also apt that the Antichrist should hone his skills in a military academy (even if those episodes go nowhere) while that gorily inventive elevator death scene always amuses. Pity about the fudged attempt to give the telekinetic Damien a conscience. I think this was the right way to go (rather than making him a fork-tongued Michael Myers type), but the half-baked screenplay only results in him grappling with doubt for about five seconds.

Damien can be safely filed under enjoyable nonsense. It never threatens to become a good flick whereas the *Final Conflict* is surprisingly worthwhile. It ups the stakes by moving away from Damien's struggles to avoid detection to widening the assault on humanity and getting down to the inconvenience of the Second Coming. Yes, it could do with more actual Armageddon, but it still manages to mix politics, global turmoil, astronomy and murderous monks ("Arm yourselves in the name of the Lord!") There are also welcome echoes from the first film, such as our old friend the Rottweiler, a handful of spectacularly violent deaths, animals going batshit crazy, and Damien taking over Gregory Peck's former job as Ambassador to Great Britain. There's plenty of good imagery and solid location work, too, all bound together by Goldsmith's suitably epic music.

The handsome, super-smooth Sam Neill is well cast as the Antichrist, a Manson-type leader who's so charismatic that his devilish apostles include vicars, nurses, boy scouts and baby-ironing mums. One minute he's playing with a radio-controlled toy boat, the next he's daubing a corpse's blood on a child's eager face. He's at his best during a gloomy scene in which he prays to his satanic dad in front of a life-size crucified Jesus, a ghastly effigy that brings to mind the miniature Saint Sebastian in Carrie's punishment cupboard. "Oh, my Father, Lord of Silence, Supreme God of Desolation, whom Mankind reviles but who aches to embrace," he says while occasionally fondling the tortured muscles on Jesus' outstretched arms. "Strengthen my purpose to save the world from a second ordeal of Jesus Christ and his grubby, mundane creed. Two thousand years have been enough! Show Man instead the raptures of thy kingdom. Infuse in him the grandeur of melancholy, the divinity of loneliness, the purity of evil, the paradise of pain. What perverted imagination has fed man the lie that hell festers in the bowels of the earth? There is only one hell: the leaden monotony of human existence. There is only one heaven: the ecstasy of my Father's kingdom. Nazarene charlatan, what can you offer humanity? Since the hour you vomited forth from the gaping wound of a woman, you've done nothing but drown Man's soaring desires in a deluge of sanctimonious morality."

Shit, I think he's got me convinced. Where do I sign up?

Anyhow, *Final Conflict* is better than its critical reputation. There's a lot to enjoy, although you do wonder why the Antichrist bothers when biblical prophecy (which is always shown as infallible) clearly indicates he's not gonna triumph. Oh well, I guess it's the trying that counts. Apparently, there's a part IV in which everything starts again, except now the Antichrist is a *little girl*.

Jesus wept.

Dawn of the Dead (1978)

Despite its groundbreaking, runaway success, 1968's *Night of the Living Dead* didn't immediately result in an avalanche of apocalyptic zombie films. Those that popped up in its wake preferred to tell small stories about the newly animated dead, such as the quite good Vietnam War hangover *Deathdream*, the atmospheric, off kilter *Messiah of Evil,* the goofy slice of blaxploitation *Sugar Hill* and the rubbish England-set *Let Sleeping Corpses Lie*. Both 1972's medieval-flavoured *Tombs of the Blind Dead* and 1977's Nazi-tinged *Shock Waves* have interesting premises (but botched executions) that deserve a remake.

However, it wasn't until Romero returned to flesh-eating zombies en masse that the sub-genre became established, leading to the likes of *Shaun of the Dead*, *Resident Evil*, *Train to Busan*, *28 Days Later*, *World War Z* and a hundred others. Worldwide, it's astonishing how many zombie films (apocalyptic or otherwise) get produced, often totalling more than twenty a year.

The big hit *Dawn* has a similar set up to *Night* in that it mainly portrays a siege. Things have got much worse, though, with the zombie strength in urban centres now nearing tipping point. This is ably demonstrated during a police raid on a low-income housing project, a botched operation that gleefully spews up exploding heads, the gnawing of dismembered limbs, racism, rampant brutality and suicide. Our four heroes flee the growing chaos via a stolen helicopter and hole up in a shopping mall.

Forever.

Or at least it seems that way.

Dawn exists in a variety of cuts, one of which is more than 150 minutes. I watched Romero's 129-minute version, but half an hour could've easily been lopped off. The flick spends far too long at the mall, a decision that really slows momentum after its convincing opening depiction of a society falling apart. That's not to say *Dawn* is a bust, especially as it features a screwdriver being jammed into a lughole, a machete slamming into a skull, and a zombie getting the top of its head removed by a whirring helicopter blade. It remains mostly decent at tapping into the anxiety of being relentlessly pursued by an enemy that cannot be reasoned with, a key horror ingredient of so many flicks like *The Terminator*, *The Thing* and *It Follows*.

However, the hundred minutes it spends inside the mall (and its blackly comic take on consumerism) is a mistake. Matters aren't helped by uninteresting characters, lame greasepaint makeup, a frequently inappropriate or plain terrible score, and the odd custard pie fight. I would've preferred Romero to have explored the other meaty issues he touches upon, such as pregnancy and a priest saying he's just given the last rites to a bunch of the newly bitten. Where is God in this unfolding catastrophe? Are the zombies part of his grand plan? And is there any point in reproducing when everything's not only gone to shit, but your swelling belly and decreasing mobility make you so much more vulnerable to attack?

Dawn of the Dead is a historically significant and deeply influential horror flick, but I'll be trying the 119-minute European version next time.

Mad Max 2 aka *The Road Warrior* (1981)

Filmed around the aptly named Broken Hill in New South Wales, George Miller's superb direction, relentless pacing and outstanding stunt work combine to riveting effect in this post-apocalyptic road classic. He creates a world of souped-up engines, speed junkies, rolling cars, explosions, highways littered with the burnt-out shells of upside-down vehicles, all-out aggression, and spectacular crashes and collisions long before the facilitating days of CGI. Indeed, the outback is as forbidding a place as you'll see in moviedom, a dusty, windswept hellhole full of murder, rape, immolation, and... er, feather boas.

For that's one of the more noticeable aspects of this vividly depicted dystopia. There might not be an ounce of sentiment or barely a trace of comedy anywhere, but it's hard to deny *Mad Max 2's* overwhelmingly camp look. Now it sure as hell doesn't have a camp *feel* – the violence and all round grim presentation of a world gone to shit ensures that – but men do prefer the company of other men. During breaks from raiding, they fuss over each other's hair. Shoulder pads, dangly silver earrings, furs, studded arm bands, face paint, lightweight chains, shaven chests, bare nipples and arse-baring chaps are all the rage. Our combatants are dressed like gladiators, traffic cops, punks or fashion show models. One of the chief baddies is a mohawked, leather-clad biker who becomes awfully upset when his mute, blonde companion is killed. Christ, even Max's dog wears a fetching red neckerchief.

This is one *flamboyant* bunch that, nevertheless, can't stop killing each other. As a result, *Mad Max 2* often plays like a massive fight between the cast of *Dynasty*, 1970s-era Judas Priest, the Village People and Blue Oyster Bar patrons zonked out of their brains from sniffing petrol fumes and angel dust.

Max is now a dog food-eating, gasoline-obsessed scavenger, travelling along a 'white line nightmare' in a supercharged V-8. Like the Man with No Name, he's a taciturn loner, indifferent to the suffering and death all around. Inadvertently, he falls in with a group of settlers, but after demonstrating his considerable survival skills against a marauding motorised gang, attempts to make him stay initially fall on deaf ears. "What is it with you, Max?" their leader asks during the flick's only speech. "What're you looking for? Everyone's looking for something. You happy out there, are you? Wandering. One day blurring into another. You're a scavenger. A maggot. You live off the corpse of the old world."

In keeping with Miller's diamond-hard preference for action over dialogue, Max simply punches this well-meaning critic in the face. Bloody hell, what a character, what a role. This is arguably Gibson's signature performance. He's pitch perfect in a fluid, kinetic movie that proved even more influential than the first. *Mad Max 2* is a lean action masterpiece, propelled by a driving score and bookended by some deeply satisfying narration.

Four years later *Beyond Thunderdome* turned up with a three-quarters empty tank and two flat tyres surrounded by goddamned snotty-nosed kids.

Aliens (1986)

"Listen up: I want this thing to go smooth and by the numbers."

So says the inexperienced commanding officer of a gung-ho bunch of heavily armed marines before they touch down on an exomoon in a bid to find out what happened to 158 colonists.

But a solitary, traumatised survivor called Newt (Carrie Henn) has a better handle on the situation. "These people are here to protect you," she's told.

"They're soldiers." The ten-year-old Newt can only shake her head. "It won't make any difference," she replies.

Hmm, we'll see what happens during this 'bug hunt'.

Alien was a haunted house in space movie that emphasised its horror underpinnings. Director James Cameron wisely gives the sequel a tweak by shifting to action/sci-fi. In fact, *Aliens* feels so much like a war film that it could have been titled *Saving Private Xenomorph*.

Ripley (Sigourney Weaver) has managed to survive more than half a century in stasis after escaping her alien-ravaged spacecraft, the *Nostromo*. You can tell she's been asleep a long time because she wakes sporting a dreadful curly hairdo like Queen's Brian May. When told contact has been lost with the intergalactic folk who've since made a home in the very place she's just fled, she warily agrees to return as an 'adviser'.

But only if every last xenomorph is zapped.

Aliens deserves plaudits for its steady build-up, especially its tense search of the colonists' deserted base, which initially throws up nothing more threatening than a pair of hamsters. Indeed, Cameron repeats Spielberg's *Jaws* trick of keeping the titular monsters hidden from view for as long as possible. Seventy minutes smoothly slide by before a xenomorph bursts out of a victim's chest. From this moment on *Aliens* turns into a clash between technology and biology. The marines have their hi-tech firepower while the xenomorphs rely on Mother Nature's savage gifts.

Cameron, who wrote the screenplay, builds on rather than repeats *Alien*. This can be seen in the way he adds nice little details to the creatures' lifestyle, such as the facehuggers' increased mobility and the alien queen laying eggs near a cocoon of imminent hosts. He also excels at creating a sense of scale, whether it's a beautiful shot of the curves of Ripley's face fading into that of a distant exomoon or panicking humans fleeing from the path of a crashing spacecraft.

Aliens is visually sumptuous and blessed with great special effects, not to mention its cool innovations like Ripley's exosuit cargo loader and those awesome robot sentries. All the same, things wouldn't work so well if it had a cast that served as little more than impending alien meals. Everyone is memorably characterised, especially the treacherous company man Burke (Paul Reiser), Ripley's refreshingly unannoying surrogate daughter Newt, the panicky Private Hudson (Bill Paxton), the female Rambo Vasquez (Jenette Goldstein), the solid, non-macho Corporal Hicks (Michael Biehn) and Lance Henriksen as a somewhat unfortunate 'synthetic'. Sorry, artificial person. Without such a tremendous cast, Cameron would never have succeeded in capturing *Aliens'* pervasive claustrophobia.

A Nightmare on Elm Street 3: Dream Warriors (1987)

Aah, poor Freddy.

Top of his game in his 1984 debut, but already wearing out his welcome in the hastily assembled, lazily named *Freddy's Revenge*. Some people get a kick out of this odd, gay-themed sequel, but I don't see it as anything other than a below average, forgettable rehash. At least we're spared the sight of a moustachioed, limp-wristed Freddy in a pink bowtie. It made a shitload of money, though, so part three's arrival fifteen months later was no surprise.

Often regarded as the best of the sequels, the overly busy *Warriors* does what it can to disguise the familiarity of its formula. There's a nice early moment that recaptures the original's creepiness when a pretty little girl riding a tricycle in Freddy's boiler-room tells a newly arrived dreamer: "This is where he takes us." It's also good to learn about Freddy's back-story ('the bastard son of a hundred maniacs') and kind of imaginative to see a kid turned into a sleepwalking puppet and led around by his torn-out arteries.

Nancy (Heather Langenkamp) and her dad (John Saxon) both return, but this just seems to emphasise how the episodic, poorly acted *Warriors* doesn't have anywhere to go or anything new to say. In reality, it's the usual bunch of naysaying adults and uncharismatic teens getting carved up by a quipping killer. There are no scares to be had, its most horrifying moment arriving when a girl swigs down a spoonful of raw coffee with Diet Coke.

And what's that Zsa Zsa Gabor cameo about?

Lethal Weapon 2 (1989)

Am I too old for this shit? I mean, I'm a mature gentleman, so shouldn't I have moved on from such high-octane buddy-cop nonsense to *The 400 Blows* or *The Sorrow and the Pity* by now?

Don't think so. The first two *Weapons* kick serious arse. Just about every scene works, although overall there are three noticeable flaws: Gibson is way too young to play a hardcore Vietnam vet unless the Special Forces recruited twelve year olds in the 1960s, his suicidal tendencies are initially overdone, and he sports one of the worst mullets in 80s cinema. Otherwise he remains a convincing action man fully deserving of his star power.

Lethal Weapon begins with a bang (or should that be a splat!) when a gorgeous, drugged-up girly takes a nudey plunge off a skyscraper. From that point on we get admirable chemistry between its leads Riggs and Murtaugh (Gibson and Danny Glover), on the money dialogue, a couple of awesome set pieces, and the scenery-chewing baddie Gary Busey, who's indifferent to having his arm barbecued. It's a near effortless watch and only a sniffy sourpuss would turn his or her nose up at such wham-bam cinema.

The sequel seamlessly continues the action, already aware of its pop culture impact when Riggs tells his longsuffering partner: "We're back, we're bad, you're black, I'm mad!" Part two tones down Riggs' death wish, instead opting for recklessness. It also ups the comedy quotient. Murtaugh's teenage daughter is now appearing in a TV condom ad, Murtaugh has to endure the longest and most memorable dump of his life and, of course, we get to meet motormouth 'Okay, okay, okay' stoolie Leo Getz (Joe Pesci). You might find this guy annoying, but his comic persona is so well drawn it's hard to believe that five minutes later in *Goodfellas* he'd be portraying one of the most psychotic villains in cinematic history.

Plot wise, Riggs and Murtaugh are after some Krugerrand-loving, racist South Africans hiding behind their Apartheid-era diplomatic immunity. Standout baddies Joss Ackland ("My dear officer, you could not even give me a parking ticket") and Derrick O'Connor ("Have your brains ever seen the light of day?") threaten to steal the show, although Patsy Kensit and her lovely firm breasts also make a warm impression.

Lethal Weapon 2 is smartly written, expertly paced stuff, full of impressive stunts, memorable scenes and winning humour.

Plaudits, too, for featuring a death by surfboard.

The Fly II (1989)

Do you remember I mentioned why people go to see sequels? The allure of familiarity, mistrust of the unknown and all that. Strangely, however, many producers seem to forget this crucial bit of the bait. Hence, it's not unusual for follow-ups to be almost bereft of everything cinemagoers liked in the first place. Look at *The Fly II*. Jeff Goldblum and Geena Davis are absent. Only John Getz reprises his role and no one knows who he is. Cronenberg doesn't direct. The writers are different. All the technical crew are new. Stuff like *Crocodile Dundee II* might be stale, but at least it managed to drag back its stars and rack up a quarter of a billion in the process. Hell, surely the sequels to *The Sting* and *Grease* fell flat on their faces because they made the massive mistake of trying to continue with a clean slate?

Well, I don't know. Maybe a near-identical *title* is enough for some folk. After all, *The Fly II* grossed almost $40million against a $6.7million budget. Perhaps such a princely sum more than satisfied its investors. What's not in doubt, however, is the sequel doesn't share the same love as its delightfully icky predecessor.

And for good reason.

Still, it starts with a dash of unpredictability. A child is born as a result of Goldblum and Davis' energetic fucking. He's quickly whisked away by the baddies at Bartok Science Industries, the hi-tech company that financed the manufacture of those cool telepods. Martin (Eric Stolz) is whip smart and grows at a superfast rate. Before long, though, he starts morphing into a juvenile version of Brundlefly.

Oh, dear. And he's just met a girl (Daphne Zuniga) and got laid.

Look, I don't mind this slightly overlong sequel, despite its mostly pedestrian acting and over-reliance on none too convincing special effects. It's not in *The Fly's* class, a largely taut, intelligent movie, but it does what it can with its body-horror leftovers. There's even a mildly affecting storyline concerning a dog that manages to raise the odd ethical question about science's relentless demand for progress. Getz, whom I just slighted, also makes a decent cameo. You might remember him from the first flick as the guy Brundlefly vomited acid over, resulting in the loss of a hand and foot. Or as Getz tells Goldblum's similarly transforming son: "I had no love for the man. He *bugged* me." True, Stolz and Zuniga are substantial downgrades on Goldblum and Davis (just compare their polite fucking), but *The Fly II* has a degree of OTT imagination throughout.

Nice last scene, too.

Indiana Jones and the Last Crusade (1989)

Raiders is imbued with magic and remains compulsively watchable. *Temple of Doom* provokes a slightly different response in that it makes me want to put my foot through the screen. Apart from the duff storyline and some surprisingly poor special effects, Indy's adventures are blighted by the combination of an infuriating prepubescent sidekick and a paramount Silly Girly in the form of Kate Capshaw. No amount of heart ripping and whacked-out dinner scenes can make up for this pair of irritants. Fair play, though, Spielberg learned from his mistakes when putting together the superior, kid-free *Crusade*. Not only is it aimed at adults, but provides a Capshaw upgrade in the form of the unfortunately named Alison Doody (who plays a duplicitous, non-screaming Nazi tart).

Most of all, however, this 1938-set instalment is rip-roaring *fun*.

This time round Indy is after the Holy Grail and its promise of eternal life. Oh, so are one or two Nazis. Their presence threatens to turn *Crusade* into a *Raiders* clone with the Grail merely standing in for the Ark of the Covenant, but given Himmler's long-rumoured interest in the occult and supernatural, it's vaguely plausible to depict these goose-stepping, power-mad wankers lusting after the Cup of Christ. Indeed, their comic book blunderings, in which they can never shoot straight or manage to employ a bit of good old-fashioned torture, prove a hoot.

Crusade opens with a slightly self-indulgent River Phoenix prologue, but kicks into splendid gear when Indy delves into a secret, semi-flooded catacomb beneath a Venetian library floor. It's a breathless escapade that features thousands of rats, a bunch of mouldering skeletons, the discovery of some crucial info, a life-threatening inferno, and a cool, Bond-like re-emergence into polite society through a manhole cover.

Crusade also boasts a good supporting cast, tremendous locations, John Williams' reliable score and, of course, the combative, sexually competitive relationship between Indy and his crusty, somewhat incompetent dad (Sean Connery). The frequent humour, both sly and uproarious, consistently lubricates while its intriguing Leap of Faith finale (that echoes *She*) does a fine job of tapping into the mystical. Full marks, too, for *Grange Hill's* Mr. Bronson turning up in a slightly less strict incarnation as Adolf Hitler.

Crusade features a couple of wild implausibilities and is not as good as *Raiders*, but so what? It's still hard to fault its imagination and sheer Hollywood vigour.

The Exorcist III (1990)

The Exorcist was a profanity-soaked horror milestone. Its follow-up was smeared in locust shit and as amusingly bonkers as they come. However, Linda Blair wasn't required for the second sequel, enabling its producers to try a new approach. *Exorcist III* is not a reboot (like the deliriously kooky *Halloween III*) but it does manage to chuck out half the bathwater and the baby's head. Its chief connection with the first two entries is that our two main characters knew Regan's doomed saviour, Father Damien Karras (Jason Miller). Otherwise this dose of satanic evil takes the form of a long dead serial killer apparently still at work.

Lieutenant Kinderman (George C. Scott) is a world-weary cop while his mate Father Dyer (Ed Flanders) is a good-natured priest. They like to go to the cinema together and afterwards gently butt heads over the world's ever-present scourge of wickedness.

"We have cancer and mongoloid babies and monsters prowling the planet, even prowling this neighbourhood," Kinderman says, "while our children suffer and our loved ones die and your God goes waltzing blithely through the universe like some kind of cosmic Billy Burke."

The Catholic response? "It all works out right. At the end of time. We're gonna be there. We're gonna live forever. We're spirits."

Excuse me while I groan. One point of view offers hard truths; the other the most hopeful fantasy. Nevertheless, it's clear there's a deep respect and camaraderie between these two men and perhaps even love.

Kinderman has got so jaded and cynical because he constantly has to clean up the worst results of human behaviour. In the latest example, a twelve-year-old black boy he vaguely knew has been killed. Actually, 'killed' is bit of an understatement. The kid was firstly injected with a paralysing agent that kept him fully conscious throughout. Then he was crucified and an ingot driven into each eye. Next his head was cut off and replaced with one from a statue of Christ.

Pretty horrible, eh?

Except we're not finished. Christ's face was changed to blackface, complete with minstrel-like, painted white eyes and mouth.

Fair play, you have to applaud such prolonged, unabashed sadism, especially as the perpetrator then has the nous to turn his meticulous handiwork into a fantastically insulting joke. No wonder Jeffrey Dahmer was reportedly a fan of *Exorcist III*.

It's moments like these that help us grasp this flick's dark potential, especially as the good scenes keep coming. Watch how a doomed priest in a confession box grows perturbed by the voice of a little old lady alongside as she starts off sounding like a pedantic pain in the arse before admitting to seventeen murders, the first being a waitress in a nearby park. "I cut her throat and watched her bleed. She bled a great deal. It's a problem I'm working on, Father. All this bleeding..."

Written and directed by the key man William Peter Blatty, *Exorcist III* is based on his 1983 novel, *Legion* (a work I need to read). Ultimately, it becomes a frustrating watch in that his film was hacked apart by the studio in a bid to make it more mainstream, partly by insisting the word *exorcist* appeared in the title. That's the reason for those clunky, obviously inserted scenes with a white-haired priest and the unnecessary exorcism finale. This is a terrible shame because before the fifty-minute mark *Exorcist III* is on course to become a classic.

However, even in it mutilated form it gets a lot right by dragging in a *Carrie*-like emphasis on blood, near-constant religious imagery, some terrifying-looking stainless steel autopsy tools, John Donne's most famous poem, the camera prowling the wet, night-time streets, senile geriatrics, black comedy, frequently pithy dialogue, those scary long flight of stone steps that Karras took his tumble down in 1973, a handful of superb scenes set in a psych ward, and the killer having a sick, mocking sense of humour and fondness for showmanship that, on my more deluded days, I like to think he stole from me.

Damn the studio and its hack job. We can only pray that a director's cut will one day emerge.

Then I might start believing life is wonderful(l).

The Silence of the Lambs (1991)

Here in Oz there are a couple of national parks in the Top End. I've visited both. One's called Kakadu (where *Crocodile Dundee* was partly filmed) and the other's Litchfield. The world heritage-listed Kakadu is the size of my home country, Wales, and a goddamned wonderland teeming with tropical wildlife. On my travels, however, I've bumped into folk hailing the much less famous Litchfield as superior. I suspect they think that by going against the consensus they're trying to present themselves as interesting, knowledgeable and discerning individuals.

Contrarians I call them on my more generous days. Yawn-inducing dicks on others.

It's the same with 1986's *Manhunter* and its very loose continuation, *Lambs*. Some people insist the former is better. They think Brian Cox's understated performance as the cannibalistic serial killer is the more memorable.

For fuck's sake, you gotta be kidding.

The box-office flop *Manhunter* is not bad at all, but *Lambs* is an indelible piece of pop culture anchored by Anthony Hopkins' mesmerising turn. The one's fava beans and a nice Chianti, the other's fish and chips with Coke.

Lambs kicks into unsettling life when we accompany the ambitious FBI rookie Clarice Starling (Jodie Foster) into the lions' den at a hospital for the criminally insane. It has to be said that you don't expect a line like "I can smell your cunt" in a major Hollywood production. Still, it's a fitting *bon mot* for this human zoo, a place where the deranged, highly dangerous inmates are in various states of distress and undress.

Except Hannibal Lecter, of course.

His glass-fronted cage at the end of the row immediately gives off a different vibe. For a start it's better lit and more orderly. Even the brickwork appears cleaner, less dank. Then there's the man himself standing to attention with his slicked back hair and penetrating gaze. Within a couple of minutes we learn he's intelligent, softly spoken, polite, playful, super-observant and uncannily perceptive. This is a cat-like, borderline supernatural presence whose eerie stillness doesn't match the horrific violence we know he's capable of, violence that can erupt in the blink of a jaundiced eye. What's also noticeable is how comfortable this guy is in his skin. He might be an absolute fucking freak who dines on torn-out tongues and tales of childhood trauma, but he doesn't do *flustered*. Even more oddly (and despite his radically reduced circumstances), he appears in charge.

Starling, however, is having a far tougher time in her cheap shoes, an uncomfortable journey that doesn't get any easier after fleeing the madhouse for some much needed fresh air. For she has to make her way in a world of men. Macho cops tower over her, obviously thinking such a Silly Girly has no place among them. Others hit on her instead of doing their jobs ("Don't you feel eyes moving over your body, Clarice?") One even tries to kill her. Even a good guy like her boss Crawford (the gaunt Scott Glenn) occasionally treats her differently because of her gender.

In a way, this is good. It forces Starling to develop resourcefulness, courage and a steely inner core. Yes, she's sensitive, self-conscious, vulnerable and occasionally sporting a face spattered by a sex offender's hurled cum, but that doesn't stop her backing down from the bunch of condescending, sexist and plain dangerous male fucks all around. Not once does she morph into a gung-ho ass-kicker, though. This, ladies and gentlemen, is how to do a Strong Female Role.

Lambs remains a tasty adult treat, its dark psychological power never less than compelling. Sure, every aspect of Lecter's daring escape (from the moment he apparently wills a pen into his hand to paramedics being unable to work out a patient is wearing a false face) is ridiculous, but *Lambs'* surfeit of brownie points elsewhere ensures we never tut-tut too much. Indeed, you know a movie has succeeded when our charming, newly liberated madman jokes he's about to 'have a friend for dinner' and we smirk along with him.

I wonder if he'll visit Litchfield on his travels.

What Becomes of the Broken Hearted? (1999)

OK, time to check in on our favourite volcanic Kiwi nutter, Jake the Muss (Temuera Morrison). When we left him at the end of *Once Were Warriors* he was outside a pub ranting at his fleeing wife with the veins bulging on his forehead after having beaten the shit out of a former mate. In other words, trying to deal with a few anger management issues.

As *Broken Hearted* opens, not a lot's changed. He remains brawny and shaven-headed but at least he's not busting heads, instead happily partaking in a pub sing-along. Then his fatal flaw – machismo – kicks in and he's giving a couple of dudes that awesome, paint-peeling stare. "All they're doing is looking at us," a mate tells him. "You're too old for that shit."

Nah, he isn't.

Jake strides over and leaves them in a bloody heap before returning to his table to carry on singing, as if having done nothing more noteworthy than taking a leak. Leopard can't change its spots and all that.

And yet *Broken Hearted* concentrates on Jake's attempt to shake off his lifelong affliction. Not that he's too successful to begin with. After all, getting wankered, hurling disobedient women around a room, and publicly breaking jaws is his speciality. He's a crude, unenlightened motherfucker. Women are the 'curse' of his life and he's forever looking to blame others for his awful mistakes. Eventually he's barred from his favourite boozer and is forced to try a new one. He gets into a fight straightaway, causing the rest of the pub-goers to back off, as if a virulent disease has entered the premises.

Bit by bit Jake gets more and more isolated, forcing him to confront a new emotion: loneliness. This pushes him into seeking out his ex-wife Beth (a barely used Rena Owen) to hesitantly try to explain his nature. "I never used to think about it before," he says. "I just thought it was normal. You know, when I was growing up, that's all I saw. The old man hitting the old lady. Uncles hitting aunties. They hit us. Sometimes everyone was hitting everyone."

Morrison's performance, in which anger and confusion drip off his burly frame, is almost as eye-catching as the first time. He's a stunted human being, all right, with an acute inferiority complex that he tries to drown in alcohol. Nevertheless, he isn't beyond hope, although he's never gonna win any father of the year awards.

Ultimately, however, *Broken Hearted* delivers a confused message about violence. It's a messy, half-decent continuation that delves into the misogynistic, self-defeating world of Maori gang culture.

T2 Trainspotting (2017)

Like *Psycho II* and *The Color of Money*, *T2* took more than twenty years to arrive.

It deserves a mention as it's hard to think of a flick so in awe of its predecessor. Indeed, it spends an overlong two hours cowering in that seminal classic's shadow, offering frequent flashbacks, reminders, re-enactments and acknowledgments. It's almost paralyzed with fear at doing anything that might veer away the original's blueprint, leaving *T2* choking on nostalgia.

Its overwhelming problem is the 'tourist in his own youth' Renton (Ewan McGregor). In the first movie he was a hedonistic, unapologetically amoral parasite. Now he's a married *accountant* who goes jogging. Are we really s'posed to root for this depressed, conscience-stricken, self-pitying sell-out? His worst moment arrives when he dredges up and modernises his epic *choose life* monologue. As he takes an awkward swipe at iPhones and Facebook, the flick grinds to a self-conscious halt.

Elsewhere, Spud is dabbling in boxing and trying to commit suicide, Begbie has grown grey and predictable, Sick Boy is blackmailing a deputy headmaster, and a redundant new character by the name of Veronica briefly goes topless.

Then there are the contrivances, such as Begbie escaping from clink at the same time Renton returns to his old stomping ground. Other episodes are plain forced, like a sing-along in a Protestant club and Kelly Macdonald popping up as a smartly dressed lawyer. The soundtrack is mostly inferior and vaguely annoying. There's still some energy in the direction but the freeze frames, snippets of animation, visual tricks and other flights of fancy feel run of the mill.

T2 is passable, but it's the celluloid equivalent of looking at a fax of the Mona Lisa. Spending time with an impotent Begbie proves about as enticing as the prospect of watching Jake the Muss help little old ladies across the road. Maybe I'm being too harsh, but I can't help suspecting a staggeringly brilliant flick like *Trainspotting* is a dynamic one-off that should be left well alone.

In that forerunner Sick Boy outlines his philosophy about vitality, especially when it comes to artistic output. "At one time," he tells Renton, "you've got it, and then you lose it, and it's gone forever."

Prophetic words when it comes to *T2* and the vast majority of sequels.

Inflatable Bikinis, Erotic Soup Bowls and Randy Nignogs

During the 70s the British film industry churned out more than twenty sitcom-based flicks, probably more than any other country in the world. I'm gonna put my cards on the table and declare the vast majority as dire.

Fucking dire.

It didn't stop Joe Public from flocking to see them, though. A handful, such as *Up Pompeii!* and *Steptoe and Son*, even produced sequels. However, the problem with most of these cheaply shot efforts is a marked inability to escape their sitcom confines. Most feel like a typical episode stretched to snapping point, especially as they were happy to recycle gags, scenes and even storylines. Then again, consuming such movies can be a bit like life itself: occasionally you have to wade through shit to find a pearl.

On the Buses (1971)

This one focuses on the 'two lecherous layabouts' Stan and Jack (Reg Varney and Bob Grant). Now I know women have a thing for pilots and firemen – hell, when I excelled at these jobs I was always fighting 'em off – but a *bus driver and conductor*? Not only that but the short, cash-strapped Stan is well over fifty and still living at home with his mum and pickled onion-eating sister while the guffawing, balding Jack is pushing middle age and a long way from matching Paul Newman's good looks. Apart from that, they're hopelessly adrift on a sea of retarded sexuality. Both suffer from bad cases of wandering eyes, double entendres, and borderline indecent assaults, although it's curious how the women's responses vary between being unaware of the leering sexism, blithely going along with the drooling attention or eagerly succumbing to their crude advances. This might have something to do with the male-penned script. Anyhow, the opening scenes set the bawdy tone by having Stan and Jack happily stare up a colleague's short skirt before making tit jokes. Five minutes later the bus is being stopped so Jack can have it away with a negligee-clad, adulterous housewife. I guess on the plus side there tends to be an earthy enjoyment of sex on both sides without guilt or embarrassment.

Stan and Jack not only lead a charmed life when it comes to avoiding arrest for sexual harassment, but also their ability to stay in the job. These are not responsible employees, a fact that their immediate boss Blakey (Stephen Lewis) is well aware of. The hapless Blakey is a terrific comic creation, a twitchy, unpopular manager with a Hitler tash that no one takes seriously. At various points he's accused of being homosexual, a cross-dresser, a knickers-snatcher and, worst of all, not getting any sex. Interestingly, he isn't sexist, does his best to protect the girls, and is far more progressive than Stan and Jack, setting the plot in motion by taking the 'diabolical' decision to hire female bus drivers (who tend to be polite, professional, middle-aged, hefty, weepy and scared of spiders).

On the Buses was the second biggest British hit of the year and so successful that two sequels rapidly followed. As you've probably gathered, this is not sophisticated entertainment. Indeed, film snobs, feminists and the politically correct will throw their hands up at this banter-filled depiction of the war of the sexes in which men don't go near a washing machine or a crying baby. Mind you, I couldn't help enjoying its funny one-liners and distinctive array of character actors. Gawd knows what that says about me.

Rating: A fairly brisk 85 minutes with a near-exhausting fixation on birds and crumpet. The sexism is exaggerated for comic effect, but I sense this might otherwise be a fairly authentic depiction of working class London life. Six out of ten.

Please Sir! (1971)

Another big local hit, this school-based flick focuses on 5C, a class of unruly teenagers that we British would politely refer to as scallywags and ruffians. They're led by Mr. Hedges (John Alderton), an idealistic, goodhearted, easily flustered sap. His colleagues include a Welsh cynic, a lovelorn ginger, a doddery, faintly clueless headmaster, a battleaxe, and an officious, toadying janitor who allegedly served in WW2.

Penned by talented writers John Esmonde and Bob Larbey (who went onto deliver the vastly superior sitcoms *The Good Life* and *Ever Decreasing Circles*) this might be plotless but it still flirts with class, gender, race, female sexual jealousy, illiteracy and religion. Like *Buses*, it's nicely performed by memorable character actors, even if it's got the usual problem of the kids being in their twenties.

Then again, this works in its favour when it comes to the extraordinary relationship between Mrs. Abbott (Barbara Mitchell), who always refers to herself in the third person as 'mummy', and her 'little soldier' Frankie (David Barry, who was pushing *30* during filming). In a classic case of overcompensation, Frankie is the school's wannabe tough guy, usually clad in a Hell's Angels leather jacket while punching his palm and flexing his shoulders. However, it's clear he couldn't blow the skin off a rice pudding, no doubt the direct result of his mother's endless babying. When the chance arrives for 5C to go on a two-week camping trip, Mrs. Abbott initially refuses permission, a stance that makes her only child threaten to set fire to her hair. Eventually she changes her mind, accompanying her sixteen-year-old son all the way to the coach. "One vital thing, Mr. Hedges," she says, clutching the teacher's arm while handing over a teddy bear. "Promise to make him do his number twos every day."

Shame there was no sequel as I could see such an intense bond ending with an alcoholic, knife-wielding Frankie dressed in his mother's clothes as her corpse moulders in the basement.

Rating: A severely padded 100 minutes, but not without its charms. Five.

Bless This House (1972)

The trials and tribulations of suburbia and the generation gap form the backbone of this feebly written comedy. Featuring a fair few *Carry On* regulars, the 'plot' appears to centre on Sid James getting a shed. Yes, it really is that exciting. Now while the incomparable Mr. James, owner of humanity's most recognisable laugh, is always worth ten minutes of your time, his hangdog face and traditionalist manner can't save a flick that rarely gets out of first gear. Instead we have to make do with the thinnest of pleasures, such as buying a second-hand car for twelve quid, the often appalling fashion, and nascent concerns about the environment and female demands for greater freedoms. Elsewhere, pratfalls and neighbourly spats are the order of the day. Blokes of a certain age, however, might appreciate the portrait of a pipe smoking, quietly exasperated father who just wants a bit of peace and quiet.

Rating: After ten minutes you get the idea. Shame it's still going after an hour. Two.

Love Thy Neighbour (1973)

When it comes to humour, I don't believe in sacred cows. Tell me a joke about rape in Auschwitz if you want. Just make it funny. And then show me pictures. Racial humour? Bring it on. There's nothing wrong with whites taking the piss out of blacks and vice versa. For confirmation see the wonderfully abrasive *48 Hrs* in which Nick Nolte and Eddie Murphy fight like cat and dog, especially the classic scene where the latter strides into a redneck bar impersonating a cop.

But, boy, oh boy, *Love Thy Neighbour's* deadening take on race (in which a white working class bigot lives next door to a black educated Tory) is like being bludgeoned for eighty-five minutes straight. There's no wit, no flair and no insight. One of its many major problems is that the main white dude is such a boring, childish, miserable twat. With his misplaced sense of superiority, he abuses Sikhs, Pakistanis and women, although his favourite target is 'nignogs', especially when it comes to their alleged breeding habits. To be fair, he's not living on a one-way street as his black counterpart (although more intelligent and mature) is equally obsessed with race. The first words he speaks are 'Hey, white boy' while a few minutes afterwards he's calling him a 'loudmouth, pale-skin poof'. An hour later nothing has changed. I don't see *Love Thy Neighbour* as racist, though. It's merely crap. Just check out the baffling opening scenes in which black and white neighbours trash each other's houses. One even brandishes an axe. It has nothing to do with anything and a sound indication of the terrible quality of writing. And yes, this was a box-office hit. I haven't been this dismayed since the derivative, nonsensical *Get Out* won an Oscar for Best Screenplay.

Rating: I think we're supposed to infer that racism is self-defeating, but it would've been nice to have chuckled at least once during such a lesson. Alas, I just stared stone-faced at the screen as a bunch of mainly poor actors went about their implausible business. Zero.

Man About the House (1974)

Despite this box-office hit being about a greedy property developer trying to snaffle up some terraced London houses, I think the only way to get through its painful ninety minutes is to instead concentrate on its presentation of the so-called permissive society. The swinging sixties have come and gone. We are at the midway point of an even more liberated decade, but *Man About the House* prefers to highlight the repressed nature of British sex.

Basically, no one's getting any. Not the married, not the young, not the attractive, not the gay, not even the oversexed. It's a world in which a man in his mid-20s tries to make progress by telling his date he was born a girl and that he's 'not had a chance to find out if it works' since the operation. Then there's a lingerie-clad, nympho neighbour who drags a potential lover into her flat to show him one of her self-made 'erotic soup bowls', the sight of whatever its sculpted interior contains causing him to shudder and run away. Another man is so averse to conjugal relations with his domineering wife that he prefers to shower affection on his budgie. The only bloke who's getting any sort of sexual contact is a married MP with a kept mistress. He, of course, merely wants to wear her gymslips.

Rating: I've picked out the best bits. Honest. Two.

The Likely Lads (1976)

Do women take you to places you don't want to go? *The Likely Lads* suggests so whether it's marriage or a crappy caravanning holiday. Working class childhood friends Bob and Terry (Rodney Bewes and James Bolam) are now pushing middle age, but hardly the most mature of adults. This is illustrated during the start in which they choose to spend their Sunday afternoon playing soccer with a bunch of lippy kids, a kick-around that results in Bob's 'strong clearance' putting the ball on a nearby roof and a fire brigade rescue after he foolishly shins up a drainpipe to retrieve it.

This public embarrassment only adds to Bob's burgeoning disillusionment. After having gone straight from living with his mum to living with a wife, he's become envious of Terry's footloose ways. Catch the scene where he meets his best mate's exotic new Finnish girlfriend at a clothing boutique while his homely wife twitters about buying an expensive dress. "What do you think, darling?" she asks, after putting the dress on and in obvious need of a compliment. Bob merely stares into space, enabling us to almost see his *joie de vivre* physically evaporate. And the eventual reply? "I couldn't give a shit."

The Likely Lads differs from many British sitcom-flicks in that it's got a proper budget. There's a lot of outdoor filming and it's nicely directed and performed. It was also written by Dick Clement and Ian La Frenais, a talented pair of writers who helped bring to life Richard Burton as a psychotic, mother-fixated gangster in 1971's *Villain*, as well as an Irish soul band in *The Commitments*, the classic first series of *Auf Wiedersehen, Pet*, and the prison sitcom, *Porridge* (see below). The anti-glamorous, Newcastle-set *Lads* remains one of their best-regarded creations. As for this big-screen effort, the comedy might get a little strained and farcical in the second half, but it's mainly an amusing step above most sitcom-flicks.

Rating: *Lads* meanders, refusing to stick with one development, but this adds to its nuances and slight unpredictability. There's a lot of excellent dialogue as it explores male camaraderie, nostalgia and disenchantment. Six.

Are You Being Served? (1977)

A master class in lame British comedy, this one peppers us with so many double entendres that a straight sentence is barely said in ninety minutes. Perhaps this emphasis on toilet humour, inflatable bikinis, rampant campness, and the bizarre immaturity generated by being near a scantily dressed mannequin is *Served's* way of trying to brush past its central problem:

setting a sitcom in a weirdly underpopulated department store is both limiting and contrived. And so once the double entendres reach their peak grating point after half an hour, the cast is shuffled off for a Spanish holiday in a bid to broaden its approach. Misunderstandings follow. Oh, and so do the fucking double entendres.

Rating: The weakest of scripts is worsened by static direction and OTT performances. Despite spending an hour in Spain, it's obviously filmed in a studio. *Carry On Abroad* is genius next to this feeble pile of shit. Zero.

Porridge (1979)

One of the major problems with bilge like *Love Thy Neighbour* and *Are You Being Served?* is the ineptness of the writing. In *Neighbour* our lovely white bigot slopes off work for an afternoon nap only for his black colleague to get a tin of house paint and coat his face while he's dozing (no doubt dreaming of the master race reasserting control). He wakes up and wanders around in blackface as everyone sniggers, somehow unable to smell his new skin colour or feel it drying. In theory, there's nothing wrong with putting a racist in unknowing blackface, but the mechanics of the process are not even remotely plausible. The start of *Served* is just as bad. A cleaner in his 70s is vacuuming the store and decides to amuse himself by sticking the hose up a mannequin's skirt. Suitably enchanted, he does it again with the next one. On the third go, he manages to inadvertently suck the panties off an actual woman, a process that would surely involve a gigantic amount of suction and his victim jumping up to allow the underwear to pass over her feet.

I dunno, perhaps I'm being picky, but *Porridge's* sharply written believability is a mighty relief. Its only flirtation with farce is a guard's curry powder-induced sneezing attack. Otherwise it's rooted in a melancholy reality that generates its abundance of laughs by acutely observing the numbing, repetitive minutiae of prison life while revelling in the smallest victory over them.

The action centres on a 'showbiz eleven' visiting Slade Prison to take part in a supposedly morale-boosting soccer match. The prisoners are hoping for the likes of Rod Stewart, Michael Parkinson and one of The Goodies, but get 'a weatherman, eight small parts and a Widow Twankey.' Nevertheless, the match is a pricelessly funny affair on a par with the gloriously pompous Brian Glover strutting around the pitch in *Kes* bullying malnourished schoolchildren. Trainer Fletch (Ronnie Barker) puts out a side that is a 'blend of youth, experience, flair and brutality' telling the lads in the moments before kickoff: "Whatever happens, don't let them panic you into playing football."

Nearly every scene in *Porridge* is written and performed to the highest standard.

Rating: A valuable record of outstanding character actors at the peak of their game, complemented by a deft script, delightful dialogue and many laugh out loud scenes. It was so successful at the British box office that it even managed to secure a US release under the title *Doing Time*. Eight and a half.

Porridge is far and away the high point of big screen sitcoms. The next year it was followed by the dreadful *Rising Damp* and *George and Mildred* spinoffs before the newly elected Thatcher decided enough damage had been done to the reputation of British film. She promptly changed the tax laws to favour high earners, enabling the many heavily taxed film stars who'd fled abroad under the earlier Labour Government to return. Suddenly blown-up, cheapo sitcom flicks were yesterday's news.

And there was me thinking Thatcher never had a day off from being a bitch.

Amazingly, this sea change wasn't the end of the story. Sitcom-movies have become a thing again. Just like the disaster movie appeared to die with 1980's lukewarm volcano drama *When Time Ran Out*, it reared its zombie-like head again at the end of the 90s with shit like *Deep Impact*, *Dante's Peak* and *Armageddon*. Mirroring this trend was the somewhat less ambitious sitcom-flick. Nearly two decades after *George and Mildred* limped toward the horizon with soiled pants, the great British public rediscovered their love of such dreck when 1997's *Bean* grossed over a quarter of a billion dollars worldwide. *Bottom*, *Absolutely Fabulous*, *The League of Gentlemen*,

The Inbetweeners, Mrs. Brown's Boys, I'm Alan Partridge, Bad Education and *The Office* subsequently tried with varying degrees of financial success to hang onto those flapping coattails.

Excuse me, while I'm sick.

The Not Quite #4: Paper Mask (1990)

When I think back over my 'career' as a teacher and journo, hardly anybody asked to see my qualifications or took the trouble to check my references. I certainly landed my first job as a trainee reporter without the slightest sniff around. I also expected to be given a form of ID to help reassure Joe Public whenever I turned up on their doorsteps, but that never happened in ten years. People just took my word that I was who I said I was, obviously swayed by my boyish charm. It made me realise how easy it would be to make shit up, especially if you were the bold type.

Paper Mask takes this concept and runs a few steps further with it, as well as reminding us that doctors are mostly arrogant fuckers.

Director: Christopher Morahan

Cast: Paul McGann, Amanda Donohoe, Frederick Treves, Tom Wilkinson, Jimmy Yuill

The story: *To be thus is nothing, but to be safely thus.* Matthew Harris (McGann) is a frustrated, doctor-envying porter at a London hospital who contracts the infection known as ambition. When a doctor colleague gets killed in a traffic accident, he decides to assume his identity so he can attend the dead man's interview for a job in a different city's A&E department...

Why it works: Bloody hell, this is one unsettling flick. On his first day as a 'doctor' Harris is so inept he struggles to put on a rubber glove while inflicting so much pain on a bloke with a gashed thumb that the patient runs away. Harris is a lucky sod, though, and a smitten nurse (Donohoe) starts showing him the ropes. Before long (and with some intensive after hours study) he's doing no worse than the other sawbones. *Paper Mask* pulls off a neat trick: we know Harris is a fink yet we half-want the bullshitting weasel to succeed.

Apart from the clumsy use of *The Great Pretender* on the soundtrack, the first eighty minutes are superb. Writer (and former doctor) John Collee obviously knows his stuff, enabling the film to ooze with telling details such as the importance of the old boy network when it comes to getting (and staying) ahead. He's also happy to show how the average doctor thinks the sun shines out of his or her stethoscope. There are some welcome touches of humour while the dialogue often veers between economical and punchy. Performances are also nicely judged. McGann, whom you might recall as Withnail's long suffering sidekick, is quietly chilling. Look at the way he doesn't hesitate while flushing an engraved watch from his parents down the bog to help obliterate his identity. He's the sort of guy who sees a tragic accident as an *opportunity*.

Donohoe makes a lovely nurse, not quite in the scrumptious class of *American Werewolf's* Jenny Agutter, but still an effective foil for our unscrupulous, arse-covering anti-hero.

Best of all is *Paper Mask's* queasy nature. Or as one slightly sozzled doctor admits at a party: "I've been qualified for five years now, and I know one, maybe two people I've killed and that's a bloody good batting average. There's no one in this room who hasn't made a mistake. If the punters don't accept that, frankly, who gives a shit?" Even a fraud like Harris can see the truth. Listen to him dismissing the standard seven years of training: "It's bullshit. They're wanking around in university for five years, they put 'em straight on the ward, they learn by trial and error."

The message is clear, folks. Do yer best to stay healthy.

The things against it: Generally speaking, for a movie to be great, it has to be great all the way through. Off the top of my head the only exception I can think of is *Psycho,* which makes the thudding mistake of wheeling on a shrink at the death to explain at length Norman Bates' deviant behaviour. *Paper Mask* has a great first hour and twenty, perfectly illustrating how far a narcissistic personality can take a man, but then lurches into implausibility, coincidence and contrivance.

Verdict: In many ways *Paper Mask* is a dark forerunner for the much better known DiCaprio conman vehicle, *Catch Me If You Can.* It explores the nature of identity, ambition, illusion, self-delusion, fakery, guilt and reputation, as well as the dangers of a little knowledge and misplaced love. It's ace at demonstrating that an appetite for dishonesty can provide the bedrock for much more cancerous behaviour. Shame about its final descent into melodrama.

Abusive Flesh Peddlers

I've got a theory that a fair few women fantasise about being hookers. Like most of my theories, it's probably shite, but I've always been fond of airing my ignorance. I really should get a Twitter account. So, anyway, why do I think some women daydream about loveless, monetised sex with strangers? Because so many actresses at or near the top of their game choose to play tarts. They're in a position to go for any script they want and yet plump for harlots. From Jane Fonda in *Klute* and Julia Roberts in *Pretty Woman* to Charlize Theron in *Monster* and Catherine Deneuve in *Belle de Jour*, it's astonishingly common for leading ladies to try their hand at being bad girl sex machines.

Now you might argue that actresses, thriving or otherwise, do not form a representative sample of women *per se*, but... but... Oh, my theory right there is fucked. Anyhow, all I'm trying to say is that successful actresses are in a position to pick roles that *appeal*.

So, now I've unequivocally proved my point, only one question remains: do men fantasise about pimping? Would we love to be in charge of a non-unionized stable of half-dressed, sexually liberated crumpet that we can both dip into and relieve of their hard-won earnings?

Hmm, think I've answered my own question...

In the pretty good 1999 doco *American Pimp* a plethora of real-life, money-obsessed parasites are interviewed. None express a moment's regret about their occupation, let alone embarrassment or shame. Their lack of self-awareness in their hyper-masculine, ultra-competitive world is even occasionally funny, such as one pimp explaining it's important to be a 'man of principles, of character, of integrity.' Some have become flesh peddlers because it was learned behaviour i.e. their dad was in the game while their mum was a hooker. Others coveted what the neighbourhood's flashy pimp was wearing or driving around in. Not unexpectedly, they didn't have too many good role models growing up.

Many pimps believe the impulse for hooking comes from the women themselves. "We ain't making hos do a goddamned motherfucking thing," one insists. "We're just introducing them to this shit and making sure they do this shit right."

Surprisingly, the pimps don't appear to grasp their misogyny. Sure, women are *bitches* and *hos*, violence is reluctantly doled out as a means to control and in response to disrespect, but none see themselves as hateful leeches that spend week in, week out dripping acid on the souls of their girls. Instead, they believe they're a kind of labour-based lubricant. These dudes possess a different mindset in which they are blind to their failings. Still, at least they feel bad when their girls occasionally get murdered by johns.

However, they do think hookers are hapless thickies in dire need of direction. Manipulation is the key. "If she don't get no instruction," one pimp says, "she's gonna be heading for self-destruction!" Another implies that without him looking after her financial affairs, she'd just fritter all her cash away on clubs, clothes and weed. "By the next weekend the bitch is starving and the rent due again," he says. Christ, it's almost as if these bloodsuckers have convinced themselves they're business managers looking after the girls' best interests.

Thankfully, *American Pimp* also gets the girls' side of things. "He's more than a pimp," Spicy from Hawaii confirms in a slightly dreamy voice. "He's an entrepreneur, a financial manager, as well as a companion. He's there to bail you out when you go to jail. He'll console you when something bad happens."

Oh, hang on, maybe some of these whores are thick after all.

All the pimps interviewed talk a good game but we don't get to see them *do* a lot, apart from offering some pretty basic advice and guidance. Plenty are adamant that pimping is not easy, but explain little about the work involved. Buying some dresses? Covering the rent? Paying a medical bill now and again? Big deal. We just see them driving around, chatting on the phone and generally being up their own arses. Or as one tells an employee while lounging in a barber's chair: "The only thing you do, bitch, is just go to work, handle my business, get my money, don't give me no problems and everything's gonna be all right."

What is clear, though, is the typical pimp is a materialist that loves to *flaunt*. Money is far more important than the sex. One is happy to make known his girls bring in up to three grand a day. Another admits taking 2-3 hours to get dressed in the morning. They love to show off photos of themselves standing next to celebrities like Trump or Al Green. All bang on about their snakeskin shoes, chunky bling and designer suits. They're players, you know?

After half an hour of *American Pimp*, their straightforward take on things comes across loud and clear. It's a doco that refuses to dilute or sanitise any aspect of their behaviour. This unapologetic bunch really do believe that taking a ho off welfare is making a contribution to society. Apart from a short segment in which ordinary folk condemn pimping, directors Albert and Allen Hughes otherwise voice no objections or criticisms of their subjects. They don't place their activities in any wider moral framework. Instead they allow the pimps to shoot their mouths off, an approach that results in ever deeper holes being dug. For example, any guy in an ordinary relationship with a woman is seen as a 'square', a quite extraordinary dismissal of the average man. *American Pimp* proves an unsettling watch, especially whenever the pimps try to underline their integrity with statements like: "I don't steal nothing but a bitch's mind."

Oh, and as for my grand theory, did I mention one gentleman in this doco confirming it? "Every bitch in their life has thought about hoing at least once," he says. "I don't care if it's your mama, your sister, your cousin. You might not wanna accept it, but every woman has at least thought about it one time."

Shit, I think like a pimp. Guess I got nowhere to go but the movies to see how it's done.

Willie in *Willie Dynamite* (1973)

The pimp is a blaxploitation staple to the point that a full on, faintly ludicrous flick like 1974's *Truck Turner* is happy to offer two murderous flesh peddlers. *Dynamite* differs in that Willie is essentially not too malicious. Yes, he still lives off women, rules them with a verbal rod of iron and occasionally doles out a backhander, but he appears much more interested in strutting around Manhattan as its most flamboyant man rather than breaking a ho's arm. This lighter, initially comedic approach is reflected during the upbeat theme song in which we're told Willie has seven women in the palm of his hand. '*It's magic how he runs his game*,' the impressed singer warbles during a bit of dubious PR, '*never treating two women the same.*'

Willie (Roscoe Orman) is a proud capitalist that wants to be the pimping top dog. His silk and satin-clad girls are on a production line, selling a sexy dream to fat cat clients. "You're making these chumps believe they're getting the thrill of their lives," he tells one underperforming ho during a pep talk. "You're not only burning a chump's body, you're setting fire to his brain. He's in the big town on big business. You gotta make him feel like he's balling the Statue of Liberty!"

Things start to get heavy, though, when he resists a business proposal from the city's number one pimp, Bell (Roger Robinson). This fur-clad dude wants to collectivise and establish territories to counter growing police pressure. Unfortunately, Willie's too much of an individualist and egomaniac to go for a more cautious, democratic approach to whoring out his girls. "I can deal with any heat," he maintains. "Also, the bitches I run are selected to win. I mean, I'm controlling some tough, aggressive, *mean*-looking animals. Now can I tell them they can only run in one part of the jungle?"

I've got a lot of time for *Dynamite*, a very competently put together movie that could've just as easily been called *Dick TNT* or *Roger Bang*. Things to enjoy include Willie's ever-changing array of ridiculous outfits, his equally outrageous purple and gold pimpmobile, a fatal catfight, and the camp, self-affected turn by Robinson. We also get a former hooker turned crusading social worker who's got the girls' interests at heart. She's a ballsy, well-written character that forces Willie to think twice about his lucrative livelihood. Mysteriously R-rated, *Dynamite* becomes unexpectedly thoughtful in its final third and is a good, gentle introduction to far nastier pimp outings.

Goldie in *The Mack* (1973)

I always thought art reflected real life. However, I might have to rethink after sitting through this whoring classic. Coz I tell you what, those good folk in *American Pimp* all seem to be acting this movie out. It's like they long ago adopted it as their bible.

Newly released con Goldie (Max Julien) is tired of gun violence, drugs, being fucked over by racist cops and praying in church with his doting mama. Still, he doesn't seem like ideal pimp material. For a start he's somewhat languid, lacking in the arrogance and motormouth departments. He's also not mean enough. Then again, he's willing to lap up advice like this juicy nugget offered by a blind former boss: "A pimp is only as good as his product. And his product is women. You got to go out there and you got to find the best ones you can find. You gotta work those broads like nobody's ever worked them before. Never forget: anybody can control a woman's body, but the key is to control her mind."

Goldie's in and keen to learn. First into the stable is part-time ho Lulu (Carol Speed). Not that she needs recruiting as she virtually begs for direction and support. "A lot of the pimps are down on me because I won't choose," she tells him. "I need a man, you know. I need somebody in my corner, not just because I'm paying him but somebody to be there. Help me, Goldie. I'm tired of being by myself."

Fucking hell, sister, ain't you heard of women's lib?

Despite having been close childhood friends, Goldie doesn't think twice about bedding her and then sticking her pussy out on the street, especially as it's clear she *wants* to be exploited. He knuckles down to work and soon he's got the requisite hat, the gold-topped cane, the flamboyant clothes and a thirty-grand pimpmobile. As for the gold at the end of the rainbow, he wants to 'walk off with the whole pot.' He's even nice to the awestruck neighbourhood kids, telling them to stick with school and try to be doctors and lawyers instead of anything like him.

Then you get to see him grooming girls and everything becomes a lot ickier. Still, the hos are thick and servile so fair enough. "I'm gonna be everything to you," he tells one gorgeous, candy-brained dreamer. "I'm gonna be your father, gonna be your friend, gonna be your lover, but you gotta believe in me. You gotta believe that everything I tell you to do is for the best."

There's no force at all. It's just smooth talk, manipulation and pie in the sky. *Then* Goldie reveals his mean streak by putting his foot up those pretty feminine arses. Elsewhere, his fellow pimps lounge around a barber shop talking about the game, being a player, hoarding money, putting bitches on the track and their overweening ambition. Fuck, it's *eerie* how *American Pimp* echoes this flick, right down to the squabbles over who owns which ho and the Pimp of the Year competition.

I often make fun of blaxploitation, partly because it's so trashy and poorly put together that it can be difficult to sit through. Then again, I also dig it because it's distinctive, politically incorrect and fun. Sometimes I find an entertaining gem like *Coffy* or a bleak anti-corruption cop drama like *Across 110th Street*. *The Mack*, however, might be the best of the lot. It's a well-written, hard-edged 110 minutes. In fact, it's so good it comes close to transcending the blaxploitation label and should be considered on its own merits. The staples are all there such as corrupt white cops, black hustlers, racism, poverty, drugs and religion, but *The Mack* never feels tired. It maintains tension throughout and is consistently inventive. Just catch the wonderfully surreal scene where an unseen Goldie is sitting in a planetarium's control booth, issuing booming instructions to a group of potential bitches that want to join his 'illustrious family.'

"The whole world is our stage," he tells them as they stare up at the vastness of the starry sky. "In this organisation there is a president, a director and a teacher. All of these offices are held by me. In this family there is no room for confusion. Anyone and anything opposing my will must be, and will be, destroyed."

Honestly, it's like he thinks he's God. Or the Wizard of Ass. Pay no attention to that mack behind the curtain.

Sidney in *Magnum Force* (1973)

Fair play, Sidney (Albert Popwell) doesn't have too much screen time in this cop classic but he sure does make an impression. You have to say that this is a man who appears to have got out of the wrong side of bed. He's particularly grumpy when it comes to one tart. She's been incommunicado all week after he set her up at a fancy hotel for a business convention. Hell, she's hoarded the green stuff before and he suspects she's done it again.

It's time to show her who's boss and maybe stop his other girls from getting any funny ideas.

The ho in question (Margaret Avery) is buzzing after her big earner. First she steals ahead of Mr. and Mrs. Well-to-do at the hotel's taxi queue before she starts counting all her lovely loot on the back seat. She's so happy she even gives the driver a flash of her knickers while squirreling away some of her ill-gotten gains.

As the cab stops outside her place, she attempts to hop out only for Sidney to materialise, shove her back in and order the driver to keep going. "I've been working like hell!" she tells him, already in a panic. "Let me show you." She retrieves a fistful of bills from her handbag but Sidney's not buying. Instead he utters the memorable quip "Let's see how much there is in the titty bank" a moment before delving down her bra.

Uh-oh, he's come up with 'Mr. Green', and our dishonest working girl is in real trouble.

Now he's checking the 'snatch bank', unbothered that the taxi driver is getting nervous at the sight of this blatant assault. Christ, not even Travis Bickle had to put up with this sort of shit on his back seat. Luckily, this cabbie's got balls of cotton wool, a condition that sees him slam on the brakes, bail and allow Sidney to carry out his plan uninterrupted. This involves struggling to remove the cap from a can of drain cleaner with his teeth as his disobedient employee struggles on his lap. Good grief, he's not going to pour that caustic stuff down…

Oh, he is.

I guess a man's gotta do what a man's gotta do. That'll teach her for nicking whitey's cab.

Sport in *Taxi Driver* (1976)

Corruption's a weird thing, perfectly capable of turning everything on its head. The most straightforward human relationship can end up back to front and upside down. This phenomenon was best illustrated to me when I covered a court case for a newspaper back in the 90s. A guy was up for sexually tinkering with his pubescent daughter and her friends. You know the type. Compliments, flashing the cash, trips in the car, naughty gulps of vodka, strip poker and drunken dares. A manipulative but not coercive slide into the worst kind of corruption. I bet he never threatened any of them.

By the time the court case rolled around, most of the abused girls had worked out it might've been better to concentrate on their homework. However, the daughter hadn't. She refused to co-operate with the cops, let alone testify. Wouldn't say one word against dear daddy. She believed he loved her and hadn't done anything wrong. She certainly loved him. Perhaps one day she imagined they were gonna run away together...

I always think of that shitkicker dad whenever I see the long-haired Sport (Harvey Keitel) doing his icky thing with Jodie Foster's Iris. He's tender with her, giving her the sort of affection and shelter a juvenile runaway is otherwise not gonna get on New York's mean streets. He might occasionally get mad and call her a bitch, but he never raises a fist. "I depend on you," he tells her. "I'd be lost without you." Just look at how he manipulates and reassures her, calling her his 'woman' and saying he hates spending time apart to attend to business.

In turn, this astrology-obsessed youngster sticks up for him, convinced he protects her from her worst impulses. She clearly enjoys his company, no doubt believing they have a future. Chances are, she's in love, unable to see through his self-interested lies because she's too young to grasp the depth of adult treachery.

But Sport is a practised con artist. Perhaps he even half-believes his committed performance whenever he's alone with her. In private, he strokes her hair, whispers sweet nothings in her ear and slow dances with her. Out on the street, however, the relationship is thrown into the sharpest of contrasts. There's no charade concerning love and commitment. Iris is merely a piece of meat to be traded. His laser-sighted focus is always on how much cash her illegal little toosh can bring in. Fifteen bucks for fifteen minutes, twenty-five for half an hour. Listen to him trying to entice a potential john like Travis Bickle (De Niro). "She's twelve and a half years old, man," he tells him. "You ain't ever had no pussy like that. You can do anything you want with her. You can cum on her, fuck her in the mouth, fuck her in the ass, cum on her face. She'll get your cock so hard she'll make it explode."

Flipping heck, how can he be so disrespectful about a fellow Libra? Not very sporting at all.

Duke in *Streetwalkin'* (1985)

When it comes down to it, you have to tip your hat at a man who inflicts fatal injuries on one of his misbehaving hos before passionately shagging another just a few metres from her inert, bloodied body. Such committed behaviour does have a certain panache, yes?

The pimp in question is Duke (Dale Midkiff). He's an out and out cunt, a glowering misogynist who reaches such a level of fury in the latter half of this little-known slice of exploitation that he appears in danger of self-combustion. In our gallery of pimps he's up there with the nastiest. *Streetwalkin'* is no classic, but it's briskly directed and for the most part engaging and smartly acted.

Cookie (a very good Melissa Leo) and her little brother run away from their drunken, hopeless mum and predatory stepdad. Duke, a practised cruiser of train stations and the like, soon spies curvy new flesh. As expected, he's all charm, offering a sympathetic shoulder, a bite to eat and the lovely chance to have sex with up to ten strangers a night. Cookie falls for him, even though his less than saintly behaviour is immediately evident. "There ain't no such thing as a bad night," he tells one of his underperforming girls on the street before spitting in her face. Like *Magnum Force's* Sidney, he's convinced whores are fundamentally dishonest when it comes to their earnings. In this case, the cocksure Duke's right, finding a wad of bills under her wig after having given her 'arse bank' a thorough check. "I work hard for my fucking money," he adds, grabbing the cash and knocking her to the pavement as a bunch of rubberneckers do nothing.

Clearly, it's just a question of how long it's gonna take Cookie to understand this guy is serious bad news. Little brother already thinks he's a creep, but Cookie is quick to defend their benefactor. "Duke looks after us," she insists. "Better learn to appreciate him."

Ah, there's that ol' mind control.

Directed and co-written by a woman, the nicely paced *Streetwalkin'* does well at depicting a whore's lot. I enjoyed its many scenes of New York's mid-80s nightlife, such as the hassling cops and the johns who are a mixture of lovelorn, hopelessly inexperienced, masochistic and downright creepy. Then there's a nightclub hangout populated with half-naked dancers, hustlers, drug addicts, competing pimps, the always welcome Antonio 'Huggy Bear' Fargas, and a tubby ladyboy in a gold bikini. The hookers are also a colourful lot, capturing a definite sense of camaraderie. One walks around the streets topless, another is a lanky pickpocket permanently encased in gaudy red lingerie, while an obese, over the hill tart futilely tries to lure customers by lifting her skirt. Duke, meanwhile, might not dress much like a pimp (although at least he's got the necklace, the earring and the fur-lined, open top car) but he does excel at being an abusive, controlling taskmaster.

Drexl Spivey in *True Romance* (1993)

I guess it's apt that Drexl ends up shot in the balls.

He's clearly not a nice guy, having murdered a couple of drug dealers and stolen their euphoria-inducing goods by the time we learn he's also an abusive pimp. As played by the excellent Gary Oldman, it's more his appearance than anything else that, ahem, catches the eye. Dreadlocked with a hideously scarred face and a fucked milky peeper, he looks almost as scary as that extraterrestrial hunter Schwarzenegger fought in the jungle. Or as he cheerfully admits: "I ain't as pretty as a couple of titties." Drexl is a diseased, unsavable sort of soul with a distressing fondness for gold jewellery, animal tooth necklaces and leopard skin outfits. At least he's a fan of *The Mack*.

Overconfidence proves his downfall. For when the none-too-happy, brand new husband of one of his former whores comes calling at his admittedly cool lair, he thinks he has his measure. "You know who we got here?" he quips to a mate. "Motherfuckin' Charlie Bronson!"

Visionary words, although I'm not sure ol' granite face ever went in for genital obliteration.

Mr. Peters in *Stella Does Tricks* (1996)

James Bolam, whom you might recall kicking a soccer ball about and sinking a few pints in *The Likely Lads*, plays the well-to-do, quietly sinister Mr. Peters. He's the sort of guy that enjoys a newspaper-covered hand job in a London public park from one of his teenage whores as she holds an ice-cream and talks about her dreams. This might make him sound seedy but, to be fair, he does use a broadsheet rather than a downmarket rag like *The Sun*.

As we've come to expect from such a bona fide flesh peddler, Mr. Peters is an expert in mind control. This is demonstrated when he asks Stella (Kelly Macdonald in a virulently anti-men, desperately poor, post-*Trainspotting* effort) why she remains under his guidance. "Because I love you," she replies with apparent sincerity. It's this sincerity that causes Mr. Peters to glance away. For this is a man both uninterested in and uncomfortable with the finer human emotions. "That's right," he eventually responds. "You do. You really do. And I make up for all the bad things, don't I? You're my girl and I look after you. But you have to pay attention to what I say. That way you're safe."

When the need arises to discipline her (e.g. after she's not long shoved a Fishermen's Friend up an abusive john's jacksy), he's careful to make this wayward Scot understand that the punishment is not only reluctantly meted out, but both her fault and in her best interest. Apart from that, he opines it will cure her occasional 'flights of fancy', those times when her mind slips from the importance of fucking strangers for money or acquiescing to their perverted demands.

"You really must concentrate, Stella," he adds. "Take part in the scheme of things. Don't make me lose you."

But Stella somehow can't quite adjust to his nurturing, despite being provided with a sizeable perk such as a rent-free flat. She wants something better and prepares to break free, a decision that only leads Mr. Peters to make an 'example' of her to his other girls by arranging a gang rape in the aforementioned flat. You might think this makes him a bit of a bastard, but he does give the bonnie wee lass a goodbye kiss beforehand and take the trouble to hold her hand throughout.

Big Tim in *Requiem for a Dream* (2000)

Things are not going well for wannabe fashion designer Marion Silver (Jennifer Connelly). She's been slinging heroin for a while with her loser boyfriend in a bid to save enough cash to open a boutique. Dealing smack, though, probably isn't the soundest business plan, especially as she's also developed a taste for the stuff. She's already having to 'borrow' cash from her shrink, a smug little tosser who feasts on her sublime physical attributes like she's a piece of steak. Disorientated and filled with self-loathing after a monetised encounter, she can only chuck her guts up and stagger home in the rain to an estranged boyfriend.

This less than loving episode, however, is merely the first bumpy downward step during her descent into sex hell. Next in line to help feed her spiralling addiction is the very lovely Big Tim (Keith David), a man who might well be in the employ of Satan. When she calls him on the phone, she doesn't even need to explain her circumstances. He just chortles, knowing full well he's hooked another twitchy, sweaty fish.

Like any pimp worth his salt, he makes sure to check out the goods firsthand. At least he's friendly, greeting her with a warm smile as she shuffles zombie-like into his upmarket pad. He offers a drink and sits alongside on the sofa, his eyes full of certainty. The small talk stretches to a good couple of sentences, punctuated by his velvety chuckles. She attempts to compliment him on his apartment's view, but after outlining a slightly dubious racial take on oral sex he indicates he'd rather get down to business. However, as she bends over his exposed penis, he picks up on her hesitation. "I know it's pretty, baby," he murmurs, "but I didn't take it out for air."

Afterward, as she numbly dresses in his bathroom, he chucks her the vital dope while mentioning 'a little gathering' in a few days' time. Marion demurs, but is reassured it'll be attended by 'all good people'. Big Tim, you see, is not a threatening chap. He much prefers to couch the prospect of soul-searing degradation in the most innocuous language. Anyhow, there's no need to get tough with a junkie in so deep. He just smiles. "I'll see you Sunday," he says, walking away naked.

What follows, of course, is an unforgettable experience both for Marion and the viewer. Big Tim, cordial to the last, realises his latest recruit is a little shy standing before the frenzied crowd of pornographic thrill-seekers in his apartment. However, it's no problem offering a bit of encouragement.

"Showtime," he whispers in her ear.

The Not Quite #5: The Devils (1971)

I love shit about repressed female sexuality. Take nuns. They're a bunch of wretched, feeble-minded cowards, women who cling to a fantasy deity and starve themselves of Earthly pleasures because they're ashamed of their pussy.

Now *The Devils* may well appear to be about religion and politics in 17th century France, but it's more to do with the way in which females that deny their sexuality are an absolute bloody menace.

Director: Ken Russell

Cast: Oliver Reed, Vanessa Redgrave, Dudley Sutton, Christopher Logue, Gemma Jones

The story: Father Urbain Grandier (Reed) finds himself in charge of the city of Loudun after its governor dies. The dastardly Baron Jean de Laubardemont (Sutton) wants to pull down its walls to help snuff out any possibility of a Protestant uprising, but the progressive, religiously tolerant Grandier tells him to piss off. A way has to be found to discredit and destroy this meddlesome priest...

Why it works: This is peak Ollie Reed, a man not only at the height of his burly powers but in the running to fill Bond's soon to be vacated shoes. He gives a good performance as the complex, contradictory Grandier, a charismatic, committed man of the cloth who's not afraid to grab as much skirt as possible while defying the corrupt, murderous authorities. Intelligent and articulate, he appreciates the religiously versed can be like a 'flock of trained parrots' (both of whom have equal chance of entering the kingdom of heaven) but fails to appreciate his own role in spreading oppressive bullshit. "If God wants you to suffer," he tells one anguished confessor, "then you should want to suffer, and accept that suffering gladly." Shit, that doesn't sound like much of a pep talk to me.

Grandier knows the heresy accusations against him by a bunch of sexually frustrated nuns are merely a smokescreen because he's a threat to church and state, but still clings to the typical religious delusion of being 'a small part of God's plan.' Likewise, he can see through the nonsense of quacks (trying to cure the plague raging all around by using cupping and stinging hornets) but can't grasp the nonsense that is Catholicism. "Turn your face toward God, my daughter," he tells one agony-stricken plague victim. "Be glad. You stand on the threshold of everlasting life." Grandier does, however, have clear insight into the machinations of power, although it's hard to feel he's locked onto anything other than a suicide mission. On one occasion he says: "I have a great need to be united with God" while at another: "Hold my hand... Like touching the dead, isn't it?"

Elsewhere, Russell comes up with some sumptuous visuals (especially its bleak closing sequence), a sprinkling of pungent dialogue, and good production values. He vividly illustrates the church's crushing power. There's also a pronounced sense that state-sponsored violence, hideous diseases and an early death are much closer to the average individual than today.

The things against it: Right from its opening scene of a play being performed on stage, *The Devils* has a theatrical feel. This is amplified by its costumes, painted faces, dissonant score, characters jabbering away to themselves, an effete, flamboyant king, Shakespearean-like comic relief and some arty directorial choices. Occasionally the casting feels anachronistic, especially one witch-hunting priest who looks like he's just stepped out of The Rolling Stones. Some humour is misplaced, such as Grandier fending off a sword attack with a stuffed crocodile. *The Devils* is very silly in places, its overheated nature undermining its frequent stretches of grimy nastiness. This is a pic crammed full of torture, rape, overflowing plague pits, and maggot-dripping skeletons broken on the wheel yet it's difficult to take seriously. What are you supposed to make of a plethora of naked nuns waggling their tongues, publicly masturbating and running around begging to be kissed? I appreciate they're pretending to be possessed by devils but at points *The Devils* feels like an X-rated *Carry on Nun*.

In fact, even pre-possession, the nuns are the biggest problem. When it comes to Grandier, they're like a bunch of silly schoolgirls trying to get a glimpse of their favourite pop star. "I can see him!" one cries, her habit all but catching fire. "He's the most beautiful man in the world!" Now there's sexual curiosity and sexual repression, but Russell's portrayal of unfulfilled womanhood is hysterical. Look at Sister Jeanne des Agnes (Redgrave), the deformed, sniggering abbess who falls in love/lust with Grandier without even meeting him. She gives an arch, crucifix-biting performance devoid of nuance and subtlety. She's a hypocritical control freak just as hungry for cock as all the rest. "Satan is ever ready to seduce us with sensual delights," she tells her girls. Moments later she's having tormented visions of licking Christ's wounds while begging God: "Take away my hump!" It's all too much: everything piles up, becomes unwieldy and falls over.

Verdict: *The Devils* is one fucking grotesque flick. It's miles over the top and (apart from the grounded Reed) mainly filled with ridiculous performances. It's almost as if he's acting in a different pic. People simply don't behave like this whether they're possessed, ambitious, jealous, repressed or insincere, especially the way they celebrate the most god-awful human suffering. Even Grandier tests our patience by remaining fantastically devout and articulate under torture.

However, I'm always going to have a soft spot for a movie that portrays religion in the worst possible light. *The Devils* shows it to be *fucked*, an irrational, fatalistic and dangerous means to control and annihilate non-conformers. It also wins brownie points for suggesting there's a fair bit of pretending involved.

Thirty Odd Years of Walken

By 1991 Christopher Walken was a major star, having secured a place in pop culture with his Oscar-winning *Deer Hunter* turn. Yet watch him drift through that year's little-seen *All-American Murder* clad in a leather jacket and a fixed expression and you have to wonder what the fuck's going on. Surely an actor of such stature should be in something a bit better than this direct-to-video *giallo* travesty?

After all, the guy was still in his prime.

Walken plays a cop called Decker in an otherwise no-name, college-set flick ridden with naff hairdos, a sappy REO Speedwagon-like soundtrack, and an almost unbroken series of implausible scenes including a cynical nympho cougar whinging about facelifts, a deaf, panties-sniffing handyman, and a gasoline-drenched cheerleader being set on fire with a blowtorch. Our wrongly accused, four-foot high hero, whose name I can't be bothered to look up, appears to be channelling *Back to the Future*-era Michael J. Fox, except he's got no skateboard and is up to his neck in murder, promiscuity and body parts. The eyebrow-raising dialogue simply provides the cherry on top ("I once knew a girl called Leslie. I called her The Squirrel because she was always grabbing my nuts.") In short, you can understand why Ken Russell was originally in the frame to direct such lurid nonsense.

Less easy to explain is Walken's presence. His character's unconventional nature is typified by the way he handles a public siege at a corner store. Here he taunts a knife-wielding perp through a bullhorn about having banged his wife. Then he breaks into song.

And yes, you did read that right.

"I never forget a face, especially if I've sat on it," he tells the agitated crim. "I hope you have the fun with her that I do. I love that little mole on her butt, don't you? And how about that sensitive left nipple? And what mouth action! I thought Jaws only moved that fast in water!" This button-pushing exercise so enrages the hubby that he lets go of his terrified hostage and rushes outside to be shot in the knee by Decker. Not that any fellow cops or onlookers bother offering a passing comment on such a dramatic turn of events.

Terrible, eh?

It's peculiar how Walken was even offered a script this bad yet alone chose to *star* in it. Then again, the next flick he wandered yawning through was a batshit crazy war drama by the name of *McBain*. After watching this pair, I think it's fair to say 1991 was not a banner year for our Chris.

But that's Walken for you. He can electrify the screen as a piss-poor daddy and unrepentant killer in *At Close Range*, but then enter into a prolonged period of churning out dreck. The man occasionally demonstrates a white-hot, Brando-like talent that also can't help disintegrating into utter disdain for his craft.

Early stuff: *The Anderson Tapes* **(1971),** *Annie Hall* **(1977),** *The Sentinel* **(1977) &** *Last Embrace* **(1979)**

Walken made his inauspicious debut in the peculiar, unexciting *Anderson Tapes* in which the newly paroled robber Duke Anderson (Sean Connery) compares safecracking to rape ("I used to pull 'em open and plunge right in!") It's a mob-tinged caper movie obviously trying to say something about technological surveillance, but finds neither the right tone nor level of action. Walken, oft-hidden behind a mask, is left without any good scenes.

It took another six years before he demonstrated his renowned ability to capture a character's off-kilter or plain weird streak when he turned up as Duane Hall in *Annie Hall*. Sitting in his gloomy bedroom like a moody teenager, he beckons his sister's boyfriend Alvy (Woody Allen) before confessing a suicidal fantasy about causing a head-on collision while driving. "I can anticipate the explosion," he reveals in an emotionless voice. "The sound of shattering glass, the flames rising out of the flowing gasoline..." And, of course, the next scene is a blank-faced Duane giving Alvy a lift to the airport as his deeply uncomfortable passenger sits alongside.

Annie Hall provided a memorable cameo, but the best that can be said about Michael Winner's incoherent horror turkey *The Sentinel* is Walken doesn't embarrass himself (unlike, for example, a leotard-clad, publicly masturbating Beverly D'Angelo and a camp Burgess Meredith throwing a feline birthday party).

Things didn't improve in the sub-Hitchcockian *Last Embrace*, a very silly, confused attempt at some sort of romantic espionage mystery. Supposedly rooted in reality, it's every bit as daft as *The Sentinel's* supernatural shenanigans. Walken plays a treacherous, bureaucratic type who does his dirty business from behind a desk. He gets to wear unflattering glasses and... oh, that's it.

No way to follow up an Oscar win, mate.

The horror gem: *The Dead Zone* (1983)

By the time *Dead Zone* came around, Walken's career was a bit wobbly. His iconic *Deer Hunter* turn had not exactly led to setting moviedom ablaze. *Heaven's Gate* became a legendary, studio-maiming bomb, not helped by Walken's unintentionally comical lead-up to his *Bonnie and Clyde*-style demise. Neither *The Dogs of War* nor the 1981 musical drama *Pennies from Heaven* found an audience whereas 1983's *Brainstorm* was a sci-fi dud whose troubled production (involving the death of Natalie Wood) was far more interesting than the final product. Five years after blowing his junkie brains out in a Saigon gambling den, Walken needed a hit.

Luckily, Cronenberg turned up with far and away the best pic he ever assembled. Given its episodic nature and incredulous goings-on, I have no idea how it works, but work it does.

It's the sad story of an everyday man whose chance of a straightforward, honest and quietly worthwhile life is snatched away and replaced by little more than visions of horrifying trauma. Just about everything he knows and trusts is lost, including his beloved girl. He doesn't do anything for this to happen, but that's one of *Dead Zone's* surprises. Right up until the climax, Johnny Smith is a passive character, a man trapped between the unconscious passage of time and a newly awakened 'gift' for dark prophecy. Movies shouldn't place such a reactive bloke front and centre yet his plight is never anything less than gripping.

Before we meet Johnny the mood is perfectly established by its opening sequence, in which confusing black markings appear on autumnal still photos. They slowly coalesce into the three-word title, accompanied by Michael Kamen's wonderfully melancholy score. Johnny's a schoolteacher and, to be honest, it's pretty clear this dude is never gonna set the world alight. With his forward-combed hair, glasses and drab dress sense, he's a bit of a dweeb. Just listen to him when his fiancée Sarah (a superb Brooke Adams) asks him in for the night. "Better not," he tells her, even though it's about to piss down. "Some things are worth waiting for." Like Duane Hall's alter ego, he drives off in his unflashy car in the rain with everything to look forward to.

Then a sliding milk tanker intervenes and the next thing he knows it's five years later and his religiously deranged mother is revealing Sarah has turned her back on him by marrying another man. The way a supine, barely comprehending Walken hoarsely delivers the line "Husband...?" from his hospital bed and covers his face is a master class in acting. Fuck, we feel his pain. Johnny has awakened from his coma, he's back in the land of the living, but everything has turned to ash. Now his existence seems to have no purpose, except to learn of dirty secrets and be confronted by psychic visions of imminent death. By doing this, *The Dead Zone* enables us to grapple with some profound moral questions.

Sarah inevitably comes back into Johnny's orbit, finding him in the hospital grounds during a bout of physical therapy. "They told me you were outside," she says. His quietly broken reply *I am* suggests he's not merely talking about his physical location. For this is a man who now stands apart from the human race, already knowing that the only way to prevent his nerve-wracking bouts of clairvoyance and find some peace is to stay far away from the ever madding crowd.

Most people plump for Walken's best performance as *The Deer Hunter*, but I'd tie it with the hapless, haunted Johnny in Cronenberg's masterpiece. The way his gaunt, pallid face continually flips between resentment, sadness, anger, fear, pain and bewilderment is bewitching. Best of all is that despite *The Dead Zone's* insistence on depicting accidents, tragedies and the worst kinds of human behaviour, it's an ace love story and a deeply life-affirming picture.

War: *The Dogs of War* (1980), *Witness in the War Zone* (1987) & *McBain* (1991)

Walken struck gold early on in the war genre but attempts to replicate his *Deer Hunter* success often resulted in him lurching around a minefield. At least the tightly edited opening forty-five minutes of *Dogs of War* are very good. Events are pushed forward with the minimum of effort, there's a lot of local colour, and it's understated, convincing stuff. Walken, who plays a mercenary tasked with overthrowing a corrupt West African regime, also gives his first starring role in a major production his best shot. Unlike later flicks, he's really trying here and by doing so generates a fair degree of charisma. Indeed, his extraordinary face resembles a cross between a pop star and a vampire. "Do you reject Satan?" a priest asks him at one point. He might say yes, but I think he'd fit in seamlessly in a satanic version of Duran Duran. There's danger in his darting eyes and litheness in his distinctive gait, all lubricated by that marvellous voice.

As you can probably tell, Walken is not the problem with *Dogs of War*. After all, he kills without hesitation and gets to feed a man a shard of glass. No, *Dogs'* mistake (despite being nicely shot and well acted by all concerned) is a serious lack of action. Ten minutes of fireworks isn't enough in a two-hour war flick. Instead it concentrates on character and the nuts and bolts of setting up such a mercenary operation. It even manages to suggest that the reason an intelligent man kills people for money in foreign countries is woman trouble. Yeah, well, I guess we all deal with a broken heart in different ways.

Dogs remains a watchable minor success unlike *Witness in the War Zone* (aka *Deadline*). This is a clumsily titled, deservedly obscure effort that requires some knowledge of the Israeli-Palestinian conflict. Walken is a duped TV news journo in Beirut having a tough time. In other words it's another reporter-in-peril flick that was all the rage in the 80s. "Here people don't kill who they want to kill," Walken is told by a fellow cameraman. "They kill who they can." This type of movie rarely works because of its passive setup in which a protagonist is chucked into a fucked-up place and gets smacked around by events way beyond his or her control. *War Zone* is no different, often feeling like a dour TV movie.

In the much more fun *McBain,* Walken starts off suffering a bout of *Deer Hunter* déjà vu. He's a blue-collar worker back in Nam getting roughed up in a bamboo cage for the entertainment of those dastardly VC. Once again, he's in dire need of saving.

And saved he is at the last second by a Colombian soldier from a different unit named Santos (Chick Vennera). This brave intervention leads to instant bonding. Then a decade or so later (in the first of a series of bonkers jumps) Santos is busy trying to overthrow a corrupt Columbian president with a ragtag army. Result? He gets executed on live TV which, somewhat understandably, upsets his little sister. She toddles off to New York to track down his old Nam buddy, McBain (Walken). Without a second thought, McBain reforms his army crew to fulfil Santos' attempted revolution. Before long, he's raising capital by knocking over a stateside drug cartel and getting ready to invade Bogotá...

Crikey, the explosion-heavy *McBain* is a mess, often playing like a drunken mash-up of *Apocalypse Now* and *Top Gun* with some gangsters thrown in for good measure. An unchallenged, somewhat indifferent Walken strides through this preposterous rubbish with a bog brush hairdo and the odd silly hat. Writer-director James (*The Exterminator*) Glickenhaus tries his best, even employing some fancy De Palma-like moves with his 360s and bird's eye views, but he's just chucking spaghetti against a bullet-ridden wall. Nothing convinces, typified by the film's many extras taking an age to respond to being shot. McBain, meanwhile, is happy to sit in a plane and use a handgun to fire through its windshield to cleanly take out a jet pilot flying alongside.

The high-octane *McBain*, as you might gather, is never dull. Bloody stupid, yes, but never dull. This is mainly because it's got some cool stunts, plentiful bursts of absurdity (that include a woeful attempt at a Strong Female Role) and a body count that outstrips *Commando*. It's even more insane than that Chuck Norris terrorist slaughterfest *Invasion USA*.

However, despite the near-relentless mayhem, my favourite bit involves a quieter moment. McBain tries to empathise with the plight of Columbia's oppressed, drug-ravaged people by telling Santos' sister that back in 69 he went to Woodstock, couldn't scrounge any food and had to sit hungry in a muddy field for three days.

Aah, the poor lamb.

A mainstream pat on the back in *A View to a Kill* (1985)

Not too many actors get to play a Bond megalomaniac, but Walken was happy to dye his hair blonde and give things a whirl. Did he do a good job?

Hmm, well, he's Max Zorin, the product of some WW2 Nazi experimentation with steroids. This tinkering has turned him into a psychopathic industrialist. Hell, you know he's mad coz he thinks it's a good idea to have the testosterone-fuelled Grace Jones as a girlfriend. When he's not pissing around with doped racehorses, he's also planning to control the production and distribution of the world's microchips. This deft business manoeuvre basically involves the obliteration of California's Silicon Valley.

So far, so good, but it's noticeable Zorin doesn't have any dialogue in the opening half hour. In fact, he doesn't have one good line until the hour mark when he hosts a business meeting aboard an airship with a potential cartel, eventually arranging to chuck a dissenter through a hatch. "Does anyone else want to drop out?" he asks the others.

To be honest, Walken gives an odd performance. He's a little hesitant, sometimes appearing on the verge of forgetting his next line. There are glimpses of his disarming smile and that instantaneous ability to transform from jovial to ice-cold, but I don't think he gets the best handle on a genuinely insane character. Or perhaps he suffers from having to play off a non-actor like Jones. She mostly glowers or hoists opponents above her head, treating the whole caboodle as an outré fashion show.

Anyhow, I doubt too many would put Zorin in their top five Bond villains. It's easy to see the awkwardness when he shoots a man dead and says to Bond: "Intuitive improvisation is the secret of genius." Not the greatest line, is it? Then there's the scene where he's laughing while machine-gunning a whole load of mine workers. This sort of hands-on slaughter might be breaking new ground for a Bond flick, but it's awfully unsubtle and unimaginative. Ditto when he tries to kill Bond with an *axe*.

Playing Zorin certainly didn't do Walken's career any harm, though, as *View to a Kill* turned into a decent-sized hit amid all the flak it took for keeping faith with the elderly Roger Moore. *View* is rubbish, but it's an amusing enough diversion with plenty of ridiculous stunts performed by obvious stunt doubles.

A rapid series of washouts: *Homeboy* **(1988),** *Biloxi Blues* **(1988),** *Communion* **(1989) &** *The Comfort of Strangers* **(1990)**

Walken's a charismatic actor, but he's sure as shit been in a lot of duds. The overlong *Homeboy* is a good example. After a stilted hour the movie hasn't even attempted to introduce a semblance of plot. Walken is a flashy, small-time crim who tries to exploit the tough, undisciplined and punch-drunk boxer, Mickey Rourke. It's a slow, flat watch, further dragged down by Eric Clapton's interminable score. Walken has little to do except stand fully clothed in a hotel bathtub listening to people fuck, make a nonsensical speech about dinosaurs, sing badly on stage, dress up as an orthodox Jew, and fail to generate any chemistry with the half-mute, equally misfiring Rourke.

By the end of the eighties it was obvious that Walken was drawn to off-centre characters, such as the WW2 veteran with a steel plate in his head that he plays in the lightweight *Biloxi Blues*. He's in charge of a bunch of newbies for ten weeks of basic training in hot, steamy Tennessee. Problem is, when it comes to drill instructors, we've been here before with the likes of *Officer and Gentleman's* Emil Foley and *Full Metal Jacket's* Hartman. Walken does his best, and the flick sure suffers when he's off screen, but everything feels tired. He's the usual mix of sarcasm, outright threats, mind games and colourful insults ("I have a nutcracker that crunches the testicles of men who take me on.") It goes without saying he knows whatever happens in his barracks, although he is capable of justifying his dehumanising approach: "Men do not face enemy machineguns because they've been treated with kindness. I don't want them *human*. I want them obedient. I'm trying to save their lives." However, his divide-and-conquer approach and push-up punishments tend to lack imagination. He's not helped by a barely average cast and Neil Simon's oft-forced dialogue.

The talky, tension-free and frequently embarrassing *Communion* has even less to recommend it. In fact, it's atrocious. I can't see it appealing to anyone except those sad whack jobs that fantasise about alien abductions, anal probes and all the rest. Walken is well cast as a faltering writer already worried about his sanity when he starts suspecting extraterrestrial life forms are whisking him away. Frankly, I would've preferred it if *he'd* started abducting the aliens. At least that would have been novel. Instead clichés abound like blinding white light, electrical malfunctions and even an E.T. light bulb finger. The interactions, dreams, hallucinations, suggestions or whatever the hell they are initially prove comical before lapsing into overlong dullness. Walken tells his doctor he's being carried off by 'big, thick kids', which surely gives a good indication of the awkward, unconvincing nature of this pseudo-sci-fi pic. At another point his worried wife accuses him of self-indulgence. Yep, that sounds about right.

Things barely improve in *The Comfort of Strangers* where Walken dusts off his weirdo act yet again, puts on a white suit and strolls around Venice. Unfortunately, his sinister character makes no sense, simply being murderous for no other reason than the movie would be even more boring if he weren't. After sitting through this slew of turkeys, I was reminded of his ridiculous cop character musing in *All-American Murder*: "How can one person fall so many times into the shit?"

Going soppy over a French whore in *Heaven's Gate* (1980)

Like *Bonfire of the Vanities*, *Gate* was one of those movies I long avoided. Bad rep, you know? Plus, it's more than three and a half hours long. Surely there should be a law capping movies at three hours? I mean, go try that bum-numbing *Apocalypse Now Redux*. Still, *Gate* is a handsome effort. Did I say handsome? I mean *sumptuous*. In every frame you can see a lot of money has been spent. It's one fuck of an authentic recreation of late nineteenth century life in Wyoming. Writer-director Michael Cimino knows how to frame a shot, too.

Shame how things unfold.

I can't decide whether the editing is terrible or non-existent. *Gate* is packed with irrelevant scenes, unintentionally funny ones, or stuff that goes on and on and on. Cimino conjures everything up with aplomb, exercising an iron control over his mammoth cast, but too often forgets about that little thing called story. Indulgent isn't the word for it. And so we have to sit through endless bouts of dancing, roller-skating, violin-playing, countryside picnics and all the banal rest while patiently waiting for a bit of murder and mayhem. It's pitiful to see talents like John Hurt, Jeff Bridges and Mickey Rourke wandering around trying to sniff out the slightest relevance.

Walken plays a xenophobic enforcer for the Wyoming Stock Growers' Association, a sinister land-owning bunch who've taken exception to the arrival of European immigrants. In a well-directed introductory scene that brings to mind Omar Sharif in *Lawrence of Arabia*, he kills a transgressor before even opening his mouth. Action is character. And boy, is there potential here with talk of a 'death list' containing the names of 125 'thieves, anarchists and outlaws' that the Association plans to kill. Unfortunately, it takes more than two hours for this plot to get underway. You think it's gonna be a prime badass role for Walken, a kind of upside-down Schindler, but after grabbing our attention by wordlessly killing an immigrant cattle rustler he then gets sucked into a dull love triangle. Worse, at some points, he looks like a moustachioed Michelle Pfeiffer.

The Ferrara connection: *King of New York* (1990), *The Addiction* (1995) and *The Funeral* (1996)

Director Abel Ferrara often makes awkward, unsatisfactory and plain weird films yet occasionally comes up with something worthwhile and in your face like 1992's *Bad Lieutenant*. He's collaborated with Walken at least four times, the pick of the bunch being the neo-noir gangster effort, *King of New York*. Walken plays Frank White, a newly released convict looking to haul his way back up to the top of the criminal pile. He shares a lot in common with Pacino's Tony Montana and Carlito Brigante. On the one hand, Frank is an intensely ambitious, trigger-happy nutter. Yet he also possesses a shaky moral code while being aware of the wasted years behind bars and the need to build a better life. "I've lost a lot of time," he tells his pretty attorney as they study the city's skyscrapers. "It's gone. From here on, I can't waste any. If I can have a year or two, I'll make something good."

Frank fixes on financing the construction of a hospital in a poor area of the city, but the viewer knows it's a pipe dream. The realities of the street are always going to intervene.

King feels right from the moment we see Frank sitting in a Sing Sing cell with his back to us. The deathly pale, snake-eyed Walken captures Frank's conflicted nature well. He's obviously intelligent, poised and refined, but doesn't hesitate when it comes to spraying blood and brains all over the shop. He moves in high society yet is not averse to a bit of *Risky Business*-style subway shagging. Most of the time he seems divorced from the manic ugliness of his mainly black gang, but never hesitates when it comes to showing his steel balls. It's like he's lost somewhere inside himself, as if he doesn't really know who he is or what he's about. There's no doubt, however, that he's always one devilish grin or calm dismissal away from the most appalling gun violence.

King is a nicely shot, fast-paced watch with fine location work. It doesn't offer anything new and sure strains credibility at points, but it has a moody style punctuated by bursts of brutality. It also boasts an excellent cast, including David Caruso and Wesley Snipes as two of the most hot-headed cops you'll ever see. Elsewhere, there are urine-soaked feet, bafflement over a tampon-packed briefcase, fire hydrant trauma, and Larry Fishburne strutting around like an ultra-vicious member of Run-DMC. *King* might fall short as a top-notch gangster flick, but it's still among Walken's better efforts.

Ferrara reverted to type with his subsequent Walken collaboration, the black and white, pro-victim blaming *The Addiction*. It wants to be an intellectual take on vampirism by having a PhD philosophy student attacked, enabling stuff like Dante, a bespectacled college professor, cello-playing, My Lai, Nazi war crimes, ethical relativism and Nietzsche-like voiceover ponderings to be chucked into the mix. If that sounds like the perfect recipe for a lack of intentional laughs, you'd be right.

Now I don't get offended by movies (which are, of course, made-up) and I struggle to sympathise with anyone who does. For me there's no such thing as bad taste. On the other hand, being a slave to accuracy usually works against any artistic vision so it makes sense to exaggerate, invert or distort. However, I do like a semblance of credibility. I'm a fan of internal logic no matter how crazy the premise. *The Addiction* trips up here by linking neck-biting to the Holocaust. Some people will find this offensive or cry vulgarity. Not me. I just think it undermines the story. Indeed, I'm gonna go out on a limb and say that such a connection is deeply... facile.

This triteness is part of the reason Ferrara's tale of egghead exsanguination ends up with no meat on the bone. It's further weakened by the blindingly obvious word 'vampire' not being mentioned while arguing that humanity is nothing more than a bunch of evil shitkickers addicted to murder. Hmm, even a jaded cynic like me struggles with such an appraisal. Mind you, *The Addiction* does succeed at depicting vampirism as a ghastly fate by showing its victims becoming unbearably pretentious.

Walken, who somehow snagged second billing for another cameo, turns up as an experienced, William S. Burroughs-reading vampire doing his best to blend in and become human again. "The entire world's a graveyard and we're birds of prey picking at the bones," he says. "We're the ones who let the dying know that the hour has come." He briefly injects some much-needed energy but not enough to save this flat, ridiculous mess, best summed up when he mentions his pride in once again being able to defecate like a regular Joe.

Walken tried his luck again a year later in the 1930s-set *The Funeral*, a Catholicism-infused, thankfully less pretentious effort. He's a patriarchal gangster, none too pleased that his obnoxious upstart of a younger brother has been gunned down. Despite top billing, Walken drifts in and out of the pic during the first hour. Instead we spend time with a suave Benicio Del Toro, a disapproving Annabella Sciorra and a red-faced, shouty Chris Penn seemingly getting fatter by the minute. Things improve a lot during the tense final stretch when Walken becomes convincingly dangerous, especially from the moment he gets his hands on a double-headed axe and starts to reveal the true depth of his loathsome, destructive hypocrisy. "Maybe one day they're gonna find me with my blood draining into the sewer," he tells a transgressor. "And when I'm dead I'm gonna roast in hell. I believe that, but the trick is: Get used to the idea while we're here." *The Funeral* is not among Walken's better known flicks, but it builds to a memorable, sledgehammer finale.

The least conspicuous turd in *Batman Returns* (1992)

I think I'm on record as disliking superhero movies. No, *hating* them. In *Batman Returns* I'm supposed to buy into a deformed dwarf crime boss having been raised by penguins in a sewer. Oh, and the dowdy, timid secretary Michelle Pfeiffer is pushed out of a high window onto the pavement and some cats nibble on her and, er... Now she's Catwoman, a super-confident street fighter in black vinyl. Not dead or disabled or anything, but a whip-cracking wisecracker.

Fucking hell, how do movies like this get made? And why do people go see 'em?

The plot of *Batman Returns* reminds me of clueless TV presenter Alan Partridge in *I'm Alan Partridge* being told his BBC show is no more before desperately pitching new ideas to a boss. His on the spot, immediately-rejected ideas include such possible viewing delights as *Inner City Sumo*, *Cooking in Prison* and *Monkey Tennis*. All ridiculous, all dismissed out of hand. And yet in the real world someone pitched an obedient-penguins-in-the-sewer scenario and a big studio spunked up the best part of one hundred mil to make it happen.

Huh?

Anyway, Walken strolls through *Batman Returns* as a corrupt industrialist. He's not engaged by his artificial surroundings, looking perplexed most of the time, but at least he's less ridiculous than his co-stars. Then again, at one point he's suspended in a cage gawping at a penguin army and I just felt sorry for him. Oh, all right, I did smile when he tried to appease a vengeful Catwoman by promising to buy her a 'very big ball of string'.

Look, I know I'm incapable of entering into the spirit when it comes to this superhero comic book shit, but *Returns* strikes me as a flat exercise in shoddy, nonsensical writing, apparently all filmed on a soundstage before an overbearing score was slapped on top. I also get amazed by the analysis such leaden, overlong junk attracts, with idiots wittering on about duality, power and other profundities. Well, for my money, this non-entertaining crap even sells children short. And Christ, it all looks so plastic, wonky and cheap. I doubt the fourth-billed Walken regretted appearing, though, as it turned into the sixth highest-grossing flick of 1992.

Walken re-teamed with director Tim Burton seven years later for *Sleepy Hollow* to claim his easiest-ever pay cheque. I don't know what it is about Burton's underwhelming movies (such as *Beetlejuice*, *Planet of the Apes* and *Sweeney Todd*) but they don't connect with me, despite their often juicy subject matter. *Sleepy Hollow*, in which Walken plays a mad mercenary killed during the American Revolutionary War, proves no different. He's an ace fighter, has a 'love of carnage', and sports a gob full of filed teeth that would make any self-respecting vampire envious. He might be dead, but that doesn't stand in his way of continuing to decapitate the terrified locals. Walken's screen time amounts to less than a few minutes, a rabid dog cameo that doesn't even require him to learn a solitary line. I'm not going to say something silly like he's the best thing in it because there's nothing wrong with the film's look or the array of British character actors employed. However, the dull, overlong *Sleepy Hollow* doesn't add up to a lot, leaving me fonder of the Headless Horseman terrifying Will Hay in coastal England sixty years earlier in *Ask a Policeman*.

Memorable cameos in *True Romance* (1993) and *Pulp Fiction* (1994)

Like most Tony Scott movies, *True Romance* is flashy and amusing enough but doesn't connect. The problem lies with Tarantino's script which can't overcome its clichés and implausibilities. There's a tart with a heart of gold, instantaneous falling in love, a supposedly mild-mannered comics store employee turning into a badass double killer at the drop of a hat, the clunky Elvis stuff, serious bodily assaults having a thirty-second-long impact, and a heavyweight Mafiosi hit man getting done over by a spunky little blonde girl. It's daft, some of the bit players wildly overact, and I wanted the miscast Christian Slater and the underwhelming Patricia Arquette as a pair of newlyweds to die.

Or at least divorce.

Still, *True Romance* moves at a fair old lick and boasts one helluva supporting cast.

Walken plays a no-nonsense Sicilian gangster on the trail of some missing coke. His solitary ten-minute scene with Dennis Hopper, the unfortunate dad of our supposedly mild-mannered comics store employee, is the best in the flick. It really is a pleasure to see these two old school faves spark off each other.

Sporting slicked-back hair, Walken is impeccably dressed with a particularly elegant stole. He finishes a cigarette and prepares to get the interrogation underway. Claiming to be the Antichrist, he tells the seated Hopper: "You get me in a vendetta kind of mood. You tell the angels in heaven you never seen evil so singularly personified as you did in the face of the man who killed you."

It's a fancy opening few lines and a lot to live up to, but the reptilian Walken manages it. This is partly down to the way he makes his eyes go flat at key moments, an ability that gives the impression he's emotionally dead. He also does this odd thing where he slowly moves his head from side to side like a reared up cobra getting ready to strike. Hopper can read him just fine – he knows he's the real deal and there's no way out – so he chooses a mocking farewell.

"Here's a fact I don't know whether you know or not," he tells Walken. "Sicilians were spawned by niggers." Walken's delayed reaction is priceless. There's no instantaneous rage or witty retort. Instead a half-smile teases his lips. He's obviously deeply insulted yet can't help being amused by Hopper's chutzpah. "Come again…?" is all he can manage before glancing around at his heavily armed henchmen. The deeply offensive theory is duly explained in detail, which eventually provokes laughter and a kiss on the cheek. "You're part eggplant," Hopper cheerfully concludes.

Hopper might be sitting down, but it's clear he's chosen to die on his feet. Walken does what he has to do and wisely bails before the movie descends into silly OTT gunplay.

In *Pulp Fiction*, Walken only gets four minutes but still leaves his mark in a flick chock-full of memorable shit. He plays Captain Koons, a former POW on a mission to deliver a prized watch to Butch (Chandler Lindauer), the young son of an air force buddy who didn't make it back from Nam. Arriving in full uniform at the child's suburban home, he sits down and calmly explains the watch's extraordinary history.

First bought by Butch's great-grandfather in Tennessee on the eve of his WW1 enlistment, it was passed to his son before he was killed by the Japs in the next global conflict. Butch's father had no better luck. He got shot down over Hanoi and spent five years in a VC-run prison camp obsessively hiding the gold timepiece from his captors.

"The way your dad looked at it," Capt Koons tells his attentive listener, "this watch was your birthright. He'd be damned if any slopes were gonna put their greasy yellow hands on his boy's birthright so he hid it. One place he knew he could hide something, his ass. Five long years he wore this watch up his ass..."

Periodically holding up the watch and pausing for dramatic effect, Capt Koons explains to Butch his father succumbed to dysentery, leaving him in charge of the watch. "I hid this uncomfortable hunk of metal up my ass two years... Now, little man, I give the watch to you."

Walken gives a subdued, deliberately straight performance. It's still a subtly funny scene, though, partly because he's telling a profane, racism-tinged story to an angelic-faced child about a supposedly lucky watch that brings nothing but terrible fortune to its owners. Butch, of course, fares no better with the jinxed timepiece, its acquisition failing to stop contact with accidental death, gun-toting gangsters, murder and gang rape.

Tarantino's influence rapidly spread throughout 90s cinema, resulting in many shoddy imitators of his hyper-aggressive, profane and blackly comic early work. Walken succumbed to this trend by popping up in 1995's *Things to Do in Denver When You're Dead* and starring in 1997's *Suicide Kings*. Neither is worth a look.

Some limited laughs: *Wayne's World 2* (1993) & *Blast from the Past* (1999)

Just like he loves to bust out the dance moves, Walken is also fond of trying his hand at comedy. First off is the lacklustre sequel to the big hit, *Wayne's World*, in which the overgrown adolescents Wayne and Garth (Mike Myers and Dana Carvey) wear ripped jeans, lust after Aerosmith and indulge in far too many movie parodies. Here Walken snags another undemanding role. The only surprise is that at no point is he seen standing on his head. He plays Bobby Cahn, a suave record producer who wants to bang Wayne's hot musician girlfriend. Bobby is the polar opposite of Wayne in that he's mature, loaded and connected. He doesn't find any of Wayne and Garth's antics funny, occasionally reduced to staring at them with mild bafflement. I have to say he has my sympathy.

Blast from the Past is one of those flicks that has an engaging (if preposterous) premise and starts chugging along OK before making a fatal mistake. Namely, it thinks Brendan Fraser is a more interesting actor. A shame, as the first forty minutes (in which a kooky, mildly amusing Walken has been raising his son in an underground fallout shelter since 1962) have promise. The decision is then made to send the bland Fraser up to the mightily changed surface. The flick gets lamer with every passing minute as we follow him on a predictable romantic adventure while wondering what Walken is up to.

Making eyes at Oscar again: *Catch Me If You Can* **(2002)**

Just over three decades after he made his forgettable debut in *The Anderson Tapes*, Walken snagged his second Academy Award nomination in Spielberg's big hit, *Catch Me If You Can*. Frankly, it's nowhere near as striking as his first Oscar nod, but at least *Catch* is a slick, decent watch. A crinkly-eyed Walken plays a con artist whose less than ideal approach to life has rubbed off big time on his teenage son, Leonard DiCaprio. I'd love to tell you about the scenes he steals or the winning lines of dialogue but there aren't any, leaving me unsure why the Academy took notice. Neither is there any weird stuff or snake-eyed threat.

Then again, perhaps I'm not used to Walken doing subtlety.

Here he's a quietly broken man who loves his son but is a poor role model. From the moment DiCaprio reveals his yen for dishonesty by impersonating a substitute high school teacher, Walken can't help but show a sneaking admiration instead of setting him straight. Before long there's barely a high status profession that DiCaprio isn't wangling his way into for thrill and material gain. "Ask me to stop," he half-begs his father. But Walken, his face hidden in silhouette, once again fails to put his foot down. "You can't stop," is the simple reply. This is not what DiCaprio needs to hear, but rather an acknowledgment of his boy's pathological lying and addiction to fantasy.

Walken's calm, understated performance fits in well with a smoothly functioning cast. His subsequent flicks have coughed up little of note, leaving me with the surprising conclusion that *Deer Hunter* and *Dead Zone* are the only classics he's starred in. Of course, with someone as talented and distinctive as Walken, there's always the hope he can pull another rabbit out of the hat. He's so unpredictable, though, that you never know whether you're gonna get the crème de la crème or a shit sandwich.

The Not Quite #6: The King of Comedy (1982)

Scorsese's cinematic partnership with De Niro is among the most legendary of the twentieth century, haemorrhaging up blood-soaked classics like *Taxi Driver* and *Goodfellas*. It wasn't all plain slaying, though. Just take a look at the headache-inducing musical *New York, New York* in which De Niro argues nonstop with Liza Minnelli. Then there's the redundant, painfully overlong *Irishman*, a 2019 flick that only tells me they should've called time with the nasty (but groovy) *Cape Fear* remake.

King of Comedy is a middling effort, loved by plenty and clearly influential. Still, it's not hard to see why it flopped by casting an over the hill Jerry Lewis while allowing De Niro his first stab at comedy. He might have just won an Oscar for *Raging Bull*, but cinemagoers were probably too used to seeing him killing people (or at least beating them up) to handle such an abrupt change in persona. *King of Comedy* also didn't help itself with an exceptionally dull promotional poster and a confusing tagline: *It's no laughing matter.*

A comedy that's no laughing matter?

Great.

Director: Martin Scorsese

Cast: Robert De Niro, Jerry Lewis, Sandra Bernhard, Diahnne Abbott, Shelley Hack

The story: In *Wayne's World*, Wayne and Garth sometimes drop to their hands and knees to worship a favoured celeb wailing: "We're not worthy! We're not worthy!" This ostentatious display might be played for laughs, but it also appears spontaneous and compulsive. Are there really dweebs out there who dissolve into a quivering mess by the mere presence of someone like Alice Cooper? Well, I guess if I consider a phenomenon like Beatlemania, that's a bloody naive question. Not only are there people who scream and faint, but there are those with much more sinister intentions.

After all, Lennon was murdered while Reagan survived an attempted assassination only a short time before the release of *King of Comedy*. Here the growth of creepy celebrity fixation is satirised in the form of Rupert Pupkin (De Niro), an aspiring stand-up comedian who desperately wants to be as famous as his hero, the late-night TV chat show host Jerry Langford (Lewis).

If at first, you don't succeed…

Why it works: The unflashy direction and performances. Christ, De Niro is excellent. You can't really forget him down in the basement surrounded by cardboard cut-outs of stars pretending to host a chat show while his mom yells at him. Neither can you forget him haunting Langford's office as he waits for his big break to somehow begin. This is a pitch-perfect portrait of a deluded, pathetic fantasist, his lust for fame so palpable you can almost see it oozing out of his pores.

Lewis also nails his role as the put-upon and abused TV host. Look at his reaction upon the overbearing Pupkin elbowing his way into his chauffeured car. Langford doesn't say much on the back seat, but the disdain and frustration is captured in the tightness of his face, his pursed lips and the placatory, non-committal replies. Langford has been here many times before and knows damn well he'll be there again. He's very good at communicating that fame is a peculiar form of hell in which you constantly have to endure people who run the gamut from ingratiating and insincere to leech-like and dangerous. To be sure, a simple walk down the street can be the stuff of nightmare ("You should only get cancer!") Quite clearly, the hoi polloi are like blind baby birds feeding on his mental and emotional wellbeing. He finally loses his rag when Pupkin turns up uninvited at his country home, leaving the audience to chortle and nod as he delivers the much-deserved line: "Did anyone ever tell you you're a moron?"

Elsewhere, Langford's office-based foot soldiers do a good job at illustrating the fine art of the brush-off. Gee, the first seventy or so minutes of the prescient *King of Comedy* are tremendous. It's an ideal companion piece to *Network*.

The things against it: *King of Comedy* is a PG flick. Oh boy, I wish it'd been aimed at adults. Then we could have enjoyed a much darker vision and greater unpredictability. As a result, Pupkin feels like Travis Bickle's nicer older brother. For all his lunacy he radiates surprising little threat. He's persistent and inept rather than dangerous. And why do we never see him perform his stand-up in New York's bars and clubs? This has always struck me as a big missed opportunity to inject pathos, cringe, grit and genuine laughs into the mix. For the most part all Pupkin does is talk and act out, but it would've been better to see him dealing with an up-close audience comprised of drunken hecklers, indifferent assholes and piss-taking MCs. At least that way we might begin to understand how hard it is to get somewhere in the world of comedy, even if you start in the right places rather than endlessly pestering an established star.

Plus, how does Pupkin support himself? A job is never mentioned. How is he so well-dressed? And why would a former cheerleader like Rita (Abbott) have anything to do with him, especially as she already knows he's a loser from school? Of course, there's a fair degree of truth that comedians are not particularly funny away from their onstage act, but you can't detect *any* humour bubbling away in Pupkin. It's obvious Rita finds him corny and boring. Just look at her face when he hands her an unrequested autograph, telling her how much it'll be worth one day.

I also don't care for Sandra Bernhard's snarling character, Masha. Resembling Bob Geldof's *Spitting Image* puppet, she's merely an amped-up female Pupkin. There's no need for her shouty character because we already have plenty of insight into the obsessive fan/stalker mindset through our main man.

But *King of Comedy*'s biggest mistake takes root through the kidnapping of Langford. Yes, this is plausible, but soon afterward things begin to horribly fizzle. This is not how cops, the FBI *et al* deal with this kind of shit. Then there's Pupkin's crowd-pleasing performance on Langford's show. Er, what? Given his lack of stand-up experience and familiarity with a TV studio, how come such a whacked out klutz is so relaxed and at home during his first broadcast before a nationwide audience? For fuck's sake, he's up to his neck in a prison-baiting criminal venture that the authorities know all about. *King of Comedy* lets itself down by abandoning Pupkin's meticulously built-up, agonising reality and instead falling headlong into his most fervent daydream. I've tried to interpret its lengthy climax as fantasy, but that doesn't work no matter how I approach it. How can it be make-believe if an exhausted Langford is watching Pupkin make it big? All I know is that as I listen to Pupkin's overlong and fucking lame brand of comedy, the movie has gone in the wrong direction while sinking ever deeper into the rankest implausibility.

Verdict: *King of Comedy* should be watched, if only to remind you how shit and phony the average chat show is. It's an often fascinating look at celebrity fan culture, happy to depict an ever-growing bunch of sad sacks who believe a photo, a handshake or some form of acknowledgement from an overpaid celeb somehow validates their existence. Why don't these people have any self-worth? Why do they act like they've got their noses pressed up against the glass? "It's not my whole life," Pupkin tells a fellow autograph hunter at the start, but it's not long before we grasp that his weird obsessions and fame-chasing fantasies are just as potent and enveloping as a serial killer's. His life is one long act in which he does everything he can to keep reality at bay. De Niro would have better box-office luck mugging for the camera in an inferior comedy like *Analyze This*, but there can be little doubt that Pupkin is a key role in his career. However, *King of Comedy*'s nonsensical, step-too-far finale betrays the movie.

Hodgespodge

Get Carter remains a fave, a bleak foray into porn, familial ties, corruption, contract killers, revenge and pollution all set in a decaying city. Often hailed as one of the greatest British gangster movies, it's the viewing equivalent of a kick in the solar plexus from a dirty, steel toe-capped boot. Amazingly, it was assembled by a youngish writer-director by the name of Mike Hodges. Christ, if the guy could put out a first-time effort this good before he was even forty, surely he'd only get better?

Alas, no.

Despite a further eight goes behind the camera, 1971's *Carter* turned out to be his nasty masterpiece. Hodges died at the end of 2022, his body of movies adding up to what I've ever so amusingly called Hodgespodge. The writing was on the wall with the immediate follow-up (and box-office disaster), *Pulp*. Supposedly a comic thriller, it shares similarities with *Carter* in that Hodges wrote it, Michael Caine is back on board, and there's gunplay on a beach. However, it's neither funny nor thrilling. To be polite, it's a fucking boring mess. Caine plays a pulp fiction writer drawn into some shenanigans involving a mystery celebrity and... Well, I'll let Caine try to explain during one of his interminable voiceovers: "This story was like some pornographic photograph: difficult to work out who was doing what and to whom." In *Carter* Caine stalked the badlands of Newcastle like a seething reptile; in *Pulp* he wanders around Malta looking distracted and/or mildly embarrassed. If you can think of a worse directorial follow-up to a classic, please name it.

Hodges then veered sharp left and had a go at sci-fi with *The Terminal Man* and *Flash Gordon*. The first is a chilly, insubstantial film full of slow, irrelevant scenes. George Segal plays a brain-damaged man whose injury has resulted in seizures and violence. He's now a paranoid psychotic 'afraid of machines and afraid that men will be turned into machines,' although he still agrees to have a computer implanted in his malfunctioning noggin. This technophobic idea is woefully underdeveloped in Hodges' script and merely results in our miscast, zonked out hero wandering around in a silly wig. Its best scene involves a woman in a sheer white nightdress being robotically stabbed to death on a waterbed to the soothing strains of Bach. Apart from that, it's a strange, uninvolving affair in which Hodges keeps a pronounced distance from his characters.

Terminal Man was an attempt at hard sci-fi, but 1980's *Flash* saw Hodges flee to the genre's opposite end with a barely believable slice of intergalactic cheese. It's the sort of OTT flick that either makes you throw your hands up and wander off in search of something competent or merrily go along with its comic book absurdities. Riddled with poor performances, exposition, crappy special effects and lousy attempts at humour, it's impossible to suspend disbelief. Somehow it wasn't made by Cannon because it would sit fine alongside such campy crap as *Masters of the Universe*.

At least *Flash* made a bit of money in the UK, but Hodges crashed back to Earth with 1985's *Morons from Outer Space*, a desperately stale sci-fi comedy devoid of anything approaching humour. At this point in his directorial career, it has to be said that *Carter* was looking increasingly like a fluke. Hodges needed to pull a rabbit out of the hat, perhaps sensing it might be wise to get back in touch with the harsh, gritty material that put his name on the map sixteen years earlier.

On paper 1987's *A Prayer for the Dying* seemed like a good choice. After all, it's about an IRA terrorist who inadvertently blows up a school bus in Northern Ireland, throws in the towel, and then gets entangled with gangsters. What's more, Hodges managed to hook Mickey Rourke to play the lead, an actor who was hot following the controversies of *9½ Weeks* and *Angel Heart*. Co-star Bob Hoskins had also caused cinemagoers to sit up and take notice with his multi-award-winning turn as an ex-con chauffeur of a 'thin black tart' in the excellent *Mona Lisa*. Would *Prayer* prove a turning point for Hodges or would the daft bugger piss on his feet again?

Well, in a nutshell, the critics savaged it and it died at the box office. However, unlike boring duds such as *Pulp* and *Morons*, I find *Prayer* strangely watchable. Admittedly, this is not because Hodges gets things right, but more to do with the way he mixes juicy subject matter like religion, politics, violence, morality, redemption and assorted nonsense.

As mentioned, a guilt-ridden Rourke turns his back on the 'glorious cause' after his school bus faux pas and flees to London. For some baffling reason a crime boss not only knows of his whereabouts, but insists on hiring him to kill a rival gangster in return for an American passport and fifty grand. Rourke's own people mysteriously want him dead while the useless police couldn't catch this 'hunted animal' unless he walked into the nearest cop shop with both hands tied behind his back. As you can probably tell, plausibility is not *Prayer's* strongpoint. I mean, who's ever heard of a London crime boss hiring an IRA assassin? Don't such scumbags have their own contacts for such dirty work? Saying all that, I do have a soft spot for this barmy flick, especially:

The cast: The chain-smoking Rourke, armed with his trusty sawn-off shotgun throughout, is fine. Some take umbrage with his Irish accent, but *Prayer* is another of those frustrating moments where you can see his talent is bigger than the project he's taken on. If he'd chosen more wisely/had more luck, he could have been the next De Niro.

Best line: "All this killing... It seems to follow me about."

Hoskins as a sincere Catholic priest. He witnesses Rourke executing a mobster in his church cemetery. Yes, I know, Hoskins playing a priest. But wait, there's more. He's an *ex-SAS* priest. A flick like *Who Dares Wins* has already shown us that any member of this elite fighting force is half-man, half-lion. Since when did they start letting in tubby little men?

Best line: "If you choose to murder people," he tells Rourke, "you may no longer consider yourself a member of the Catholic Church." Hmm, mate, for a priest you sure as shit don't have much knowledge of how Catholicism has operated for two thousand years.

Alan Bates as a smartly dressed, courteous gangster boss/undertaker who's usually far more respectful to the dead than the living. Bates seems to know the material isn't very good and adjusts his performance accordingly, deciding to have fun instead. And so he's nice to grieving old ladies, takes great pride in his facial restoration work, and isn't embarrassed to publicly reveal his cash-stricken mum used to hump 'perfect strangers' outside pubs for five shillings a time. Of course, being a gangster he does like to dish out a bit of aggro. If you steal from him, he will pin your hands to the wall. Bates' enjoyable, tongue in cheek performance is one of *Prayer's* strengths.

Best line: "It wasn't even dark." Bates expresses his sadness about a young woman's rape and murder as he prepares to make her beautiful again.

Christopher Fulford as Bates' bluster-filled, misogynistic younger brother. Fulford is an excellent example of a TV actor that wandered onto a movie set and somehow didn't get thrown off. He has one expression here and that's a scowl. Somehow he thinks a combination of this glare, a slicked back hairstyle and some angry gesticulating is enough to convince people he's mean. Mind you, he can act tough with the ladies, as exemplified by a sexual assault upon a brothel madam. This crude display angers Rourke, forcing him to grab the hapless Fulford by the earlobe and lead him away like he's six years old.

Best line: "I do what I fucking want when I fucking want!"

Sammi Davis as Hoskins' blind niece. Davis, like just about all movie blind girls, is super-nice, sincere and weirdly upbeat. And, of course, it takes her an entire two conversations to fall in love with Rourke after he shows he's a dab hand with the church organ.

Best line: "I think he's a very gentle, understanding man." This appraisal brushes aside her knowledge Rourke is an experienced killer, suggesting blind girls are just as susceptible to bad boy charm as their seeing counterparts. Witness the brothel madam, obviously grateful for her chivalrous rescue to the point her snatch is nearing ignition point. After admiring a tattoo on Rourke's arm, she places a hand between his legs and asks: "Have you got one down here?"

A pre-stardom Liam Neeson as a redundant IRA man. Believes Rourke is a 'danger to the movement' since the botched bombing. Poor old Neeson. He has nothing to do, except look pained while trying to persuade Rourke to return to Northern Ireland. His role makes no difference to anything. Don't worry, mate, the parts will get better.

Best line: "Thanks for putting me in this predicament." I think this was adlibbed with Hodges in mind.

A rubbish fight: Hoskins' church is desecrated by some spray-painting, fire-starting hooligans. Bates, of course, is behind the kerfuffle. When the cardigan-wearing Hoskins challenges him in a pub, three goons take him outside to administer a pasting, except Hoskins goes all Sonny Corleone with a dustbin lid. Daftness reigns supreme as Bates' men fail to get one punch in. Still, it has to be said that Bates does surround himself with particularly ineffective hard men. From his driver to his brother they all get done over at some point. A couple even end up nude and humiliated. How do you become a crime lord when your hired help is so bad?

Then again, Rourke is no slouch when it comes to incompetence. At the start he spectacularly cocks up a British Army bombing before carrying out a graveyard hit unaware that both a priest and one of Bates' men are in the cemetery looking on. If the Harlem Globetrotters had also been passing through, I suspect he might not have noticed.

The worst rape attempt of all time: Before I watched *Prayer* the worst attempted rape I'd seen was Kris Kristofferson as a biker in the otherwise terrific *Bring Me the Head of Alfredo Garcia*. He gatecrashes a picnic, pulls a gun and leads a woman off to do the bizzo. He rips through her top, slaps her and then… wanders away to sit in the long grass. The topless woman is so confused by his apathy she follows him. Don't her nice, big tits do anything for him? Then her old man turns up and puts two bullets in the still sitting Kristofferson. Frankly, he deserved such a fate for giving all those honest, hardworking rapists out there a bad name.

Fulford, however, makes an even bigger twat of himself. Initially, he goes down the guffawing route, taking time out to spray-paint the blind girl's face while obviously savouring his imminent conquest. As she tries to flee in her nightie bumping into walls and stuff, he follows her around her house singing *Three Blind Mice*. In other words, all good so far. He gets her in the darkened living room before contriving to get stabbed in the stomach by a pair of scissors. There's incompetence, there's macho bluster, and then there's not only failing to overpower a blind girl but getting done in by her. Doubly pathetic. Fulford would have to be one of the most rubbish gangsters ever. His only success was snarling, swearing and finger pointing which, I imagine, doesn't impress you much.

In short, *A Prayer for the Dying* is goofy fun but a long way from a directorial return to form, even if I did enjoy the heavily metaphoric scene in which a terrified Rourke clings to a giant suspended crucifix. However, *Prayer* is infinitely preferable to Hodges' next effort, 1989's little seen *Black Rainbow*. This one is a boring, jumbled mess about a psychic and her alcoholic dad. Not even the welcome sight of Rosanna Arquette's bare breasts can save it. Much better is *Croupier*, a casino-flavoured flick that followed almost a decade later. Clive Owen is our titular character, a cynical, vaguely sociopathic, wannabe novelist who ends up dealing blackjack and spinning the roulette wheel. His interior monologue gives everything a noir tinge. Just listen to him after he's beaten a punter at blackjack: "A wave of elation came over him. He was hooked again, watching people lose." Hodges proceeds surely with a top-notch supporting cast, full-frontal nudity, and a simmering sense of enigma. *Croupier* is mostly good, making it his second best movie.

In 2003 Hodges came full circle with his final film, *I'll Sleep When I'm Dead*. It's a moody crime pic that centres on a gangster returning to his hometown to investigate his brother's death. Sound familiar? Sadly it's nowhere near as good as his debut, but Hodges makes a fair fist of things in the opening twenty minutes. Here we get minimal dialogue, a badly beaten guy being pissed on, heroin labelled a 'cunt's drug', and that reliable nut job Malcolm McDowell dragging a cocksure, drug-dealing wide boy off the streets and wordlessly launching into a bout of anal rape. *I'll Sleep* begins to drift in its second half, though, let down by a lack of action, a curdled romance, lots of loose ends and a central performance that can't hold a candle next to Michael Caine's reptilian panache.

No matter. Hodges gave us *Get Carter* and for that I'll be forever grateful.

The Not Quite #7: Dead Man's Shoes (2004)

"God will forgive them. He'll forgive them and allow them into heaven. I can't live with that."

So says our heartbroken, self-loathing main man in an ominous voiceover at the start of this revenger. And, of course, he finds 'them' and does a wee bit more than issue a stern telling off.

Sounds like formulaic stuff, yes? And to a point it is, but *Shoes* is still a long way from the simple exploitative thrills of watching Bronson hunt down cocky, loudmouthed punks on the streets of L.A. Indeed, if you've tired of such stone-faced, trigger-pulling antics, you could do worse than give this British cult flick a whirl.

Director: Shane Meadows

Cast: Paddy Considine, Toby Kebbell, Gary Stretch, Stuart Wolfenden, Neil Bell

The story: Richard (Considine) is an ex-paratrooper back in town to set right the somewhat unsporting treatment meted out to his mentally disabled younger brother by a king bully called Sonny (Stretch) and his goons. Face-painting is just the start.

Why it works: The depiction of Sonny's drug-dealing gang. This is one bunch of thick, incompetent chavs. Pranks, binge-drinking, acid trips and leeching form the basis of their useless days. "*Janet loves al fresco fun so why not join her as she spreads herself wide in the open air,*" one chav reads aloud from a porno mag before pausing to ask a mate the meaning of *al fresco*. "Al fresco...?" comes the reply. "That's up your anus, isn't it?" Perhaps the most telling symbol of their small-time ridiculousness is their main form of transport, a clapped-out, green and white Citroen 2CV. In essence, it's a clown car, although at least they listen to gangsta rap in it. Bronson might manage a one-liner or two in his flicks to help lubricate the carnage, but *Shoes* prefers black comedy and queasy laughs.

Shoes' rural flavour (it was filmed in England's Peak District) also offers a less run-of-the-mill setting for a revenge thriller. Rolling green fields, a farm and a castle are just some of the locations used, often accompanied by a semi-acoustic, folksy or choral soundtrack. These atypical choices effectively contrast against the stabbings, expelled brains and occasional dismemberment served up by our deranged hero.

What works against it: The casting. Unfortunately, someone decided Considine should be the avenger and Stretch the abusive thug. Don't think so. Considine is a decent actor but doesn't convince as an army man on the warpath. He snarls, swears and threatens but I never really bought it. The way he carries himself also lacks that distinctive military bearing. On the other hand, Stretch is a former light middleweight boxing champion. Fourteen years after he won a WBC title he's still clearly in shape. In particular, there's an eyeball to eyeball confrontation on the street between the two during which the six-foot-two Stretch looks like he could kick the shit out of the shorter man without even breaking sweat.

Apart from the bungled central casting, plausibility also gets strained. Our ninja-like avenger shows his hand very early on, having decided on a campaign of psychological warfare first. This quickly sows the seeds of panic but it results in a case of six fully aware chavs against one little bearded guy. Somehow they fail to lay a glove on him, even after he tells them he's living at an old farmhouse. They then rock up to his place with a telescopic rifle and *one bullet*. Now I know this lot are deliberately portrayed as thickies, but bringing such a severe lack of ammunition is... well, thick. After all, the guy has murdered one of them the night beforehand with an axe and left the phrase 'One Down' daubed in blood on the wall by the corpse. He fucking well means business, all right, so why don't they rush him with pickaxe handles, flee town, tip off the cops or try to run him over in their clown car? Or better still buy a box of bullets.

In addition, I have no idea why our punisher is frequently wearing a gasmask.

Verdict: In some ways *Shoes* is as simplistic as the likes of *Death Wish II*, although it has a much quirkier feel and the odd surprise. The black humour probably undermines attempts to build tension, but is far and away the flick's most memorable aspect, especially when drugs get ingested. *Shoes* also demonstrates that killing people left, right and centre isn't the most fulfilling of pastimes. Bronson would surely chafe at such a depiction; he'd most definitely tut and roll his eyes at the way things play out during the finale.

Good God, What Were You Thinking, Girl?

There's an extraordinary scene at the end of the pretty good 1981 slasher *Eyes of a Stranger* in which Jennifer Jason Leigh's blind deaf-mute character has just regained her sight after being sexually assaulted and beaten in her home by a serial killer. The teenager has managed to turn the tables and shoot the vicious bastard, enabling her to stand in front of a bathroom mirror to see herself for the first time since she was abducted and hideously traumatised as a child. Now a woman, she takes her hand (that's bright red from the serial killer's blood) and wipes it down her cheek before dipping a couple of fingers into her mouth. Then (with downcast eyes and an impossible-to-read face) she opens her torn blouse to wordlessly fondle a pink-nippled breast.

At this point, I'm willing to listen to your interpretation of such a queasy little sequence coz I sure as hell am flailing. Is it supposed to be some sort of eroticised portrait of violence? A delayed sexual awakening? Or is the character weirdly grateful for the latest assault in that it's enabled her long lost vision to return?

All I do know is that it immediately underlined Leigh's decade-long fondness for plunging into the most unpleasant subject matter, stuff that invariably riffed on violation, nudity, sexual uncertainty, passivity and the most appalling brutality. As her star rose during the 80s you could never accuse Leigh of plumping for safe, middle of the road characters. Blandness was anathema. Her roles were markedly sexual, taking in everything from childhood abuse to prostitution. Even in something as tame as 1984's *Grandview, U.S.A* she plays an adulterous tramp who beds a washing machine salesman and indulges in mild bondage while insisting on being called 'Miss Baby Doll'. Pick one of her 80's efforts and, chances are, she'll be smoking, nudey and R-rated. Indeed, this was a girl with a perverse fondness for having control wrenched away, a partiality that often saw her turned into the plaything of male aggressors.

Meg Ryan, she wasn't.

Virgins

Early on Leigh had a strong attraction for portraying virgins. In her 1982 breakthrough hit, *Fast Times at Ridgemont High*, she might have been gloriously upstaged by the bikini-shedding Phoebe Cates, but she still played her part in a worthwhile ensemble comedy that's essentially a study of fragile bullshitters. Here she's a fifteen-year-old high schoolgirl and part-time waitress that wants to know about sex. This involves copying her best friend's blowjob demonstration on a lucky carrot in the middle of the school cafeteria, an impromptu display that causes all the boys to applaud. Not that it answers all her questions. "When a guy has an orgasm," she asks, "how much comes out?"

Soon she's repeatedly lying about her age to hook up with a 26-year-old guy, eventually having her cherry lovelessly popped in a baseball dugout while staring at the graffiti-daubed ceiling. By Leigh's standards, this is quite a tender introduction to sex. *Fast Times* remains much more sweet-natured than most of her early flicks, but she's still an underage girl dealing with everything from premature ejaculation to abortion.

Easy Money followed, a dismal Rodney Dangerfield comedy in which she marries a Puerto Rican and freezes on her wedding night. "I dunno what to do," she says. Well, girl, I suggest watching your other films. By the end her frigidity has given way to insatiability in an awkward storyline that fits in fine with all the other blundering on show.

Somehow *Easy Money* was a hit unlike 1985's medieval mega-flop, *Flesh and Blood*. Director Paul Verhoeven had the last laugh, though, as his eye-opening effort has endured to become a cult flick. Not that it's any good. It's an increasingly bonkers mix of black comedy, frequent nudity, religious lunacy, rampant ignorance, the Black Death, pillage, sexual violence, dismembered dogs flying through the air, casual murder, and all-round sheer bloody horror. One minute it's unapologetically nasty, the next it's a swashbuckling romp, and then it's like Verhoeven couldn't give a flying fuck about the slightest plausibility.

Never mind. I enjoy it, especially the way the effortlessly cool Rutger Hauer strolls around like some kind of rock 'n' roll soldier. It also provided Leigh with her first starring role as a virginal aristocrat who's sex-obsessed from the first moment. "How do you behave when you're all alone with a man?" she asks her chubby lady-in-waiting. "Will you show me how it's done?" When her maid demurs, Leigh simply orders her to fuck her lover in the bushes while she watches. She's now added voyeurism to her smorgasbord of sexual quirks, although she doesn't seem too impressed by what she perves on, eventually beating them with a branch and demanding they stop.

Then again, this is one fucking weird girl. Shortly afterward, she demurely meets her intended husband and curtsies before digging up a mandrake beneath a pair of rotting hanged corpses. "Eat it and we'll love each other forever," she tells him while proffering half the vegetable under the executed men's dangling legs.

I could be wrong, but this might be Leigh's idea of romance.

Getting splatted

Surprisingly, Leigh was only murdered once in the 80s (although there were strangling and drowning attempts in *Flesh* and 1987's *Sister, Sister*). Still, what she lacked in quantity, she made up for in memorability in 1986's hugely entertaining *The Hitcher*, a horror-thriller that was met with howls of protest over its violence and full on approach. Believably cast as a trusting, down-to-earth waitress working at a truck stop in the middle of nowhere with dreams of moving to California, she gets involved with C. Thomas Howell as he tries to flee the demonic madman Rutger Hauer. As usual it's mainly a reactive role, typified by her horrifying fate. Abducted, gagged and tied between the cab of a Mack truck and its trailer with our stylish maniac revving the gas, it's an agonisingly drawn-out scene. Or perhaps I should say *stretched*. "She's sweet," Hauer says after a horrified Howell has clambered into the cab to try to bargain for her life. Yes, Mr. Hauer, she is, she's really sweet, so surely you're not gonna take your foot off the…

Oh, you are.

Rape

Well, this is the area in which Leigh excelled during the 80s, playing a victim of sexual assault no less than *five* times. You have to say that's proclivity rather than mere coincidence. Following *Eyes of a Stranger*, she's raped at length by Hauer in *Flesh and Blood* as women and children cheer him on. It's a full frontal piece of exploitation, made ickier by Verhoeven's curious presentation which is a long way from the traditional understanding that rape and its aftermath are not very nice. "You won't get me to scream," she tells Hauer as he settles down to his sadistic business. "If you think you're harming me, you're wrong. I like it. I *like* it!" Then she wraps her legs around his back, causing him to frown while his thrusting pelvis understandably slows. Is this how a virgin reacts to rape? Well, in Verhoeven's less than sensitive world, yes.

Things shortly get even murkier when she starts wooing her rapist. Of course, this could be a survival tactic, but her relationship with Hauer is blurred all the way through. At points, she definitely appears smitten. Whatever the case, she's soon rubbing a foot into his crotch beneath the dinner table while sparking jealousy in his prostitute 'wife' and sexual competiveness from another wannabe rapist. Then there's the bath scene after her merry band of outlaws have conquered a castle in three minutes flat. Just watch her smiling and standing stark naked on its candle-adorned rim with both hands above her head looking down at her recent violator. "The whole world belongs to us," she says with apparent glee. You have to say this is a confident, bold actress. Hauer would probably agree. "I've always wanted a girl with soft skin," he says after she jumps into the steaming water. A moment later he's pulling her toward him by her nipples.

Three years after her bout of medieval madness Leigh starred in one of her worst films, *Heart of Midnight*. It wants to be the 80's answer to Polanski's *Repulsion*, a glorious black and white flick that delved into male abusers, female sexual repression, insanity and latent violence. *Midnight* does its best to be daring but it's merely overlong, boring, laughable, incoherent and technically inept. Leigh plays a repressed, traumatised, mentally unstable young woman who inherits a seedy nightclub/ brothel from her dodgy uncle. Five minutes later three punks (including a young Steve Buscemi) see her undressing at a window and decide that's all the invitation they need. "Tell me you wanna fuck me," Buscemi demands while lying on top of her as a fellow rapist takes Polaroids. We later learn Leigh is a victim of childhood sexual abuse and almost scratched a boyfriend's eye out for going too far. "I don't even like sex," she says at one point. Hmm... You might not like it, girl, but its more extreme manifestations sure have a thing for you.

The 'best' was yet to come, though. Leigh first played a hooker in 1986's widely panned *Men's Club*, a small part that paved the way for Peak Leigh in 1989's *Last Exit to Brooklyn*. If you're ever curious about what it's like to take a swim in the cinematic equivalent of a toilet bowl, this one's for you. Set in 1952, Leigh plays a hardened bitch in an undersized bra on the streets of New York. Her first scene sets the unwavering tone in which she's slapped by a pimp, eventually bawling at a concerned passerby: "Go fuck your mother! I hear she's a good hump!" Leigh is tits-deep in a world of homophobic bullies, heroin, savage beatings, incandescent industrial relations, paid sex, self loathing, closet gays, robberies, and marital rape. Just about everyone hates everyone and I'm not sure there's a single sympathetic character in the whole shebang.

Leigh is an aggressive, bleached blonde bottom feeder, a skanky ho happy to lure johns into getting robbed. Toward the end she appears to lose her mind, drunkenly ripping her top open in a crowded bar while saying: "How do you like my tits?" Not surprisingly, she's pushed around and pawed before being taken outside and thrown into the back of a wrecked car. "Come on, you bastards," she bawls at the dozens of men queuing up, "I'll fuck you blind!" I have no idea if this prolonged gang rape is supposed to cast such an obnoxious character in a more sympathetic light, but it did make me wonder if Leigh ever attended her movie premieres with family.

Last Exit was Leigh's final 80's flick. In later decades the sleazy concentration of passive abuse fell away, but she couldn't help having another go at hooking in 1990's *Miami Blues* and 2004's *The Machinist* while also getting to watch her thirteen-year-old self give daddy a handjob in 1995's awful *Dolores Claiborne*. Clearly, old habits die hard. Now in her sixties, I guess that means there's still a chance of getting to see her play a geriatric gangbang victim.

Spinning Plates

From Bing Crosby's silky crooning in *The Road to Singapore* to Mark Wahlberg's seven-inch, floppy rubber cock in *Boogie Nights*, it's clear that the musical stars of the day have always fancied their big screen chances. Perhaps after topping the charts it's the most natural of moves. Then again, maybe such success merely prompts their insatiable egos to crave box-office validation, cinematic immortality and world domination. Or as a steely-eyed Madonna puts it during that artistic treasure *Shanghai Surprise*: "You have no idea of the depth of my determination." This no doubt Herculean effort to conquer both fields explains why I'm neither a pop star nor movie idol; such pursuits are bound to get in the way of my afternoon nap.

Despite her Golden Globe for *Evita*, the aforementioned Madonna is, of course, a prime example of how ridicule-inducing such celluloid adventures can go. Not that she's alone. Just catch the legendary Bob Dylan twitching and scampering through the mid-seventies western *Pat Garrett and Billy the Kid*, looking so confused that his expression often resembles a horse trying to work out why someone has shat in its nosebag. You could also take a peep at the equally legendary Vanilla Ice riding into town in *Cool as Ice* almost matching Clint Eastwood's smouldering intensity and yen for havoc in *High Plains Drifter*, albeit with fluorescent clothing and a reverse baseball cap.

However, although big shots such as Barbra Streisand, Cher or Will Smith tend to mix mediocrity and outright crap, it doesn't stop those fickle gods of fortune rewarding them with Oscar glory. Win or lose, it's pretty easy to tell that the world will never be enough for some of these musician-actor types.

Sinatra in *From Here to Eternity* (1953), *Suddenly* (1954), *The Man with the Golden Arm* (1955), *The Manchurian Candidate* (1962) & *Von Ryan's Express* (1965)

The WW2 drama *Eternity* was a big Oscar winner with Sinatra a beneficiary. It's aged poorly, its one-time racy elements now not even noticeable amid the lukewarm soap suds. Sinatra's a flaky but hard-headed soldier in Hawaii, although he's so scrawny he looks like a glorified boy scout. His performance as a 'tough monkey' picked on by 'fatso' Ernest Borgnine is barely adequate, not helped by a script that requires him to be half-cut most of the time. A late attempt at pathos falls comically flat. Frankly, that Best Supporting Actor Oscar suggests Sinatra got his Italian mates to make the Academy members an offer they couldn't refuse. *Eternity* is a meandering, unconvincing pic that even stuffs up the Jap assault on Pearl Harbor by not only tacking it on the end but making it appear less significant than the love lives and careers of some self-absorbed bores. It does a good job, however, of reminding me that the army must be the most ridiculous organisation on Earth.

Sinatra provided support in *Eternity* but he's centre stage as a dapper villain in the comically bad, suspense-free *Suddenly*. He wants to assassinate the president, taking over a suburban home that provides a perfect vantage point after somehow learning of Eisenhower's planned train stop at a no-name Californian town. Not long afterward he's revealed his unmarried parents were alcoholics that dumped him in a children's home, he killed 27 men in WW2, and he's all out of the milk of human kindness. "Show me a guy with feelings," he barks, "and I'll show you a sucker!" Now he's gonna gun down America's top dog for a shit load of cash from a mysterious employer because Eisenhower is 'just another man.'

Unfortunately, the most telling moment arrives when the name of John Wilkes Booth (a stage actor and Abraham Lincoln's killer) is brought up, prompting Sinatra to retort: "I'm no actor!"

Hmm....

Can you tell I'm not warming to this guy's thespian abilities? He's so small for a start. In every scene with cop Sterling Hayden he's cricking his neck to look at his face. Sinatra's tough guy character is far too composed and talkative, not helped by flat direction and a theatrical feel. Even an eight-year-old child yells at him: "You stink!" Sinatra doesn't give off the slightest air of danger, gun in hand or not.

Sinatra, more than a decade into his movie career by 1955, proves much better as a guilt-ridden, twitchy loser with a nutso wife in the Chicago-set *Man with the Golden Arm*. Here he drops the absurd tough guy act and instead plays an ex-con addict trying to make good while surrounded by hustlers, drunks, strippers, card sharks and unsympathetic cops. "The monkey's gone," is the first thing he says to a mate upon his release from clink, but that's a moot point given he now lives in the same neighbourhood as his former dealer, Louie (Darren McGavin). "Monkey's never dead," Louie tells him. "You kick him off, he just hides in the corner waiting his turn."

Golden Arm is surely one of Hollywood's first depictions of drug addiction, even if the word 'heroin' is oddly never used (whereas 'fix', 'hooked' and 'junkie' are). It's a tad overlong, occasionally clunky and features one amusingly OTT performance, but I otherwise enjoyed its gallery of lowlifes and depiction of 50s drug use. Louie might be an arch manipulator, but he's also suave and intelligent. Apart from that, he thoughtfully provides a syringe, spoon, and his own apartment to shoot up in. He even does the injecting himself, all for a few bucks. A quite splendid service, really, and I think today's dealers could learn a thing or two from such old-fashioned chivalry.

After heading an ensemble cast in the financially successful, overlong and hideously dull heist flick *Ocean's 11*, Sinatra went onto play a brainwashed soldier returning from the Korean War in the well-regarded political thriller *The Manchurian Candidate*. Like amnesia, I find cinematic depictions of brainwashing, such as *Shutter Island* and *Get Out*, awfully hard to swallow. The McCarthy-flavoured *Candidate* plays like a boring, daft as fuck combination of a hypnotist's seaside magic show and a padded, below par *Twilight Zone* episode. There's also very little action, although we do get a nightmare-afflicted Sinatra karate-chopping his way through a table in yet another unconvincing display of machismo. This leaves us to be entertained by Ol' Blue Eyes wandering around sweaty, shaky and half-dazed like a Commie-programmed puppet-robot suffering a nervous breakdown. Honestly, if you want a bit of dry-cleaned brain action, you're better off with John Hurt in *1984* or the first season of Showtime's *Homeland*.

Much better is Sinatra's biggest 60's hit, the straightforward, well-directed *Von Ryan's Express*. Here he plays a downed pilot imprisoned in an Italian POW camp in 1943. At one point I was steeling myself for things turning into a *Great Escape* knockoff in which a brown leather jacket-clad Sinatra tries to emulate Steve McQueen. Them's too big boots to fill, Frankie. Wisely, the flick heads in a different direction when those wishy-washy Eyeties capitulate and a resourceful Sinatra and his merry band of men commandeer a north-bound train. *Express* has some faults, like people getting knocked cold/killed too easily or being unable to decide whether machine gun fire causes a victim to bleed. I also wasn't keen on a wimpy chaplain donning the enemy's uniform at key points to impersonate an authoritarian German commander (and provide some laughs). Still, Sinatra's antics are easy to digest and I quite like the scene where he struggles to hold onto his professional resolve as an Italian floozy slips on a pair of stockings in front of him. *Express* isn't as good as Frankenheimer's 1964 classic, *The Train*, and lacks the flair and cool characters of favoured WW2 romps, such as *Kelly's Heroes* and *Dirty Dozen*, but its martial score, convincing production values, occasional bite and action-packed finale make it perfectly watchable.

Elvis in *Jailhouse Rock* (1957) & *King Creole* (1958)

There's a scene in *True Romance* where Christian Slater admits that if he were forced to shag a man, he'd pick Elvis.

Fair enough.

Let's face it: Elvis was a handsome dude, almost as desirable as Dolph Lundgren in *Rocky IV*.

Or so I'm told.

Elvis wasn't just a good-looking bastard, though. This hugely talented upstart dripped charisma, created groundbreaking music, and developed a cult of personality that is likely to last as long as western civilisation.

But could he act and make good movies?

Well, to begin with, *yes*. Like the rest of his life and career, it all became bloated, mediocre, insane and *too much*, but the guy fucking well rocked in his early days. Take *Jailhouse Rock*. Its main surprise is that it doesn't go as expected. It's a straightforward narrative, but at the same time it isn't some fawning, glorified pop promo.

Elvis plays Vince Everett, a bloke that soon finds himself in mighty big trouble for inadvertently beating to death a lady-abusing twat in a bar. In its fast-moving opening quarter of an hour we get a well-staged fight, incarceration, and news that a coast to coast TV show is going to be broadcast from the prison two and a half minutes after Vince arrives. Vince struts his stuff in front of the cameras and the next day the place is flooded with fan mail from fifteen-year-old girls, happy to reveal their vital statistics and phone number. Hmm, wonder if any were from Priscilla…

Vince has a palpable edge. He's impulsive, confrontational, sullen, sneering, testy, rude, arrogant and sarcastic. Just like me on a good day. He's also very loose with his fists, happy to punch out any guy in the way whether that's a screw or a record label boss. As for the ladies, he calls a woman he's just met in a bar 'pretty well stacked' while a fair bit of the time he appears to be staring at their tits with heavy-lidded appreciation. "How dare you think such cheap tactics would work with me," one girl objects after he grabs her on the street and forcibly pashes her. "They ain't tactics, honey," he replies. "That's just the beast in me."

Rock on.

In *King Creole* he's an overage New Orleans school kid and 'pretty fresh boy' on the cusp of crime, a singing career and bedding two hotties. Like Vince Everett, he's rebellious and handy with his fists, although that doesn't stop an occasional slide into melodrama and corniness. Just watch him stride into a five and ten store armed with a guitar. He so mesmerises everyone that no one notices his accomplices nicking everything from wristwatches to a bicycle. Still, *King Creole* is an enjoyable watch with some nicely drawn characters.

Things hot up when this singing busboy crosses paths with laconic gangster Maxie Fields (a young Walther Matthau) who's not beyond jealously telling his hard-drinking girl: "I'll break every finger you got." Matthau is terrific and I did enjoy him smashing a chair over Elvis' head. Then again, Elvis does well against more experienced actors. Indeed, *Creole* might be his best-ever shift. He nails each scene whether telling a girl at the local cathouse that she'd have to pay him or wielding a pair of broken bottles against some local hoodlums. And if you've got any doubts about the guy's magnetism take a gander at him jumping on a bar and launching into *Trouble* accompanied by a black, bowler-hatted backing band while busting out those suggestive moves.

The sixties lay gaping before Elvis, a decade in which he employed a Nic Cage-like work rate to pump out twenty-seven movies. And if you think I'm gonna sit through that avalanche of tosh after the fun *Jailhouse* and *Creole*, you've got another thing coming.

Jagger in *Performance* (1970) & *Ned Kelly* (1970)

Art and commerce have a weird relationship. On the face of it, it makes perfect sense to slap a pop star into a feature film, sit back and watch his or her fans gobble up the tickets. Who needs marketing when you've got a built-in audience? Such an approach worked a treat for the likes of Presley, Prince and The Spice Girls (whose slapdash *Spice World* is more of an example of commerce than art).

So why didn't it work with Jagger? Why do some pop stars like Britney Spears and Mariah Carey fall flat on their pretty faces? After all, at the beginning of the 70s, Jagger was white hot, a gossip column mainstay, an artist at the peak of his startling powers, and a lightning rod for controversy, the counterculture and rug-wrapped, naked ladies. Perhaps the financial failures of *Performance* and *Kelly* were down to the flicks not being very good. But, hang on, *Purple Rain* and *Spice World* were not very good. Maybe Jagger's efforts were too weird, dark and experimental for mainstream taste. Then again, poor distribution and advertising could have scuttled them.

Whatever the case, the man couldn't have done much worse in trying to kick-start a movie career.

Performance, actually filmed in 1968, is by far the weirder of his early efforts. It starts by crosscutting images of a supersonic jet flying overhead, a Rolls Royce travelling through the serene English countryside, lots of thrusting arses, and naked women being slapped and choked to a discordant score. In other words, it's not hard to tell this one's a wee bit fucked.

Indeed, its arty directorial choices and rapid-fire editing will either fascinate you or turn you right off. Now I don't normally go in for pretentious or avant-garde stuff, but *Performance* has a definite *feel*. It has a tremendous opening half-hour and is so strange at points that it's impossible to be bored. I also imagine its depiction of wisecracking but slightly dim and sadistic gangsters complaining about TV violence or looking at homosexual porn influenced Tarantino and especially Guy Ritchie's early work. The goddamn thing has mighty big balls, all right, but whether it holds together is another matter.

The slim, good-looking (but old-fashioned) James Fox is a 'mad dog' gangster who steps on the toes of his London boss once too often, forcing him to improvise and hide out at the mansion of a reclusive rock star. Here we meet Jagger, who utilises his extraordinary face and somnolent, debauched demeanour to maximum effect. Christ, just watch him perform the excellent song *Memo from Turner*. He's like an incarnation of a drugged-up, shagged-out Pan, giving the impression he's tried all Earthly perversions and long wearied of them. This lethargy is reflected in his speech. He might read aloud from literary texts but barely manages to say anything coherent. Not that he has to while indulging in threesomes on his four-poster bed or wandering around his darkened, bohemian, heroin-haunted micro-world plastered in wet five-pound notes. The hard as nails Fox isn't impressed with Jagger's 'freak show', anyway. "Comical little geezer," he tells this satanic beatnik. "You'll look funny when you're fifty."

Now while the extraordinary *Performance* is ahead of its time, it might just be a load of weird bollocks. The handsome-looking *Ned Kelly*, on the other hand, is simply a load of tension-free bollocks. Still, it shows what allure Jagger had in that this was only his second feature film and he was already being teamed with an Oscar-winning director. Unfortunately, Jagger's miscasting, and writer-director Tony Richardson's jumpy, uninvolving screenplay and half-jokey approach, severely undermine the gritty nature of this real-life tale. This should be a dynamic story of mistreatment, multiple cop killings, bank robberies, bushranger life and an execution yet far too often we're left listening to a plethora of leaden folk songs or watching Jagger look awkward on horseback. He's supposedly portraying a charismatic, feared outlaw but his slight stature, unconvincing beard and wavering Irish accent instead somehow manage to give the impression of an effete Amish leprechaun. *Performance* showed he could project a strong whiff of decadence and corruption, but when it comes to bare knuckle brawling and the tough guy stuff he's about as convincing as Sinatra.

David Essex in *That'll Be the Day* (1973) & *Stardust* (1974)

I went into the PG-rated *Day* expecting a nice little coming of age story set in late-50s Britain. Instead I got the handsome, husky-voiced, outwardly affable David Essex going from virgin schoolboy to schoolgirl rapist. Indeed, this is a study in misogyny in which Essex can't even give his mum a fair shake.

Essex plays the teenage Jim MacLaine. Instead of sitting his university-entrance exams, he runs away to the seaside to become a deckchair attendant. He's clever but alienated and shiftless, perhaps the result of an absentee father. At the seaside he meets the older Mike (a surprisingly good Ringo Starr), a man that isn't exactly a role model when it comes to honesty and chivalry ("The one with the big knockers is mine!") In fact, Mike is a super horny Teddy Boy who plays crazy golf because it's 'good practice for getting things into holes.'

Bit by bit, Jim's behaviour worsens. Despite his success with the ladies, there's no joy in him. He's a coward, a man out for himself, and an increasingly cocky drifter. Essex isn't the most energetic performer but he captures a disaffected quality and makes a good fist of disguising a contemptible character in this low-key, melancholy drama. Like the later *Quadrophenia*, it offers excellent period detail.

Day's sequel, *Stardust*, also became a hit. It's now 1963, Kennedy's just been offed, and Jim has started a band. This seems like a good move in that not too long later he's enjoying a threesome with two busty blondes and buying a Spanish castle. *Day* was rooted in kitchen sink realism, but *Stardust* feels more like a wannabe musician's fantasy, especially the speed with which Jim gets noticed by a record label and played on the radio. Plausibility isn't helped by all his songs being crap. Despite the good direction and R rating, *Stardust* struggles with its uneven script, Essex's much weaker performance, and an absence of engaging characters. Mind you, I won't be forgetting a disgruntled Jim feeding an acid tab to a mate's pregnant Airedale Terrier in a hurry.

Bowie in *The Man Who Fell to Earth* (1976), *The Hunger* (1983), *Merry Christmas, Mr. Lawrence* (1983) & *Labyrinth* (1986)

Bowie always had an otherworldly quality so playing a humanoid alien in his feature film debut was a smart move, especially given he'd been practising for a good couple of years as Ziggy Stardust. In fact, his deathly pale skin, different coloured eyes, androgynous persona, hairless, stick-thin body, air of detachment and pronounced lack of threat occasionally manage to suggest Bowie *isn't* acting. So he's perfectly cast in *Man Who Fell to Earth*, but I can't work up much enthusiasm for anything else in Nicolas Roeg's wonky, earnest and overlong sci-fi drama. The acting across the board is sub-par. Bowie has precious little to do or say in this tale of corruption, defeated by the meandering, disjointed narrative and array of irrelevant scenes. Even with the graphic nudity, it's a pretentious, turgid mess, although many see it as Bowie's best film.

Better is the sleek, Goth-tinged *The Hunger*, a moody flick that plays like some stylish horror pop video, complete with billowing lace curtains, dry ice, fluttering doves, plentiful silhouettes, curling cigarette smoke and rain-spattered window panes. Like *Man Who Fell*, Bowie is another unearthly creature obsessed with appearance. Here he's a two-century-old, rapidly ageing vampire attacking roller-skaters and murdering violinists in a bid to salvage his not-quite eternal youth. It's no good, though. Twenty minutes earlier he'd been an ultra-cool nightclub patron picking up a hot chick and enjoying a face full of titties, but now his hair has fallen out, he's covered in liver spots and he's barely got the strength to get out of his chair. "You said forever," he tells his vampire-creator Miriam (Catherine Deneuve) with a definite accusatory edge to his hoarse voice. "Kiss me. Think of me as I was." Bowie might play second fiddle to Miriam's lesbo antics, but he's still one of the better aspects of Tony Scott's directorial debut. *The Hunger* is all blood and no meat, but Bowie manages to generate a degree of pity during the effective ageing sequences in which he ends up as feeble as *Texas Chainsaw's* grandpa.

In *Merry Christmas, Mr. Lawrence* he plays a British soldier captured by those nasty Japs during WW2. Early on he's described in a courtroom as a 'very difficult man'. Flipping heck, that's an understatement. He's actually the personification of The Stiff Upper Lip.

Or a parody of it.

This is a man who clings to his principles, can stoically bear any ill treatment and is unafraid of death to an extraordinary degree. He's variously described as a 'born leader', 'soldier's soldier' and so on. After a mock firing squad execution (in which he refuses a blindfold and blanks are used) he immediately declares: "That's a good one!"

If you're starting to think I don't have a very high opinion of *Merry Christmas*, you'd be right. Yes, it's a sporadically interesting examination of extreme culture clash and unbending mindsets but for a flick set in occupied Java, there isn't enough action. What violence there is doesn't convince and the whole thing feels like a stiff, overlong play. At some points, it's diabolical. Now while Bowie's gaunt enough to portray an underfed POW, his character comes across as ridiculously obstinate. Plus, there's a fair bit of unintentional humour in watching him pretend to shave, have an imaginary cup of tea or actually eat flowers in defiance of his captors. The affable Tom Conti (The 'Lawrence' of the title) isn't much better, always bouncing back from the routine abuse he witnesses and suffers. It's like the movie is trying to tell us that good manners and dignity will wear down and defeat the most monstrous tyranny, even if you end up with a sun-baked head. *Bridge on the River Kwai* managed to convince with its decorum-at-all-costs-in-the-face-of-adversity schtick, but *Merry Christmas* just made me long for a *Monty Python*-style character or two to wander into the throng and break up the over-earnestness.

Unlike his occasional musical collaborator Jagger, Bowie was determined to make it as a movie star. By 1986 he'd already compiled a fair body of work before putting up his hand for Jim Henson's puppet extravaganza, *Labyrinth*. In case you don't know, this is the one where he sings and dances in a puffy shirt and package-revealing grey leggings in a room full of grooving puppets while tossing a baby in the air. Not as cringe-inducing as *The Laughing Gnome* or trying to lead concert-goers into prayer at the Freddie Mercury Tribute Concert, I know, but pretty damn close.

Bowie's blank-faced performance is only part of the problem, though. "How are you enjoying my labyrinth?" he asks at one point. Well, to tell the truth, mate, I ain't. *Labyrinth* simply isn't a good movie. It lacks inspiration, feeling both derivative and repetitive. The sets and special effects look cheap. The humour falls flat while the whole thing never comes close to taking flight. Now mysteriously a cult movie with ongoing talk of a sequel, *Labyrinth* should be buried in the Bog of Eternal Stench.

Its weak, hasty setup sees gawky teenager Jennifer Connelly wish her infant brother away. Goblin King Bowie obliges, forcing her to negotiate the titular maze to get him back, while apparently not caring he's up to his Motley Crue hairdo in mediocrity. Bowie also contributes a handful of songs in line with his post-*Let's Dance* slump before the poorly written *Labyrinth* drags itself to an underwhelming finale. At least the baby has the good sense to occasionally look embarrassed.

Olivia Newton-John in *Grease* (1978)

"Got any porno?" Debbie Harry asks in *Videodrome*. "Gets me in the mood." Good line, but I doubt Newton-John ever said anything like it during her movie career. She might've been known as Olivia Neutron-Bomb after the release of the image-altering, multi-million selling *Physical*, but in reality has any late twentieth century woman projected such wholesomeness? Think of the girl next door and it's hard not to picture this ultra-cute, amazingly successful singer. Straightaway during *Grease's* blissful beach opening her dominant character trait sees her fight off Travolta's ardent advances. "Don't spoil it!" she cries, resisting his kisses before no doubt scampering off to church.

Gawd, talk about a professional virgin.

Throughout this 1950s-set monster hit she wanders around in a long skirt with a cardigan draped over her delicate shoulders, demurely clutching a ring binder against her chest. She doesn't smoke and will hiccup after one swig of dessert wine. Sincerity, courtesy and femininity are her forte, resulting in the slightest trace of dirt being repelled at a distance of at least three metres. Oh, that porcelain skin, downcast eyes, wondrous smile and air of naiveté! In short, she's a paragon of virtue. Is this why I prefer to watch the majority of *Grease* dressed as the Gimp, pacing and grunting in front of the screen as my knuckles drag against the carpet?

Still, if you think I'm on some anti-Olivia rant here, you're wrong. In a flick packed with theatrical performances and surprisingly crude dialogue, she provides a grounded, effective counter. The chemistry with Travolta (doing his best heterosexual impersonation) is palpable. She might not be able to match his charisma, but at least she gets to belt out a few world-class pop songs, including *Hopelessly Devoted to You* while wearing a hair band and a flowing, pure white nightdress that's so long you can't even glimpse a toe. Heaven! However, when she vamps it up in the final ten minutes ("I need a man!"), I tend to rip off my Gimp outfit and collapse sulking on the sofa.

Diana Ross and Michael Jackson in *The Wiz* (1978)

Despite belonging to that poxy genre known as the musical, 1939's *The Wizard of Oz* is a fave. Built on the most vivid imagination, it features tremendously quotable dialogue, a shining example of a Strong Female Role, impressive special effects, mostly great songs and, of course, one of moviedom's best villains. No flick has stood the test of time better or permeated popular culture to such an extraordinary degree.

Then there's *The Wiz*, a terribly written, all-black remake in which the white 'talent' had the good sense to stay out of sight behind the camera. Jesus fucking Christ, after ten minutes I wanted to reach in and slap everyone with the admonishment: "Stop being so goddamn silly!" Graham Chapman, good sir, your nonsense-hating presence is required.

The plain-looking Diana Ross, who was approaching her *mid-30s* when this ludicrous abomination was filmed, is about as miscast as anyone I've ever seen. She continually overacts, either staring wide-eyed at the rampant absurdity all around or looking like she's about to piss her pants over the most trivial of incidents. "I'm acting like a baby," she sings at one point.

The effervescent, vaguely manic Jackson fares a little better, but he still gets attacked by a pair of carnivorous trash cans. Decked out in a drab costume and a woollen afro with the tip of his nose browned, he looks like a downmarket Scary Spice after her schnoz has been dipped in shit. In common with Ross, his songs are so boring you barely listen to the lyrics. When he speaks, his breathy, high-pitched voice makes it sound like he's not long been kicked in the balls.

Chuck in unimaginative choreography, the sheer ugliness of the urban-flavoured sets, and nonsensical elements like the awful Ross being whisked off to Oz by a snowbound New York tornado, and this one adds up to more than two hours of outright embarrassment for all concerned, especially heavyweight director Sidney Lumet. It's so bad I even wanted Toto to get run over.

Sting in *Quadrophenia* (1979)

Sting has had a spotty movie career, his enthusiasm understandably dampened by failing to win rave notices for turning up in a codpiece in 1984's incomprehensible mega-flop *Dune*. He staggered on for a bit with a meatier, arm-breaking role alongside Tommy Lee Jones in the Newcastle-set dud *Stormy Monday* before finally doing something right as a bar owner in the big hit *Lock, Stock and Two Smoking Barrels*.

Back in 1979 he made his debut in the bloody excellent *Quadrophenia*, an on-the-money exploration of a curious case of British racism in which sharply dressed, scooter-riding Mods can't get along with leather-clad Rockers on motorbikes. Sting arrives on a customised scooter sporting bleached blonde hair and a long leather coat, immediately causing everyone to be half-blinded by his charisma. Well, he is called Ace Face. Not long afterward this flash bastard takes to the dance floor and mass gawping ensues. Committed poseur he might be, but he's not averse to smashing a shop window, pulling a bobby off his horse or laying into a Rocker or two. Then again, he might not be as cool as he makes out. A lovelorn Toyah also pops up but disappointingly sticks to dancing and drugs.

The nicely filmed *Quadrophenia* is a superb recreation of mid-60s UK life. It effortlessly captures authenticity with its array of pasty faces, distinctive accents, foul-mouthed dialogue, dead-end jobs, wet streets, brawls and pill popping, not to mention the way it handles the generation gap, some funny black humour, an overall sense of drabness and the exuberant ridiculousness of disaffected youth. It also benefits from The Who's banging soundtrack while casting a bunch of appropriately-aged, memorably-faced youngsters, the vast majority of whom went onto other movies and/or long running TV careers. And while it's always nice to see Razors from *Long Good Friday*, I could have done without those lengthy shots of Ray Winstone's submerged cock.

Meat Loaf in *Roadie* (1980), *Fight Club* (1999) & *The 51st State* (2001)

I've always found it impossible to dislike Meat Loaf. His music is as bombastic, OTT and ridiculous as it gets yet is also distinctive, wholehearted and memorable. It shouldn't work but it does. Unfortunately, his debut starring role in *Roadie* definitely doesn't work. He plays a good ol' Texan boy roped into the music business despite knowing nothing about it, as typified by a less than inspired guess that Alice Cooper is one of Charlie's Angels.

Meat Loaf tries too hard with his wide eyes and exaggerated reactions, but even if his acting were better he'd still be sunk by this quarter-baked movie's clumsy, rambling, knockabout nature and the way it throws in everything from armadillos to UFOs. Most of its cameos and in-jokes have been lost to time. *Roadie* aims for quirkiness but gets mired in tedium in less than half an hour.

After *Roadie* crashed and burned at the box office, Meat Loaf kept trying to spin those plates by instead concentrating on supporting roles. Or perhaps no producer would trust him with a starring turn again. *Fight Club* was far and away the most successful product of this strategy and, along with *Rocky Horror*, remains his best-known flick. Here you have to give him credit for picking such an unglamorous role. He plays a former champion bodybuilder whose unchecked steroid use has resulted in a pair of 'bitch tits' so big that they make Christina Hendricks' divine double look like an A cup. Oh yeah, he's also developed testicular cancer and had his nuts chopped off.

A memorable set-up, yes?

Shame his blubbering, none too bright character doesn't go anywhere, even after he gets sucked into a local chapter of Fight Club. Nonetheless, perhaps I should be grateful he's one of the few sincere characters in this plodding, ultra-cynical movie.

Things don't improve in *51st State* (aka *Formula 51*). Now while Meat Loaf's performance in *Roadie* was a little forced, *everything* about *51st State* is forced. This action comedy has an interesting cast and desperately wants to be in the same class as the likes of *Pulp Fiction*, *Lock, Stock* and *Trainspotting* but is sunk by its tired, profanity-peppered script and derivative underpinnings. Meat Loaf makes little impression as a scaly-faced drug lord called The Lizard, even if he does wear slippers emblazoned with cute silhouettes of his reptilian moniker. He gets double-crossed and almost assassinated (or 'truly ass-invaded' as he puts it), a turn of events that transforms him into a vengeful, bellowing type. I dunno, maybe I'm too familiar with the guy's real-life genial personality to buy into his mean character in this predictable clodhopper. To be honest, I've come to the conclusion he never improved as an actor, although I suspect he still would've made a more convincing Dorothy than Diana Ross.

Debbie Harry in *Videodrome* (1983)

I went to see the reformed Blondie in the late nineties, enabling me to notice something blindingly obvious about Ms Harry. The poor lass ain't much of a dancer. Great voice, fantastic songs, a brilliant all-round contribution, but a long way from mastering Madonna-like exertions. Oh well, guess you can't have everything. I mean, where would you put it?

But is Harry's acting better than her dancing?

I'd say about the same in that both lack commitment and animation. In *Videodrome* she plays Nicki, a kinky radio show host who considers having a needle stuck through an earlobe as foreplay. She's also into self-harming and watching porn, a predilection that brings her into contact with sleazy small-time TV boss Max Renn (James Woods). "We live in over-stimulated times," is her explanation for her less than conservative behaviour. It's music to his ears. Two minutes later she's stubbing out a fag on herself.

Videodrome is probably the pick of Cronenberg's body horror stuff from the controversial first phase of his career. Like *Shivers*, *Rabid*, *Brood* and *Scanners*, it's built on fascinating subject matter, as well as providing some sort of explanation/defence for the Canadian director's partiality for dark, twisted shit ("Better on TV than the streets.") Unlike those earlier efforts, however, *Videodrome* doesn't prompt me to lapse into boredom, puzzlement or sniggers. It's not as good as his later *Fly*, but it's got plenty to say about TV addiction, the consumption of 2D sex and violence, and those perennial moral panics. Harry (effectively obliterating her Blondie identity with dark hair) is hardly pivotal to its minor success, but I quite liked her cooing 'Come to Nicki' before a hallucinating Woods sticks his head through the TV screen into her giant mouth.

Prince in *Purple Rain* (1984)

I like some Prince songs such as *Thieves in the Temple*, *Sign o' the Times* and a fair chunk of the mega-selling *Purple Rain* stuff. He had something, all right, but too often I find his music tinny and unconvincing. I also got embarrassed by the guy's self-indulgent sulking, like writing the word *slave* on his face and changing his name to a symbol. Frankly, if a record company made me a multi-millionaire chick magnet and gave my music a worldwide presence, I'd cut them a bit of slack. Big picture and all that. Plus, Prince was very short and it's hard to take such people seriously.

Anyhow, he made his acting debut beneath a lopsided, poodly hairdo in the poorly edited *Purple Rain*. There's not much of a storyline here. Calling himself The Squid, sorry, The Kid, his dad slaps him around whenever he's not snubbing female band mates or butting heads with a rival musician who wants him ousted from the nightclub they both play at. Of course, there's also a besotted girl, but as she's busty and topless she gets a pass, even if she can do little more than lovingly stare at him with tears in her eyes. The Kid tries hard to be moody and enigmatic, but this is tricky given he still lives with his mum and dad, wears high-heeled boots and a frilly shirt, and mainly comes across as a large, camp child that loves nothing more than playing dress up. At least he's managed to take the stabilisers off his purple, customised motorbike.

For the most part the multi-award winning $70m hit *Purple Rain* is a padded concert movie. Prince is an energetic performer on stage but fairly stiff off it. Wait till you see him try to do *enraged* while storming after his abusive dad. He's about as threatening as a candyfloss meerkat. Saying that, even a half-decent thesp would be sunk by *Purple Rain's* pitiful level of writing. Frankly, I found it dull, its value likely to rest on how much you value Prince's music when the guy was at his commercial peak.

Madonna in *Shanghai Surprise* (1986)

Just as we can safely assume Madonna is a superior singer to Sean Penn, I guess her former hubby is the better actor. However, I do believe she won an award for The Most Unsexy and Overlong Masturbation Scene courtesy of the amusingly bonkers *Body of Evidence*.

For the record I enjoy Madonna's warbling. I've got a lot of time for fun stuff like *Material Girl* and *Papa Don't Preach*, as well as her more sophisticated, electronica-infused efforts such as the *Ray of Light* album. Phenomenally successful and enduring, her impact on the late twentieth century can only be denied by the blindest of haters. I'll chuck my hat in the ring by also declaring her an artist of some note.

Unfortunately, her Nazi-like ambition to conquer the world saw an inevitable sideways shift into the movies, a mad craving that refused to even begin to take into account her acting limitations. The result? One disaster after another. Now Madge might have survived box-office bombs like *Who's that Girl* and *Swept Away*, but both the 6th Army's rout at Stalingrad and Hitler's subterranean, bug-eyed descent into suicide were probably more dignified.

So, anyway, to the 1938-set *Shanghai Surprise*. It's some sort of attempt at a screwball comedy, a flick that caught an almighty bunch of flak back in the day. I don't know why. It's not good or anything but it's not boring like *Purple Rain*. For starters I was intrigued by Penn's sexual proclivities. Here he laments the lack of nipples on his latest half-finished piece of body art, gets whipped by a Chinese hooker's long hair after gulping down a load of aphrodisiacs, and declares mumps 'more fun' than having an insistent, half-naked Madonna in his bed. Not long later he publicly lets slip that he's 'never lonely with a pair of silk stockings.'

Surprise is ropey as hell, not helped by its dire George Harrison plinky-plonky, faux-oriental soundtrack and barely intelligible lyrics. The flick is also bizarrely devoid of any occupying Jap soldiers. Meanwhile, missionary nurse and 'pious lady' Madonna is trying to track down a shitload of opium to help wounded Chinese soldiers. We don't get a glimpse of this lot, either. Nevertheless, I enjoyed quite a few scenes from *Surprise's* continually misfiring script, especially a credibility-defying one involving a pair of interactive wicker baskets. The movie even boasts a decent ten-minute opening in which we get panicky flight from the imminent Jap invasion, blown-off hands, an opium smuggler being shot in the back, and *Withnail's* less than svelte Uncle Monty doing his own stunt work. Madonna, with her 'twin pagodas' and 'haven of celestial bliss', is plastic throughout, simply unable to sell the slightest bit of emotion, but she's not the worst performer. Still, it's noticeable that *Surprise* starts dipping quality-wise as soon as she turns up. "I do not intend to be made a fool of," she tersely informs Penn a few minutes after they meet.

Well, good luck with that, dearie.

The Kemp brothers in *The Krays* (1990)

I never liked the pretentiously named Spandau Ballet, a very successful London band that scored a number one hit in 1983 with the god-awful ballad, *True*. 'This is the sound of my soul,' vocalist Tony Hadley trills at one point. Yeah, well, mate, if that's what your soul sounds like, enjoy your time in hell.

Brothers Martin and Gary Kemp, however, started to make up for their band's deficiencies by doing a fine job impersonating those lovable Cockney rascals, the Kray twins. In particular, their eyes suggest a boundless appetite for malice, the possibility of a telepathic connection, and creeping insanity. They also like going batshit crazy. These volcanic outbursts might result in the impalement of a transgressor's pinioned hand while accompanied by a demand for gratefulness or a pub interior being raked by submachine gun fire. Their menacing joint persona is effectively contrasted against their softly spoken, well-groomed appearance and bashful, often charming nature, especially in front of their doting mum. This incongruence is captured early on when the jealous, unstable Ronnie (Gary) picks a fight at one of their successful nightclubs. He quickly pushes a nonentity out into the street, only to be surprised by the clearly scared guy brandishing a flick-knife. "There's no need for violence," Ronnie counters with a disarming smile. "We're all acting like a bunch of kids here." Once the knife has been dropped, Ronnie whips out a sword and forces it horizontally into his victim's mouth to inflict a Joker-style grin.

Still, we get little explanation for the depth of such OTT malevolence. *The Krays* is happy to show a war-torn childhood in which the boys cower underground during the Blitz while being told lurid tales about Jack the Ripper, but such colourful East End episodes hardly provide a basis for their later murderous cruelty. Perhaps some people are simply born nasty cunts. There's no doubt, though, that the brothers end up like the two-headed baby they find exhibited in a jar of formaldehyde at a 1950s circus freak show: imprisoned, reviled, and endlessly gawped at.

Ice Cube in *Boyz n the Hood* (1991)

I know how white I am when I try to listen to gangsta rap like N.W.A's *Straight Outta Compton*. *Crazy motherfucker* this, *pussy ass nigga* that and a bit of *dirty ass ho* and *fuck the police* thrown in for good measure... Boy, its potty-mouthed hyper-aggression gets awfully tiring after a few minutes. Don't these young urban gentlemen ever rhapsodise about rainbows and sunsets? Or, er, maybe even try to track down a melody and have a go at singing? *Straight Outta Compton* is the aural equivalent of being surrounded by angry, finger-pointing men while their crack-addicted neighbours have a bust-up and the gun-toting police kick over a ghetto blaster outside and bawl at everyone through a bullhorn to calm the fuck down.

After the massive success of *Compton*, one of N.W.A.'s main men, Ice Cube, decided his subtle charms might also be deployed to enrich moviedom. He made his debut in the smoothly directed but occasionally clunky crime drama *Boyz n the Hood* as a poetry-loving intellectual. Oh, all right, that's not true. In a big surprise, he's actually a mouthy ex-con by the name of Doughboy. He might only provide support, but his scowling, beer-guzzling presence fits in fine with an excellent cast.

Just like *Once Were Warriors* concentrates on male Maori dysfunction, *Boyz* tackles black on black violence on the garbage-strewn, blood-spattered streets of South Central L.A. It's very good at depicting self-defeating machismo and how gun murders have their roots in the most trivial of incidents, such as a contemptuous look, a simple car ride or territorial pissings. The drug-dealing Doughboy is a less favoured son in the shadow of his college-bound brother. It's quietly amusing how he barely says one intelligent or encouraging thing throughout. Still, he's not beyond hope or sympathy, although it's clear he's a layabout with a somewhat unenlightened view of the ladies. Or as he informs a homey: "Can't learn shit talkin' to no stupid-ass bitch." In a performance that veers between disdain and insults to packing heat and all out aggression, it's beyond a resentful thickie like Doughboy to see the big picture and do something as simple as back down. The boy can't even play dominoes nicely.

Whitney Houston in *The Bodyguard* (1992)

So far, I suspect my biggest achievement in life has been to avoid prison. In fact, I'm already thinking of having that success immortalised on my gravestone: *Here lies Dave. He avoided prison.*

Brings a tear to your eye, don't it?

I guess what I'm trying to say is that it's pretty damned hard to get somewhere in life, let alone start breathing some rarefied air. That's why I never quite grasp how lucky fuckers whose dreams have come true promptly piss it all away and end up as a punch line. Take Whitney Houston. Just look at her beaming and twirling in her 1987 video *I Wanna Dance with Somebody (Who Loves Me)*. I hate to use a cliché like 'full of life' but, well, go look at that vid. Young, sexy, talented, charismatic, happy... The girl made it, all right. And then 25 years later she's an emaciated, erratic, drugged-up half-joke slipping under that lukewarm bathtub water at the Beverly Hilton, inadvertently checking out in a slightly more dignified manner than a constipated, hamburger-engorged Elvis falling off the bog at the age of 42 with a stopped ticker.

I mean, things ain't s'posed to go that way, are they?

Of course, it's impossible to imagine the level of fame Whitney achieved and what it does to a person's psyche and emotional wellbeing (an insane altitude nudged even higher by the monster success of *The Bodyguard*) but you do wish she could've said *this isn't working anymore and maybe it's time to do something else*. You see, the thought of Whitney's demise always saddens me. Aah, if only she'd employed me on her staff and listened to the wise counsel of an absolutely fucking nobody...

Anyway, back in 1992 her popularity went into overdrive when the public spunked up more than $400m to see her feature film debut while going gaga over its stratospheric hit, *I Will Always Love You*. However, *Bodyguard* often plays more like a two-hour ego massage for that epitome of bland handsomeness, Kevin Costner. He's a deadly serious, ultra-competent, ex-secret service bodyguard prepared to take a bullet for a client. And, of course, despite being a teetotal square and having one of the 90's naffest haircuts, he proves irresistible to a gorgeous, multi-millionaire pop star. "I've never felt this safe before," a post-coital Whitney dreamily says while lying in his manly arms. "No one could get by you." Surprisingly, she doesn't add: "And what a great big cock you have!"

Whitney won a Razzie for her diva-like role, but this strikes me as unfair. As expected, she is convincing during the songs. She also manages to handle stuff like being flirty, capricious, sarcastic, charming, snarky and defiant quite well. She even chucks in the odd surprise by turning the air blue on more than one occasion ("No fucking freak's gonna run me off stage!") I also liked her laying into Costner while hung-over as he smugly sips his orange juice. "Probably never had a heavy night in your whole damned disciplined life," she snaps from behind dark glasses. "You're a self-righteous sonuvabitch!"

Nevertheless, the movie has flaws, like her staff deciding to call in Costner rather than the cops after she's sent dozens of whacked out letters and someone breaks into her mansion and shoots his wad over her bed. *Bodyguard* is sporadically good at capturing the madness of mega-celebrity life but slips up by having her appear unrecognised at length in a public bar. Is she a superstar or not? The stalker is also characterised to a non-existent degree while there's a bafflingly unnecessary rescue of a child. None of this is Whitney or her dazzling teeth's fault, though. Yes, *Bodyguard* is romantic, clichéd, OTT pap, at times both implausible and ridiculous, but I must admit I enjoyed it. It's as Hollywood as it gets.

The Spice Girls in *Spice World* (1997)

Gary Glitter had a cameo in *Spice World* before his rapid fall from grace resulted in its removal. After watching this leaden travesty, I can only assume he feels at least he dodged one bullet during an otherwise very unfortunate time.

Like the vastly overrated *Hard Day's Night*, *Spice World* is pure fluff and just as difficult to sit through. To be fair, it's not aimed at a middle-aged grump like me and the girls do mock themselves, but there's no artistic reason for its self-indulgent existence, except to capitalise on the group's success and promote the next song. Or as one of them says in a girl power-undermining aside: "My money's my best friend." *Spice World*, filmed a year before Ginger fucked off from her so-called besties, is more a series of sketches than an actual narrative, packed with flat cameos, fantasy inserts, impersonations and a prevailing inability to dredge up a laugh from anywhere. Its only surprise is to present the girls from the first frame onward as unfailingly dumb and trivial. Most disappointingly, at no point do they have a lingerie-clad pillow fight. All in all, I would have preferred the Glitter cameo kept and the Spice Girls edited out. Twenty-five years later *Spice World* is only gonna appeal to the gormless tweens that pestered their parents to see it in the first place.

Eminem in *8 Mile* (2002)

Feisty little white fucker best sums up Rabbit, Eminem's character in this Detroit-set drama. He gets in a bouncer's face, fires paintballs at a cop car, bounces back from a beating and tries to make a rapping name for himself in a black, hyper-masculine world. "This is hip hop," he's told by a black opponent in an onstage rap battle. "You don't belong. You're a tourist." Seconds later, Rabbit chokes, unable to respond with even one word in this public dissing contest, and is laughed off stage. His mind-numbing factory job and dreary trailer park home life don't offer much respite, either. Mom's a bit hopeless and her new boyfriend is a dick. Only two things keep him going: protecting his vulnerable little sis and a pervasive dream of snagging a record deal.

I have to say there's something faintly daft about grown men taking part in rap battles in which they colourfully insult each other in rhyme. Yes, it's a healthy release of negative energy and requires an amazing burst of quick thinking, but surely serious rappers prefer to murder rivals in a drive-by? After all, that's the way it's been done for decades. How else do you get respect and show you *really mean it* in such an ocean of machismo? *8 Mile* wants to be all urban and gritty, but it's built on polystyrene. Rabbit not only possesses the wrong skin colour, but sticks up for gays. What sort of rapper is this? In real life me thinks he'd end up in a stew.

However, despite *8 Mile's* inherent silliness, the non-smiling, beanie-clad Eminem is good. Sure, he's essentially playing a version of himself, but as Prince showed, this isn't as straightforward as you'd think. He holds the centre well in a dick-swinging flick that feels like a cross between *Saturday Night Fever* and *Blue Collar* while not being as good as either. Its climactic rap battle wants to be the equivalent of Rocky vs. Apollo but falls about eight miles short. Still, it offers an occasionally interesting glimpse into a different world, and it's a shame Eminem never followed up its runaway success.

Right, time for my nap.

Don't miss out!

Visit the website below and you can sign up to receive emails whenever Dave Franklin publishes a new book. There's no charge and no obligation.

https://books2read.com/r/B-A-UYN-EKYEC

BOOKS 2 READ

Connecting independent readers to independent writers.

Also by Dave Franklin

Iceberg Movies Guide
Rooney Eats It! A Brit's Take on Pimps, Child Deaths and Other Fun Movie Stuff

Ice Dog Movie Guide
Go Fuck an Iceberg! A Brit's Take on Guns, Tits and Other Fun Movie Stuff
Smile, You Sonuvabitch! A Brit's Take on Catfights, Serial Killers and Other Fun Movie Stuff

Straitjacket Blues
Straitjacket Blues: Stories of Unease
Straitjacket Blues 2
Straitjacket Blues 3
Begin The Madness: The Straitjacket Blues Trilogy

The Goodreads Killer
The Goodreads Killer
The Goodreads Killer 2
The Goodreads Killer 3
The Goodreads Killer: The Trilogy

Welcome to Wales, Girls
Welcome to Wales, Keiko
Welcome to Wales, Paola
Welcome to Wales, Kylie

Standalone
Camaraderie
English Toss on Planet Andong
Girls Like Funny Boys
Shelter: A Supernatural Short Story
Manic Streets of Perth
To Dare A Future: A Novel of Rage
Looking for Sarah Jane Smith
Evil Arse Soup: Three Ultra-Dark Comedies
Blundering Blokes
We Should Be More Like Fish: A Medieval Novella
Bawdy Blokes: Three Porno Funnies
Then Came The Last Days Of May
Nice Man Jack
Riders on the Storm and Other Killer Songs
Saving a Child from God
Near-Life Experience: A Gripping Tale of Anxiety
Eaters of Evil Spirits
The Muslim Zombies
A Promise of Pain: A Collection of Dark Psychological Writing

About the Author

Dave Franklin is a Brit who lives Down Under. He has also written ten novels ranging from dark comedy and horror to crime and hardcore porn. His naughty work includes *Looking for Sarah Jane Smith* (2001), *Begin the Madness: The Straitjacket Blues Trilogy* (2014), *The Muslim Zombies* (2018) & *Welcome to Wales, Girls: A Violent Odyssey of Pornographic Filth* (2018).

www.ingramcontent.com/pod-product-compliance
Lightning Source LLC
Chambersburg PA
CBHW070138100426
42743CB00013B/2748